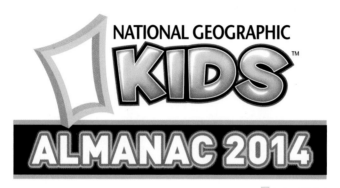

NATIONAL GEOGRAPHIC

NATIONAL GEOGRAPHIC
KIDS™
ALMANAC 2014

Emperor penguins in Antarctica travel
across sea ice to their nesting colony.

National Geographic Children's Books
gratefully acknowledges the following people for their help with the
National Geographic Kids Almanac 2014.

Curtis Malarkey, Julie Segal, and Cheryl Zook
of the National Geographic Explorers program;
Truly Herbert, National Geographic Communications;
and Chuck Errig of Random House

Awesome Adventure

Jen Bloomer, Media Relations Manager,
The National Aquarium in Baltimore

Amazing Animals

Suzanne Braden, Director, Pandas International

Dr. Rodolfo Coria, Paleontologist, Plaza Huincul, Argentina

Dr. Sylvia Earle,
National Geographic Explorer-in-Residence

Dr. Thomas R. Holtz, Jr., Senior Lecturer, Vertebrate Paleontology,
Department of Geology, University of Maryland

Dr. Luke Hunter, Executive Director, Panthera

Dereck and Beverly Joubert,
National Geographic Explorers-in-Residence

"Dino" Don Lessem, President, Exhibits Rex

Kathy B. Maher, Research Editor,
NATIONAL GEOGRAPHIC magazine

Kathleen Martin, Canadian Sea Turtle Network

Barbara Nielsen, Polar Bears International

Andy Prince, Austin Zoo

Christopher Sloan

Julia Thorson, translator, Zurich, Switzerland

Dennis vanEngelsdorp, Senior Extension Associate,
Pennsylvania Department of Agriculture

Wonders of Nature

Anatta, NOAA Public Affairs Officer

Dr. Robert Ballard,
National Geographic Explorer-in-Residence

Douglas H. Chadwick, wildlife biologist and contributor to
NATIONAL GEOGRAPHIC magazine

Drew Hardesty, Forecaster, Utah Avalanche Center

Culture Connection

Dr. Wade Davis,
National Geographic Explorer-in-Residence

Deirdre Mullervy, Managing Editor,
Gallaudet University Press

Super Science

Tim Appenzeller, Chief Magazine Editor, NATURE

Dr. José de Ondarza, Associate Professor,
Department of Biological Sciences, State University
of New York, College at Plattsburgh

Lesley B. Rogers, Managing Editor (former),
NATIONAL GEOGRAPHIC magazine

Dr. Enric Sala, National Geographic Visiting Fellow

Abigail A. Tipton, Director of Research (former),
NATIONAL GEOGRAPHIC magazine

Erin Vintinner, Biodiversity Specialist,
Center for Biodiversity and Conservation at the
American Museum of Natural History

Barbara L. Wyckoff, Research Editor,
NATIONAL GEOGRAPHIC magazine

Going Green

Eric J. Bohn, Math Teacher, Santa Rosa High School

Stephen David Harris, Professional Engineer,
Industry Consulting

Catherine C. Milbourn, Senior Press Officer, EPA

Brad Scriber, Senior Researcher,
NATIONAL GEOGRAPHIC magazine

Paola Segura and Cid Simões,
National Geographic Emerging Explorers

Dr. Wes Tunnell, Harte Research Institute for
Gulf of Mexico Studies, Texas A&M
University–Corpus Christi

History Happens

Sylvie Beaudreau, Associate Professor, Department of History,
State University of New York

Elspeth Deir, Assistant Professor, Faculty of Education,
Queens University, Kingston, Ontario, Canada

Dr. Gregory Geddes, Lecturer, Department of Global Studies,
State University of New York–Orange,
Middletown-Newburgh, New York

Dr. Fredrik Hiebert, National Geographic Visiting Fellow

Micheline Joanisse, Media Relations Officer,
Natural Resources Canada

Dr. Robert D. Johnston,
Associate Professor and Director of the
Teaching of History Program,
University of Illinois at Chicago

Dickson Mansfield, Geography Instructor (retired),
Faculty of Education, Queens University,
Kingston, Ontario, Canada

Tina Norris, U.S. Census Bureau

Parliamentary Information and Research Service,
Library of Parliament, Ottawa, Canada

Karyn Pugliese, Acting Director, Communications,
Assembly of First Nations

Geography Rocks

Glynnis Breen, National Geographic Special Projects

Carl Haub, Senior Demographer, Conrad Taeuber Chair of Public
Information, Population Reference Bureau

Dr. Mary Kent, Demographer,
Population Reference Bureau

Dr. Walt Meier, National Snow and Ice Data Center

Dr. Richard W. Reynolds,
NOAA's National Climatic Data Center

United States Census Bureau, Public Help Desk

Dr. Spencer Wells,
National Geographic Explorer-in-Residence

Contents

Your World 2014

8

Awesome Adventure

18

Amazing Animals

36

CONTENTS

Going Green   206

History Happens   224

Geography Rocks   256

Two new snowboarding events will be featured at the 2014 Olympic Winter Games in Sochi, Russia—snowboard slopestyle and snowboard parallel special slalom. In this photo, athletes compete in women's snowboard cross at the 2010 Olympic Winter Games in Vancouver, Canada.

Your World
2014

NATIONAL
GEOGRAPHIC
KIDS

DIGITAL EXTRAS!

SCAN THIS PAGE!
GET BONUS MOBILE
CONTENT! Download
the free NG Kids
scanner app. Directions
on inside front cover.

Shark-Tracking
ROBOT

A robot that surfs on the waves is being used by scientists to track the movements of great white sharks.

"WAVE GLIDER" ROBOT

How do you locate great white sharks in the ocean? You track them with a surfing robot, of course! That's what scientists are doing off the coast of California, U.S.A., in an attempt to keep tabs on the elusive sea creatures. The solar-powered "Wave Glider" robot—which looks a lot like a giant yellow surfboard—floats around in the Pacific Ocean picking up signals from tagged sharks up to 1,000 feet (330 m) away.

The signals are then sent by satellite to researchers on land who analyze the data to map out the sharks' whereabouts. That way they can get a better understanding of the sharks' daily lives and movements. Even cooler? All of the data picked up by the robot is available on a free app for iPods, iPads, and iPhones. Meaning you, too, can follow the ferocious fish with a swipe of your finger. Fierce!

Panama Canal:
100th Anniversary

PANAMA CANAL, AUGUST 1914

MODERN-DAY PANAMA CANAL

Every year more than 14,000 ships make the trip from the Atlantic to the Pacific through the Panama Canal, which celebrates its 100th birthday in 2014. Completed in 1914, the 40-mile (65-km) canal changed the way goods move across the world by offering ships a more direct route between two major oceans. In 2014, the canal will mark its major milestone with a makeover, including a new lock system to allow even bigger ships to pass through this engineering marvel.

STRIPED FOREST

A toxic waste spill in western Hungary has left people seeing red, literally. After millions of gallons of waste from an aluminum factory burst through a dam, a thick, rust-colored sludge blanketed forests and fields. Now, a red line remains, serving as a permanent reminder of the country's worst chemical accident.

11

MARS ROVER
CURIOSITY

MARTIAN
LANDSCAPE

ANCIENT
STREAMBED

SHINY SOIL
FOUND ON MARS!

Talk about a bright moment for Mars: A recent soil
sample collected by NASA's rover Curiosity revealed shiny
pebbles in the red planet's dirt. Scientists think the bright
rocks are probably native Martian mineral flecks, and hope
the sample will help them discover more information about
the planet's terrain. So far, Curiosity, a six-wheeled robot
about the size of a Mini Cooper car, has also stumbled upon
an ancient streambed, indicating that water once flowed
on Mars. These types of clues are helping researchers piece
together whether the red planet ever supported life.

GORILLAS ESCAPE TRAP!

YOUNG GORILLAS IN RWANDA DISMANTLE A TRAP. THE WEEK BEFORE A SIMILAR TRAP HAD KILLED A GORILLA NAMED NGWINO.

A poacher was no match for two young gorillas who destroyed a pair of traps in their forest home in Rwanda in Africa. The camouflaged traps—usually set out for antelopes by bush-meat hunters—are dangerous for young mountain gorillas, who often aren't strong enough to free themselves. But not for Rwema and Dukore, two young gorillas who worked together to break the branches surrounding the traps and loosen their nooses. Trackers at the nearby Karisoke Research Center think the gorillas may have learned how to dismantle the traps by watching humans do the same.

SOLAR FERRIS WHEEL

What's more awesome than taking a ride on a giant Ferris wheel? How about if the ride is actually helping the environment with every loop you make? Eco-friendly amusement rides—like the Pacific Wheel on Santa Monica Pier in California, U.S.A.—are popping up, promoting the use of clean, sustainable energy. Some, like the Pacific Wheel, are powered by solar energy, while other outlets use biofuel (think french-fry grease and used vegetable oil) to make the rides go 'round. Helping the environment has never been so fun!

13

Floating VACATION

From a shiplike hotel to a research station for studying ocean animals, the Utopia is many things—but it's mostly just cool. Still in the concept stage, this large floating world will rest on four legs that extend and float about 50 feet (15 m) below the surface. These legs will minimize how much of the vessel actually touches the water, reducing wave motion. When it's not a home for marine biologists, it will accommodate tourists. Take a helicopter, boat, or mini-submarine to it, then lounge in its guest suites, pools, and restaurants. There will even be a movie theater. The best part is the top deck, where a 360-degree observatory high above the water's surface will make you feel as if you're on top of the world.

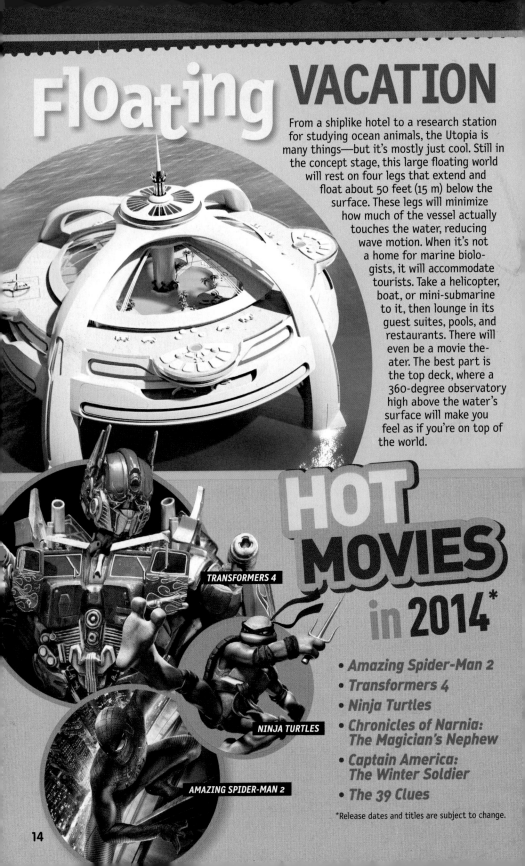

TRANSFORMERS 4

NINJA TURTLES

AMAZING SPIDER-MAN 2

HOT MOVIES in 2014*

- *Amazing Spider-Man 2*
- *Transformers 4*
- *Ninja Turtles*
- *Chronicles of Narnia: The Magician's Nephew*
- *Captain America: The Winter Soldier*
- *The 39 Clues*

*Release dates and titles are subject to change.

14

Stratos EXTREME Free Fall

One Giant Leap! Imagine standing at the edge of space and taking one giant leap before plummeting 24 miles (39 km) down to Earth below. That's just what professional skydiver Felix Baumgartner did as part of the Red Bull Stratos Project, setting a world record for highest and fastest parachute jump and becoming the first person to break the sound barrier without vehicle power in the process. But this jump wasn't just a daredevil's stunt: Scientists working on the project hope that they'll be able to advance aerospace technology that will help future space missions. Everything from Baumgartner's superprotective space suit to his high-tech parachute can be adopted by astronauts and scientists as they continue to explore life above Earth in the future.

Cool Events in 2014

Global Belly Laugh Day

It's a great day to get in some good laughs. LOL!

January 24

Australian Sand Sculpting Championships

Artists gather in Surfers Paradise, Queensland, Australia, to create stunning sand sculptures.

February

XXII Olympic Winter Games

Hundreds of athletes travel to Sochi, Russia, to go for the gold on the snow and ice.

February 7–23

XI Paralympic Winter Games

Physically challenged athletes from around the world compete in events like wheelchair curling and ice sledge hockey.

March 7–16

World Oceans Day

Celebrate everything you love about the great blue sea today!

June 8

FIFA World Cup Brazil

The world's best soccer teams go head-to-head in Rio de Janeiro, Brazil. Goooooal!

June 12–July 13

International Talk Like a Pirate Day

Arr, matey! Practice your pirate-speak!

September 19

Origami Day, Japan

Try your hand at the Japanese art of paper folding.

November 11

AWESOME 3-D ART

Look out below! This young man may look like he's dangerously close to falling into a deep ravine, but in reality, he's leaping over solid ground. 3-D murals, like this one in China, are popping up on sidewalks all over the world. These amazing exhibits, depicted in 3-D form, are bringing a brand-new twist to the term "street art."

sports funnies

OLYMPIC EDITION

Olympians totally inspire us ... but they can definitely make us laugh, too. In honor of the 2014 Winter Games, here are two athletes from past Olympics caught in the act of being, well, funny!

SET UP THE BOWLING PINS—I'M GOING FOR A STRIKE

YIKES! THIS ICE IS CRAWLING WITH COCKROACHES!

Sweden's Anja Paerson takes a victory slide after winning gold at the women's slalom skiing competition at the 2006 Winter Olympics in Italy.

Emily Hughes of the United States performs in the figure skating competition at the 2006 Winter Olympics in Italy.

17

Awesome Adventure

Three skydivers perform a head-down flying maneuver. Jumpers travel at speeds that can reach more than 150 miles an hour (241 kph).

DARE TO E⟩

Do you have what it takes to be a great explorer? Read the stories of three

ELEPHANT MOM WITH HER CALF

KRITHI KARANTH

THE CONSERVATION BIOLOGIST

Wildlife protector Krithi Karanth talks about a heart-pounding encounter with an elephant.

"Once while walking down a curving road at a wildlife park in India, we came face-to-face with a group of elephants. Not wanting to disturb them, we began to back up. Most of us knew to stay calm and quiet. But one person in the group who wasn't used to encountering wild animals created some noise. Startled, an elephant looked up. Normally, these creatures are gentle giants, but some become defensive when scared. This one started stomping toward us! We got out of there fast. My job does have some risks, but I love it."

Want to be a CONSERVATION BIOLOGIST?

STUDY: Biology, geography, and mathematics

WATCH: *The Truth About Tigers*

READ: *My Life With the Chimpanzees*

ADVICE: "Find a career you love. The rest will fall into place."

Want to be a PHOTOJOURNALIST?

STUDY: Photography, journalism, and sociology

WATCH: National Geographic's *The Photographers*

READ: *National Geographic* magazine

ADVICE: "You have to be driven by a love of telling the story. And if that's not there, something's missing."

THE PHOTO-JOURNALIST

Chris Rainier, who travels the world documenting everything from indigenous cultures to war, explains what it takes to capture such unique images.

"When everyone else is running away, you've got to run towards the danger. That is where you will find the images. I tend to scout out areas that are a landscape, urban or natural, and then have events unfold in that area. And so you're capturing things as they happen…it's very important for me to capture all the acute micro-details. You cannot be just an observer. You want to dive in; you want to taste it and smell it. If you participate, your photography and your storytelling will be even more powerful."

XPLORE

famous adventurers, and see how you can get started on the same path.

PAUL SERENO WITH A CAST OF *DELTADROMEUS*

THE PALEONTOLOGIST

Paul Sereno on discovering a nearly complete skeleton of *Herrerasaurus*, one of the earliest dinosaurs:

"The Ischigualasto Valley in Argentina stretches about 75 miles (121 km). We had spent several weeks on this harsh terrain looking for more complete remains of the earliest dinosaurs. Nobody thought we'd succeed. But just as the team was preparing to leave, I decided to look in one place we'd missed. Here, I noticed vertebrae eroding from a sandstone ledge. My eyes followed the neck bones right up to the base of a dinosaur skull. It was truly amazing. I felt as if I had found a 230-million-year-old needle in a monstrous haystack."

RAINIER'S PHOTO OF A HULI MAN OF PAPUA NEW GUINEA IN SING-SING FESTIVAL DRESS

CHRIS RAINIER

Want to be a PALEONTOLOGIST?

STUDY: Science, art

WATCH: The *Jurassic Park* series

READ: *National Geographic Kids The Ultimate Dinopedia*

ADVICE: "Be active, be productive, and test your limits."

Island Adventure
Cayman Islands

AN UP CLOSE ENCOUNTER WITH SOUTHERN STING-RAYS AT STINGRAY CITY

Swimming with stingrays, snorkeling in coral reefs, and crouching face-to-face with blue iguanas are just a few of the wild encounters that 15 *National Geographic Kids* readers experienced in the Cayman Islands. The explorers are winners of the annual NG KIDS Hands-On Explorer Challenge (HOEC), an essay and photo competition.

THE EXPEDITION TEAM visited Grand Cayman and Cayman Brac, two of the three islands that make up the Cayman Islands, a British Overseas Territory in the western Caribbean. As they hiked and explored, swam and sailed, the HOEC kids took photographs of fish, live conchs, mangroves, iguanas, birds, coral, and more—using the Nikon cameras they also won. One of the animals the kids got to know was the blue iguana—found only on Grand Cayman.

The kids explored caves that dotted the limestone cliffs of Cayman Brac. Local people have taken refuge in these caves for decades during hurricanes.

STINGRAY CITY, a sandbar off Grand Cayman Island, is a site where stingrays gather around visitors as they wade in the warm, tropical waters.

"I was nervous about getting into the water with them," admits Maddie Lloyd of Flower Mound, Texas, U.S.A., "but once I did, I loved feeling their smooth, soft texture."

AN ENDANGERED BLUE IGUANA THRIVES AT A RESERVE.

WATCHING FISH FROM THE SUBMARINE *ATLANTIS*

IN AN AVIARY, A BIRD LANDS ON A NGK EXPLORER'S HAND.

SAILING ON A CATAMARAN FOR A DAY OF SNORKELING

MYSTERY IN THE SKIES

What happened to Amelia Earhart?

PILOT AMELIA EARHART AND HER COPILOT FRED NOONAN REVIEW A FLIGHT CHART.

A Lockheed Electra airplane took off into the sky over the Pacific, with no sign of trouble ahead. At the controls was famous American pilot Amelia Earhart, the first woman to fly solo across the Atlantic Ocean. Alongside her sat Fred Noonan. Together, they planned to fly 2,556 miles (4,113 km) from the island nation of Papua New Guinea to Howland Island in the South Pacific Ocean, the third-to-last leg in a trip around the world. The date was July 2, 1937. That was the last time anyone ever saw them.

Earhart's disappearance remains a mystery. Now, more than 75 years later, new research is shedding light on what may have happened during that fateful flight.

SPLASH AND SINK
The most widely accepted explanation for what happened to Earhart is that her plane crashed into the ocean. According to a U.S. Coast Guard boat keeping radio communication with the Electra during the flight, Earhart said she was searching for the island but could not find it—and that she was running low on fuel. No underwater wreckage has been found, but searches continue. A recent expedition used a deep-sea sonar system to scan a wide area around which the Electra likely went down, but it did not find any sign of a plane.

CRASH LANDING
Others think the Electra landed on the remote Pacific atoll Nikumaroro and that Earhart and Noonan lived as castaways. Newly discovered evidence found on Nikumaroro—such as fragments of glass made in the U.S. and a cosmetics jar—have caused speculation that Earhart lived there for an unknown amount of time before she died. But despite multiple expeditions to the island, no plane or other conclusive evidence has been found.

LEGACY
Other less likely theories—including one claiming that Earhart acted as a spy during World War II and then changed her identity—are still floating around, offering extra ideas for what happened. As the search for answers continues, one thing remains certain: Amelia Earhart will always be one of the most celebrated aviators in history.

CRYSTAL

A ONCE HIDDEN CHAMBER REVEALS GIGANTIC, ICICLE-LIKE CRYSTALS.

It looks like a mysterious alien hideaway, with crystal structures about the height of a three-story building jutting straight into the air and crisscrossing overhead. But Mexico's Cave of Crystals isn't science fiction. It's a real cave that miners discovered only 14 years ago. And scientists had never seen anything like it.

SECRET WORLD

In 2000, miners looking for lead and silver beneath Mexico's Naica Mountain began pumping water out of a flooded chamber. They were shocked when they found a hidden gallery of giant, icicle-like crystals beneath the watery depths almost a thousand feet (300 m) below the Earth's surface. Some of the crystals measured up to 37.4 feet (11.4 m) tall.

The Cave of Crystals is like no other cave in the world, but the massive glittering formations aren't the only things that make it unique. Most caves stay cool, around 60°F (16°C). But the Cave of Crystals rests atop what was once bubbling magma (hot, liquid rock). The leftover embers can make the mine hotter than the Sahara and wetter than a rain forest.

"It's like being in a sauna, only it's a thousand feet underground," says Juan Manuel García-Ruiz of the Spanish National Research Council in Granada, Spain. "As soon as I entered the cave I was dripping with sweat. My glasses fogged up from the humidity and I couldn't see."

The Cave of Crystals is made of a mineral called gypsum. Geologists call the cave's crystallized form of gypsum "selenite," after Selene, the Greek goddess of the moon. "They have the brightness and whiteness of moonlight," says crystal expert Juan Manuel García-Ruiz.

CAVE

How a Crystal Cave Grew

The superhot water that used to fill the cave contained molecules, or tiny particles, of chemicals. When those molecules bumped up against each other, they sometimes stuck together. Other molecules floating past glommed on as well, and a crystal would start to grow. Over half a million years, the crystals grew—adding the thickness of a human hair every 100 years—until they reached the size they are today.

DEATH-DEFYING SCIENTISTS

Harsh underground conditions are what allow the incredible crystals to grow into miniature Washington Monuments. Brave scientists put themselves in danger to study the cave, hoping to discover things such as the age of the crystals and whether tiny life-forms are living among them.

One Italian research team is developing cooling and breathing equipment to help scientists remain in the cave for long periods of time. "It's dangerous to stay too long," García-Ruiz says. "After ten minutes, I felt like I was boiling on the inside."

But to García-Ruiz and other scientists, the incredible experience inside the mysterious cave is worth the risk. "You think you're looking at icicles, but when you touch them they're hot because it's 140°F (60°C) in there," he says. "When I first saw the cave, I was so happy that I laughed out loud like a crazy man!"

15 THINGS TO DO BEFORE YOU GROW UP

1 START YOUR OWN BUSINESS.

2 MAKE A FRIEND WHO IS A DIFFERENT RACE OR RELIGION THAN YOU ARE.

3 WRITE A ROCK SONG.

4 BECOME AN EXPLORER. GET A MAP AND PUT PINS IN EVERY PLACE YOU VISIT. TRY TO VISIT A NEW LOCATION—SUCH AS A CITY OR A NATIONAL PARK—EACH YEAR.

5
ORGANIZE A "YEAR IN THE LIFE" PHOTO ALBUM ABOUT YOUR FAMILY.

6 CONVINCE YOUR PARENTS TO MAKE ONE BIG CHANGE TO HELP THE ENVIRONMENT.
- DRINK TAP WATER INSTEAD OF BOTTLED WATER.
- CHANGE TO COMPACT FLUORESCENT BULBS.
- WALK INSTEAD OF DRIVE IN YOUR NEIGHBORHOOD.

7 APOLOGIZE FOR SOMETHING YOU DID A LONG TIME AGO. (C'MON, YOU *KNOW* THERE'S SOMETHING!)

8 BE A MUST-HAVE GUEST. LEARN TO JUGGLE, TELL JOKES, OR WHISTLE.

9 BE AN EXCHANGE STUDENT IN ANOTHER COUNTRY.

10 STAY UP ALL NIGHT (WITH YOUR PARENTS' PERMISSION).

11 MASTER ONE DISH FROM ANOTHER COUNTRY EVERY MONTH AND SERVE IT TO YOUR FAMILY.

12 LEARN A FOREIGN LANGUAGE.

13 MAKE A VIDEO ABOUT SOMETHING MEANINGFUL TO YOU: YOUR SPORTS TEAM, A VOLUNTEER CAUSE, A FESTIVAL, OR YOUR TOWN.

14 EAT AN EXOTIC FRUIT, SUCH AS NASHI (ASIAN PEAR) OR YANG TAO (KIWI).

15 RECORD YOUR RELATIVES TELLING YOU THEIR FAVORITE MEMORIES. THEN WRITE THEIR STORIES IN A MEMORY BOOK.

DEEP-SEA Explorer

Ocean explorer **James Cameron,** who also directed movies such as *Avatar* and *Titanic,* tells about diving **6.8 miles (10.9 km)** to the bottom of the Pacific Ocean's Mariana Trench, **the deepest part of the ocean.**

"The DEEPSEA CHALLENGER descends fast, about 500 feet (153 m) per minute. As I dropped down from the surface, it got dark very quickly—I was in complete blackness in about two or three minutes. But with the sub's lights, I could see little jellyfish and some plankton, and because the sub was going through the water so fast, they were racing through the light. If you've ever driven a car in a snowstorm at night, that's exactly what it looked like.

DEEPSEA CHALLENGER UNDERWATER

"Imagine six or seven SUVs sitting on top of your thumbnail. That's a sense of the pressure outside the sub. If the DEEPSEA CHALLENGER sprung a leak down there, the water would squirt in like a laser, cutting right through everything inside the sub— myself included. The sub would collapse like a soda can that has a bank vault dropped onto it.

"I always knew I wanted to explore. Follow your dreams, follow your passions. There is still a tremendous amount left to explore on this planet."

27

AVALANCHE!

One by one, the three **skiers cautiously move across and down the** snow-covered mountain. **Janet Kellam** skis last. When she reaches the middle of the slope, she realizes the snowpack is much more dangerous than it had seemed.

"The whole slope shatters like a pane of glass—I see it cracking around my feet," she says. She suddenly falls. "You just think, 'It can't be happening.'"

Search dogs smell **avalanche victims** under the snow and **show rescuers** where to **dig.**

But it was happening. Kellam was caught in an avalanche—a massive, potentially deadly snowslide that thunders down the side of a mountain. An expert avalanche forecaster, Kellam had been observing snow conditions in Idaho's Smoky Mountains. As she tumbled down the mountain, she feared she might become one of the 30 or so people who die in avalanches every year in the western United States.

ANATOMY OF AN AVALANCHE

"We think of snow as being this nice, soft, fluffy material," says Karl Birkeland, an avalanche scientist with the USDA Forest Service National Avalanche Center. "But when it builds up, it can destroy buildings and topple giant trees like twigs. Avalanches can travel downhill at more than 150 miles an hour [241 kph]." Avalanches typically occur when new, heavy snowfall piles on top of a weaker layer, causing it to collapse and send snow sweeping down the mountainside. Other common avalanche triggers include overhanging blocks of snow that fall, or even humans—usually backcountry snowshoers, snowmobilers, or skiers like Kellam.

SWEPT AWAY

As Kellam approached the flat valley floor after sliding down the mountain, the snow shoved her down and buried her. Remembering that most avalanche fatalities are caused by suffocation, Kellam immediately tried to dig an air pocket in front of her face. But she could barely wiggle the tips of her fingers. Kellam had to trust that her two colleagues would find her.

A cubic yard (0.76 m³) of **mountain snow** weighs about **660 pounds** (300 kg).

QUICK RESCUE

Eventually Kellam heard a familiar crunch above her—boots on snow! Her colleagues had watched her until she disappeared. They switched their avalanche transceivers to receive and followed the signal from the transceiver Kellam wore. They located her under the snow using a search probe and dug her out with a shovel within five minutes. Buried avalanche victims begin to suffocate after 15 minutes. After just five minutes, Kellam's face had turned blue.

Later, the forecasting team learned that heavy winds had loaded snow onto the slope—something that weather instruments missed. Had they known that, they would have steered clear of the dangerous area. Kellam says her training and equipment saved her life. "But the bottom line is that you don't want to get caught in an avalanche to begin with," she says.

HOW TO SURVIVE A
KILLER BEE ATTACK!

1) Buzz Off
Killer bees—or Africanized honey bees—only attack when their hive is being threatened. If you see several bees buzzing near you, a hive is probably close by. Heed their "back off" attitude and slowly walk away.

2) Don't Join the Swat Team
Your first instinct might be to start swatting and slapping the bees. But that just makes the buzzers angry. Loud noises have the same effect, so don't start screaming, either. Just get away.

3) Don't Play Hide-and-Seek
Hives are often near water, but don't even think about outlasting the bees underwater. They'll hover and attack when you come up for air, even if you try to swim for it.

4) Make Like Speedy Gonzalez
Killer bees will chase you, but they'll give up when you're far enough away from the hive (usually about 200 yards [183 m]). Take off running and don't stop until the buzzing does.

5) Create a Cover-Up
Killer bees often go for the face and throat, which are the most dangerous places to be stung. While you're on the run, protect your face and neck with your hands, or pull your shirt over your head.

HOW TO SURVIVE A
BEE STING!

1. De-Sting Yourself
First, get inside or to a cool place. Then, remove the stinger by scraping a fingernail over the area, like you would to get a splinter out. Do not squeeze the stinger or use tweezers unless you absolutely can't get it out any other way.

2. Put It on Ice
Wash the area with soap and water and apply a cool compress to reduce swelling. Continue icing the spot for 20 minutes every hour. Place a washcloth or towel between the ice and your skin.

3. Treat It Right
With a parent's permission, take an antihistamine and gently rub a hydrocortisone cream on the sting site.

4. Hands Off
Make sure you don't scratch the sting. You'll just increase the pain and swelling.

5. Recognize Danger
If you experience severe burning and itching, swelling of the throat and/or mouth, difficulty breathing, weakness, or nausea, or if you already know you are allergic to bees, get to an emergency room immediately.

29

EXTREME ACTION SPORTS

Forget soccer and softball: Some athletes go above and beyond when it comes to their sport of choice. These activities take a ton of skill—and plenty of guts, too. Here's a roundup of some *extreme*-ly out-there sports!

BASE JUMPING

SPECIAL GEAR
Parachute

WHY IT'S EXTREME
Instead of leaping from an airplane, BASE jumpers parachute from fixed objects, including buildings (B), antennas (A), spans (S), such as bridges, and Earth's formations (E).

EXTREME IRONING

SPECIAL GEAR
Iron, ironing board, and wrinkled clothes

WHY IT'S EXTREME
Thrill-seekers iron their laundry while performing an extreme sport, like riding on a moving car or scuba diving.

SNOWKITING

SPECIAL GEAR
Skis, large kite

WHY IT'S EXTREME
Skiers use large kites to propel themselves across snow and ice—and off of mountains.

FLARE SURFING

SPECIAL GEAR
Surfboard, flares

WHY IT'S EXTREME
Surfers create a fiery display while they ride the waves by attaching flares to the backs of their boards.

STILT JUMPING

SPECIAL GEAR
Jumping stilts

WHY IT'S EXTREME
Stride up to nine feet (2.7 m) with these spring-loaded stilts that you can walk, jump, and jog in.

UNDERWATER HOCKEY

SPECIAL GEAR
Hockey puck, stick, swimming pool

WHY IT'S EXTREME
Players hold their breath as they dive to the bottom of the pool to go after the puck and push it to the goal.

MY SHOT

Calling all shutterbugs! Budding photographers can send their favorite pics to National Geographic Kids My Shot (ngkidsmyshot.com), where you can share, view, and rate cool images, like these taken by kids like you. So, what do you see through that lens? Break out your camera and start snapping away!

Bubbles!
gabriela

My leopard gecko
RCH9797

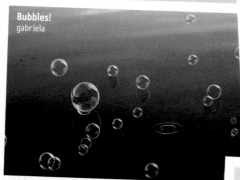

Canyonlands National Park
HikerChik

Two puffins
Blueberry Eyes

Carnival eyes!
aubs21

Flowers looking up
kk4jas

TIPS FROM A PRO
How to Take Great Photos

As far as the eye can see, there are photographs waiting to be captured or created. Life swirls around us without stopping, but as a photographer, you can put a frame around moments in time. A lot more goes into taking a good photograph than just pushing a button, though.

Learn how to use a camera, but most of all, learn how to think like a photographer. Here are some valuable tips from expert photographer Neil Johnson to help you get started on your way.

COMPOSITION

• Making your subject the focus of attention does not mean that you have to put it in the middle of the frame. Placing the subject slightly off center can help lead the viewer into the picture.

SUBJECT

• When taking pictures of animals, getting down to their eye level and moving in close will improve your photographs.

• When taking pictures of people, try to get them to forget about the camera and just go about doing what they enjoy.

LIGHT

• When lighting a subject, it is important to consider not only the direction of the light (front, side, or back), but also the color of the background.

• Light does not always have to fall on the front of your subject.

• On-camera flash is most useful for subjects that are 10 to 15 feet (3 to 4.5 m) away.

QUICK TIPS!

• **Get close.** A lot of cameras have zoom features, but nothing beats being right there next to your subject.

• **Experiment with the different modes** on your digital camera, like portrait, sports, and macro. See what works and what doesn't.

• **Don't spend too much time** looking at the pictures on your digital camera—doing this drains the batteries! Download your photos instead.

• **Stay still,** especially if you're using a camera phone. The steadier you are, the clearer your shot will be.

STUMP YOUR PARENTS

AWESOME ADVENTURE QUIZ

See if your parents are up to speed by quizzing their knowledge on all things adventure. (All questions are based on information in this chapter.) ANSWERS BELOW

1 Researchers say Mexico's Cave of Crystals feels like what?
a. a sauna
b. a desert
c. a damp basement
d. a hot tub

2 **True or false?** Aviator Amelia Earhart was attempting a trip around the world when she disappeared.

3 Which of these is not a real extreme sport?
a. underwater hockey
b. extreme ironing
c. flare surfing
d. pig juggling

4 How fast can an avalanche travel?
a. 65 miles an hour (105 kph)
b. 150 miles an hour (241 kph)
c. 225 miles an hour (362 kph)
d. faster than a speeding bullet

5 What should you do if killer bees attack?
a. run
b. pull your shirt over your head
c. don't swat or scream
d. all of the above

6 Where would you find a blue iguana?
a. Australia
b. Cayman Islands
c. Mexico
d. Indonesia

ANSWERS:
1. a; 2. True. She was on the third-to-last leg of a trip around the world. 3. d; 4. b; 5. d; 6. b

HOMEWORK HELP

How to Write a Perfect Essay

Need to write an essay? Does the assignment feel as big as climbing Mount Everest? Fear not. You're up to the challenge! The following step-by-step tips will help you with this monumental task.

1. BRAINSTORM. Sometimes the subject matter of your essay is assigned to you, sometimes it's not. Either way, you have to decide what you want to say. Start by brainstorming some ideas, writing down any thoughts you have about the subject. Then read over everything you've come up with and consider which idea you think is the strongest. Ask yourself what you want to write about the most. Keep in mind the goal of your essay. Can you achieve the goal of the assignment with this topic? If so, you're good to go.

2. WRITE A TOPIC SENTENCE. This is the main idea of your essay, a statement of your thoughts on the subject. Again, consider the goal of your essay. Think of the topic sentence as an introduction that tells your reader what the rest of your essay will be about.

3. OUTLINE YOUR IDEAS. Once you have a good topic sentence, then you need to support that main idea with more detailed information, facts, thoughts, and examples. These supporting points answer one question about your topic sentence—"Why?" This is where research and perhaps more brainstorming come in. Then organize these points in the way you think makes the most sense, probably in order of importance. Now you have an outline for your essay.

4. ON YOUR MARK, GET SET, WRITE! Follow your outline, using each of your supporting points as the topic sentence of its own paragraph. Use descriptive words to get your ideas across to the reader. Go into detail, using specific information to tell your story or make your point. Stay on track, making sure that everything you include is somehow related to the main idea of your essay. Use transitions to make your writing flow.

5. WRAP IT UP. Finish your essay with a conclusion that summarizes your entire essay and restates your main idea.

6. PROOFREAD AND REVISE. Check for errors in spelling, capitalization, punctuation, and grammar. Look for ways to make your writing clear, understandable, and interesting. Use descriptive verbs, adjectives, or adverbs when possible. It also helps to have someone else read your work to point out things you might have missed. Then make the necessary corrections and changes in a second draft. Repeat this revision process once more to make your final draft as good as you can.

Amazing Animals

A ring-tailed lemur baby clings to its mother's
back at Berenty Private Reserve in Madagascar.

WHAT IS Taxonomy?

Since there are billions and billions of living things, called organisms, on the planet, people need a way of classifying them. Scientists created a system called **taxonomy**, which helps to classify all living things into ordered groups. By putting organisms into categories we are better able to understand how they are the same and how they are different. There are seven levels of taxonomic classification, beginning with the broadest group, called a domain, down to the most specific group, called a species.

Biologists divide life based on evolutionary history, and they place organisms in three domains depending on their genetic structure: Archaea, Bacteria, and Eukarya. (See p. 175 for "The Three Domains of Life.")

Where do animals come In?

Animals are a part of the Eukarya domain, which means they are organisms made of cells with nuclei. More than one million species of animals have been named, including humans. Like all living things, animals can be divided into smaller groups, called phyla. Most scientists believe there are more than 30 phyla into which animals can be grouped based on certain scientific criteria, such as body type or whether or not the animal has a backbone. It can be pretty complicated, so there is another, less complicated system that groups animals into two categories: vertebrates and invertebrates.

Chinese stripe-necked turtle

SAMPLE CLASSIFICATION
KOALA

Domain:	Eukarya
Phylum:	Chordata
Class:	Mammalia
Order:	Diprotodontia
Family:	Phascolarctidae
Genus:	*Phascolarctos*
Species:	*cinereus*

TIP
Here's a sentence to help you remember the classification order:
Dear **P**hillip **C**ame **O**ver **F**or **G**ood **S**oup.

BY THE NUMBERS

There are 10,820 vulnerable or endangered animal species in the world. The list includes:

- **1,139 mammals**, such as the snow leopard, the polar bear, and the fishing cat.

- **1,313 birds**, including the Steller's sea eagle and the Madagascar plover.

- **2,049 fish**, such as the Mekong giant catfish.

- **807 reptiles**, including the American crocodile.

- **829 insects**, including the Macedonian grayling.

- **1,933 amphibians**, such as the Round Island day gecko.

- **And more**, including 20 arachnids, 596 crustaceans, 236 sea anemones and corals, 164 bivalves, and 1,693 snails and slugs.

COOL CLICK

For more information about the status of threatened species around the world, check out the International Union for Conservation of Nature (IUCN) Red List:
iucnredlist.org

Vertebrates Animals WITH Backbones

Fish are cold-blooded and live in water. They breathe with gills, lay eggs, and usually have scales.

Amphibians are cold-blooded. Their young live in water and breathe with gills. Adults live on land and breathe with lungs.

Reptiles are cold-blooded and breathe with lungs. They live both on land and in water.

Birds are warm-blooded and have feathers and wings. They lay eggs, breathe with lungs, and usually are able to fly. Some birds live on land, some in water, and some on both.

Mammals are warm-blooded and feed on their mothers' milk. They also have skin that is usually covered with hair. Mammals live both on land and in water.

Bird: Bald eagle

Fish: Clown anemonefish

Invertebrates Animals WITHOUT Backbones

Sponges are a very basic form of animal life. They live in water and do not move on their own.

Echinoderms have external skeletons and live in seawater.

Mollusks have soft bodies and can live either in or out of shells, on land or in water.

Arthropods are the largest group of animals. They have external skeletons, called exoskeletons, and segmented bodies with appendages. Arthropods live in water and on land.

Worms are soft-bodied animals with no true legs. Worms live in soil.

Cnidaria live in water and have mouths surrounded by tentacles.

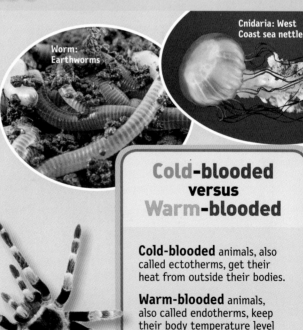

Worm: Earthworms

Cnidaria: West Coast sea nettle

Arthropod: Red-kneed tarantula

Cold-blooded versus Warm-blooded

Cold-blooded animals, also called ectotherms, get their heat from outside their bodies.

Warm-blooded animals, also called endotherms, keep their body temperature level regardless of the temperature of their environments.

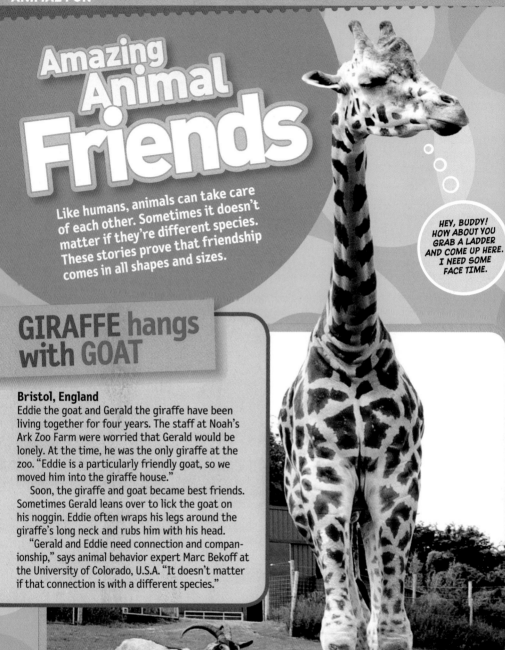

Amazing Animal Friends

Like humans, animals can take care of each other. Sometimes it doesn't matter if they're different species. These stories prove that friendship comes in all shapes and sizes.

HEY, BUDDY! HOW ABOUT YOU GRAB A LADDER AND COME UP HERE. I NEED SOME FACE TIME.

GIRAFFE hangs with GOAT

Bristol, England

Eddie the goat and Gerald the giraffe have been living together for four years. The staff at Noah's Ark Zoo Farm were worried that Gerald would be lonely. At the time, he was the only giraffe at the zoo. "Eddie is a particularly friendly goat, so we moved him into the giraffe house."

Soon, the giraffe and goat became best friends. Sometimes Gerald leans over to lick the goat on his noggin. Eddie often wraps his legs around the giraffe's long neck and rubs him with his head.

"Gerald and Eddie need connection and companionship," says animal behavior expert Marc Bekoff at the University of Colorado, U.S.A. "It doesn't matter if that connection is with a different species."

RACCOON adopts CAT

WHO IS THIS MASKED MAN?

Warstein, Germany

Raccoons usually hang out with their mom and siblings, but not in this case! This raccoon seems to have taken in a cat, who cuddles with the raccoon and its family as they lounge on rocks, and snoozes with them in a cave. The masked gang even lets the kitty have first dibs when feeding time rolls around.

Most cats are solitary, and raccoons can be territorial. So rangers at Wildpark Warstein tried to remove the cat several times. But the feline always returned to the welcoming paws of the raccoon family. "Raccoons often live in families," park chief Henning Dictus says. "I think the raccoons see the cat as part of theirs."

YES, I LOVE YOU. BUT KISSING ME IN PUBLIC IS NOT COOL!

DOG loves OWL

Cornwall, England

Before Bramble the owl takes to the sky for her daily flight, Sophi the English springer spaniel clears her for takeoff by licking the bird's beak. The Eurasian eagle owl and spaniel became best friends when two-week-old Bramble arrived at Ancient Art Falconry. "Sophi sniffed and licked the chick," says Sharon Bindon, the dog's owner, who also runs a sanctuary for birds of prey.

"Soon Bramble hopped down, toddled over to Sophi, and started following her everywhere."

They're still practically inseparable, even though in the wild this friendship would never exist. A wild owl would prey on small mammals such as mice, rabbits, and even foxes, which are about Sophi's size.

CRITTER CREATIONS

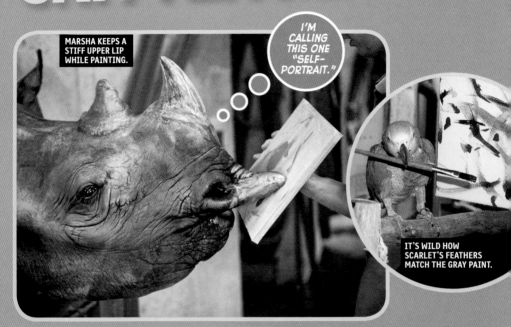

MARSHA KEEPS A STIFF UPPER LIP WHILE PAINTING.

I'M CALLING THIS ONE "SELF-PORTRAIT."

IT'S WILD HOW SCARLET'S FEATHERS MATCH THE GRAY PAINT.

Marsha the black rhino paints with her upper lip. Wiley the grizzly bear steps in paint and lumbers across a canvas. Then there's Midgie the sea lion, who paints with a brush in her mouth, then "signs" her work with a noseprint.

It's all part of an enrichment program at the Oklahoma City Zoo, in Oklahoma, U.S.A. Animals there express their wild side through art. Scarlet the African grey parrot makes masterpieces with delicate strokes, holding a small brush with his beak. "But if the canvas isn't set up when he's ready, watch out," says zoo spokesperson Tara Henson. "Scarlet will paint whatever's closest: a wall, a trash can ... even his keeper walking by."

PIG IN BOOTS!

A pig's funny-looking snout helps the animal dig.

MOST PIGS LOVE WALLOWING IN THE MUD—BUT NOT CINDERS! WHEN SHE REFUSED TO PLOD THROUGH PUDDLES, HER OWNERS FIT HER WITH TINY BOOTS TO PROTECT THE PIG'S HOOVES.

ANIMAL MYTHS BUSTED

Some people mistakenly think adult opossums hang by their tails, or that porcupines shoot their quills. What other misconceptions are out there? Here are some common animal myths.

MYTH Elephants are afraid of mice.

HOW IT MAY HAVE STARTED People used to think that mice liked to crawl into an elephant's trunk, which could cause damage and terrible sneezing. So it makes sense that elephants would be afraid of the rodents.

WHY IT'S NOT TRUE Although elephants do get anxious when they hear sounds they can't identify, their eyesight is so poor that they could barely even see a mouse. Plus, if an elephant isn't afraid to live among predators such as tigers, rhinos, and crocodiles, a mouse would be the least of its worries!

MYTH Goldfish only have a three-second memory.

HOW IT MAY HAVE STARTED While an adult human's brain weighs about three pounds (1.4 kg), an average gold-fish's brain weighs only a tiny fraction of that. So how could there be any room for memory in there?

WHY IT'S NOT TRUE Research has shown that goldfish are quite smart. Phil Gee of the University of Plymouth in the United Kingdom trained goldfish to push a lever that dropped food into their tank. "They remembered the time of day that the lever worked and waited until feeding time to press it," Gee says. One scientist even trained goldfish to tell the difference between classical and blues music!

MYTH Bulls charge when they see red.

HOW IT MAY HAVE STARTED Traditionally, a red cape is part of a bullfighter's colorful costume. When the bullfighter flashes the cape at the bull, the bull charges.

WHY IT'S NOT TRUE Movement actually makes a bull charge. "I've seen bulls chase everything from red to blue to plaid," says Temple Grandin of the Colorado State University in Colorado, U.S.A. "It's the motion of the bullfighter's cape, not the color."

PLAY like a DOLPHIN

A dolphin's day always includes some time spent clowning around. Dolphins can turn almost any floating object into a toy. Some dolphins drape themselves in seaweed; others toss it into the air and try to catch it. Amazon river dolphins play catch with coconuts. Male dolphins sometimes carry objects when trying to woo females. A male will pick up a branch, a rock, or a clump of weeds and twirl in a circle in an attempt to impress the ladies!

Sometimes dolphins use objects as tools, not just as toys. Some bottlenose dolphins off the coast of Australia protect their noses with sponges as they dig in the ocean floor for food. Dolphins have also been observed pushing massive shells to the water's surface. Then they give the shells a shake to force out fish hiding inside.

Dolphins don't necessarily need props for fun. They can chase one another in a game like tag, jump acrobatically, and cuddle with a playmate. Dolphins even get a kick out of playing with other species. They tease eels to coax them out of their holes and prod puffer fish to make them inflate. Play nice, dolphins!

MY FINNED FRIEND

MAJA KAZAZIC HAD BECOME used to living with pain—and feeling different. As a teen, Maja lost her leg after she was badly injured during the Bosnian civil war. But even after treatment, an uncomfortable prosthesis—or artificial body part—made every movement painful.

Maja's life changed when she met Winter, a dolphin at Clearwater Marine Aquarium in Florida, U.S.A. Winter had lost her tail in a crab trap as a baby. Maja felt a connection with the tailless dolphin.

When Winter got a high-tech tail to help her swim, Maja wondered if a similar product could help her be pain free. The aquarium put Maja in touch with the company that made Winter's prosthesis. Maja received a new leg out of the same materials that helped Winter. Soon the pair were swimming together—one with a new leg, the other with a new tail!

DOLPHINS' COOL MOVES

Sure, they're great swimmers, but check out the other abilities that make dolphins **ALL-STAR AQUA ATHLETES.**

SPIN CYCLE
Spinner dolphins rotate in the air—like a football—as they leap.

TAIL WALKING
In this stunt, a dolphin stands on its fluke and scoots across the water. It's a common trick dolphins perform in captivity.

BENDY BODY
Amazon river dolphins have very flexible necks that they use to snake their way through tangled underwater branches.

OCEAN SUPERSTARS

The fascinating lives of 6 sea turtle species

Think all sea turtles are the same? Think again! Each of these species stands out in its own way.

1 GREEN SEA TURTLE: THE NEAT FREAK

In Hawaii, U.S.A., green sea turtles choose a "cleaning station"—a location where groups of cleaner fish groom the turtles by eating ocean gunk, like algae and parasites, off their skin and shells. In Australia, the turtles rub against a favorite sponge or rock to scrub themselves. Neat!

2 KEMP'S RIDLEY: THE LITTLE ONE

They may be the smallest sea turtles, but they're not so tiny: Adults weigh as much as many ten-year-old kids, and their shell is about the size of a car tire. They're speedy, too: It takes them less than an hour to dig a nest, then lay and bury their eggs.

3 **OLIVE RIDLEY: THE ULTRA MOM**
Every year, hundreds of thousands of female olive ridley sea turtles take over beaches to lay their eggs and then bury them before disappearing back into the sea. Call it safety in numbers: With thousands of turtles swarming the shoreline, they're sure to overwhelm any predator.

4 **LEATHERBACK: THE MEGA TURTLE**
These giants among reptiles have shells about as a big as a door and weigh as much as six professional football players! Their size doesn't slow them down, though. A leatherback can swim as fast as a bottlenose dolphin.

5 **HAWKSBILL: THE HEARTY EATER**
What's the hawksbill's favorite snack? Sponges! These turtles gobble about 1,200 pounds (544 kg) of sponges a year. The turtles can safely eat this sea life, which is toxic to other animals. That means there are plenty of sponges to snack on!

6 **LOGGERHEAD: THE TOUGH GUY**
The loggerhead sea turtle's powerful jaws can easily crack open the shells of lobsters, conchs, and snails to get at the meat inside. Some loggerheads swim a third of the way around the world to find food.

Meet the
PENGUINS

Check out 10 of the world's coolest penguin species.

Rockhopper

Both northern and southern rockhopper penguins are expert climbers. They use their sharp claws to hop and scramble up steep cliffs to nest. The two species live in the subarctic. Only northern rockhoppers are endangered.

Little

More than a half million tourists a year watch the nightly parade of these blue-gray, football-size penguins from New Zealand and Australia returning to their burrows after foraging at sea.

Adélie

Adélie penguins must win a deadly game of freeze tag while crossing thin ice in Antarctica. Leopard seals lurk below, watching for movement. If an Adélie sees a predator, it "freezes" until the danger passes.

Emperor

Emperor penguins are the largest species—as tall as a seven-year-old kid. They can dive 1,853 feet (565 m) straight down and hold their breath underwater for up to 22 minutes.

Galápagos

Instead of fighting frostbite, these penguins battle sunburn. That's because they live on the Galápagos Islands at the Equator. They shade their feet with their flippers to avoid sunburn.

Gentoo

When a gentoo parent returns from hunting subantarctic seas, it races away from its chicks. But hungry chicks will follow. Once a chick is fed and full, it won't bother chasing its parent anymore.

Royal

Royal penguins spend about four months each year eating and sleeping at sea—somewhere between Australia and Antarctica.

Macaroni

Every October, about 18 million macaroni penguins nest on the hillsides and cliffs of Antarctic and sub-atlantic shorelines. Macaronis have the largest population of all penguins.

African

The only species that breeds on the coast of Africa, the African penguin faces land predators such as leopards, rats, snakes, and mongooses. It is known for its mating call, which sounds like a braying donkey.

Yellow-eyed

Unlike penguins that nest together in crowded colonies, yellow-eyed penguins hide in coastal forests and shrubland far from any other penguin's nest.

SuperShark AWARDS

FASTER THAN A SPEEDING BULLETFISH, LEAPING SMALL BOATS IN A SINGLE BOUND . . . it's Super Shark! Most of the 450 to 500 shark species go about their lives in secrecy, but a few stand out. Here are some of the world's super sharks.

Fantastic Fish

Whale sharks are the world's largest shark—and fish. Possibly reaching lengths up to 65 feet (20 m), it's larger than two city buses. Weighing up to 74,970 pounds (34,006 kg), it doesn't just tip the scales, it smashes them!

When threatened, a swell shark doubles its size by gulping water. Once safe it makes a doglike bark and burps out all the water.

Best Burp (and bark)

During the day, as many as 36 nurse sharks pile on top of each other as they rest in caves and crevices.

Best Dog Pile

Peewee Predators

One of the smallest sharks, the dwarf lanternshark is only 6.6 to 7.8 inches (17–20 cm)—about as long as a pencil.

Speed Chaser

Shredding the water at 31 miles per hour (50 kph), a shortfin mako shark is the world's fastest shark. Makos are faster than bottlenose dolphins (22 mph/35 kph) and killer whales (30 mph/48 kph). Their speed makes them too fast for most predators— except humans.

High Jump

A shortfin mako can leap 20 feet (6 m) above the water surface. That's higher than a giraffe's head.

Mystery of the Disappearing FROGS

Frogs survived the catastrophic extinction of the dinosaurs. But strangely, the world's frogs and toads have suddenly begun to disappear. Some species that were common 25 years ago are now rare or extinct. And individual frogs are showing up with deformities such as too many legs. Scientists are not sure exactly what is going on.

But scientists do agree that because frogs drink and breathe through their thin skin, they are especially vulnerable to pesticides and pollution. A deformed frog often indicates that all is not well with the environment. And frogs live just about everywhere on Earth.

Frogs are amphibians, which means "double life." They generally hatch in water as tadpoles and end up living on land as fully formed frogs. Frogs' skin must stay moist, so they're usually found in wet places.

Because frogs are so sensitive to environmental changes, they act as an early-warning system.

Their dwindling numbers may be a sign that our planet is not as clean and healthy as it once was. By studying how frogs are affected by the environment around them, scientists may be able to predict—and sound an alarm—that a neighborhood needs to cut back on lawn fertilizers or that a chemical-dumping factory should clean up its act. The hidden message in frogs' familiar peeps and croaks? "I'm jumpy for a reason!"

SOME FROGS GLOW WHEN THEY EAT FIREFLIES.

CALLING ALL FROGS

Frogs bark, croak, cluck, click, grunt, snore, squawk, chirp, whistle, trill, and yap. Some frogs are named for the noise they make. A chorus of barking tree frogs sounds like a pack of hounds on a hunt. The carpenter frog sounds like two carpenters hammering nails, and the pig frog grunts like—you guessed it—Porky's cousin! The male Australian red-eyed tree frog (top of page) inflates his throat pouch, which helps make his female-attracting calls louder.

5 COOL THINGS ABOUT KOALAS

A koala doesn't look like the kind of creature that keeps campers awake at night or dines on food that would give you a serious stomachache. There's a lot more to these living "teddy bears" than cotton-ball ears and a laid-back lifestyle. Check out five amazing things about these wild, loud, and lovable creatures from Australia.

1. Loudmouths
Imagine a burp so loud it brings you to your knees, followed by a snore that rattles the rafters. Combine them and you have the typical bellow of a koala. Why so noisy? Male koalas grunt with gusto to broadcast their whereabouts to distant females or to scare rivals.

2. Toxic Diet
Koalas eat one to two pounds (450 to 900 g) of eucalyptus leaves each day. The leaves are not only poisonous—they're tough to digest and provide little nutrition. But koalas have a specially adapted digestive system that extracts every drop of energy from the leaves while neutralizing their toxins.

3. Mistaken Identity
The Europeans who first settled in Australia mistook these tree dwellers for a type of bear, and the name "koala bear" stuck. However, a koala is actually a marsupial—a type of mammal that protects and nurtures its tiny newborns in a pouch.

4. Feisty Guys
A koala may look like a stuffed animal, but you'd be sorry if you tried to cuddle a wild one. Their long, sharp claws—supremely adapted for climbing trees—are used as daggers when two male koalas argue over territory or a mate.

5. Awesome Moms
Born blind, hairless, and no bigger than a jelly bean, a baby koala spends six months sleeping and drinking milk in its mother's pouch. Eventually, it will poke its head out to eat pap—a poopy soup from its mother that builds resistance to eucalyptus poison. When the joey leaves the pouch, the mama koala carries it on her back or belly as she climbs trees and teaches the tiny koala by example.

The Fox Next Door

T he sun starts to set in northern Virginia, U.S.A., and a red fox wakes up, ready to search for dinner. She steps silently through the bushes, following an appetizing scent to a wooden fence. The red fox squeezes through a narrow gap in the fence, then leaps over the edge of . . . an open garbage can. She tears through a plastic bag and snatches some scraps of grilled chicken. As the fox climbs out, the garbage can tips over with a crash. Backyard lights turn on, but the sly fox has already disappeared with her meal.

RED FOXES COULD BE MOVING

URBAN WILDLIFE

This dinnertime scenario is becoming more and more common across the United States. Cities and suburbs are spreading into the countryside, swallowing up red fox habitat. But instead of moving, these clever wild animals learn to thrive near people. "Red foxes can be scavengers or predators, whatever they need to get food and find den sites," says Vicky Monroe, a wildlife biologist in Fairfax County, Virginia, U.S.A., which is just outside

PEOPLE MUST NEVER FEED FOXES AND SHOULD ALWAYS MAINTAIN A DISTANCE FROM THEM. WILDLIFE BIOLOGIST VICKY MONROE ADVISES COVERING GARBAGE CANS AND BRINGING PETS AND PET FOOD IN AT NIGHT.

Washington, D.C. To avoid people, skillful red foxes hunt at night in backyards, gardens, and city parks. Although rabbits as well as mice and other rodents are their favorite fare, red foxes will eat birds, frogs, snakes, grasshoppers, and even berries. A hungry red fox will also jump into an open Dumpster or garbage can for tasty leftovers or nibble on pet food that is left out on the porch.

MOVING IN

As winter begins near Denver, Colorado, U.S.A., two red foxes pair up to mate and raise a family. Needing a place to nestle, the foxes sneak under a porch. This is prime real estate, hidden from people, with plenty of rodents nearby. They'll stay here until their six pups, or kits, start to explore the world. By October, the members of the red fox family will leave the safety of the porch, each in search of its own den site.

The clever red foxes find creative accommodations. They have been known to squeeze through gates, scale high fences, and break into sheds and garages. One scientist says he knew of a red fox that found its way into a college sports stadium and slept on the field during the off-season.

STREET SAVVY

In the woods, a red fox is prowling for new territory. Other foxes have marked their range here already, so this male ventures farther away where there will be less competition for

LOCATION, LOCATION, LOCATION
Red foxes are the most widespread meat-eating mammals in the world. Their natural range covers much of the Northern Hemisphere.

INTO YOUR NEIGHBORHOOD.

food. The red fox wanders to a suburban park. His search is over; here he will live closer to other foxes than he would in the countryside, but there is plenty of food and no predators in sight.

But that doesn't mean this fox is out of danger. His ears pick up a sound he recognizes. He freezes at the park's edge. He sits and waits. A car zooms past. Satisfied that the threat is gone, the fox trots across the road, slinking into the bushes on the other side.

Why did the fox cross the road? Because people put it there.

CANINE COUSINS
They are small and seem catlike, but red foxes are relatives of dogs, wolves, and coyotes.

55

Meerkat CITY

Meerkats always have something to do. These mongoose relatives live in busy communities, with no time to sit around being bored. In their family groups of up to 40 members, everyone pitches in to get all the jobs done.

A SENTINEL KEEPS WATCH.

Guards

Meerkats are very territorial. Guards, called sentinels, are always on the lookout for rival meerkats that try to move in on their territory. If a sentinel (left) spots any intruding meerkats, it sends out an alarm call. The whole group gathers together and stands tall to try to scare away the rivals. If that doesn't work, meerkats quickly decide whether to fight or retreat.

Predators such as eagles or jackals rate a different warning call. If a sentinel spots the predator first, it lets out an alarm call that sends all the meerkats scurrying into the nearest bolt hole—an underground safety den where the eagle can't follow.

Babysitters

Within a meerkat group, the alpha, or leader, female and the alpha male are usually the only ones that have babies. When their babies are too young to follow along while they search for food, meerkat parents have to go without them. So they leave their pups with babysitters—other adult meerkats in the group. The pups stay inside their family's underground burrow for the first three weeks of life, protected and cared for by the babysitters.

Diggers

Picture yourself looking for a tasty bug to eat (below) when suddenly you hear the alarm call for "eagle." You dash left, you dash right, and you finally find a bolt hole.

Bolt holes provide fast getaways for meerkats in danger. Members of the group cooperate to make sure bolt holes are properly dug out, that nothing is blocking the entry, and that there are enough bolt holes in every area.

Meerkats are built to be superdiggers. All four of their paws have long, sturdy claws that they use like rakes. They dig to find food, such as lizards and other small reptiles, insects and their larvae, and scorpions.

DIGGING FOR FOOD

HOME SWEET BURROW

WILD DOGS OF AFRICA

The puppy-dog eyes and pleading squeals of a five-month-old African wild dog named Cici can mean only one thing: dinnertime. An older sister in Cici's pack responds, dragging over a meaty impala bone. In African wild dog society, puppies have all the power. "It's up to the older siblings to take care of the puppies," says Micaela Gunther, a scientist who studies wild dogs, including Cici's family. "The doting grown-ups even deliver toys, such as a strip of impala skin perfect for puppy tug-of-war." Imagine your big brother or sister working hard to hand you snacks and games while you eat, play, and rest all day.

DOG DAYS

Like wolves, wild dogs live in a pack of up to 15 dogs. Pups stay in the pack for about two years. Then some may break off to start packs of their own, while others stay with their mom and dad.

When the pups are newborn, every member of the pack works together to provide for them. At first the puppies stay near the den, often under the watch of a babysitter while the pack hunts. Returning pack members throw up meat for the pups. Sound gross? Puppies love these leftovers.

PACK ATTACK

By the time the pups are six months old, they join the pack on hunting expeditions. First they learn how to stalk prey, and eventually they participate in the kill. Single 60-pound (27-kg) dogs rarely catch larger prey on their own, but a pack of 20 proves that there really is strength in numbers. Together they can take down a zebra or wildebeest weighing up to a thousand pounds (454 kg).

Hunting wild dogs often pursue herds of gazelle for miles, fresh dogs trading places with tired ones. Eventually the weakest of the chased animals tires. The dogs surround it and attack from every direction. This teamwork is bred from the pack's intense social bonding, such as the daily greeting ceremonies and puppy play sessions. Team-building is the reason wild dogs spoil the pups, who grow up united and ready to contribute to the strength of the pack.

6 Tips Every Polar

Life in the frozen wilds of the Arctic Circle isn't exactly easy, even if you're a polar bear, the world's largest land-dwelling predator. To withstand the subzero temperatures, snow-covered landscapes, and day after day without sun, you're going to need to put all 1,500 pounds (680 kg) of your muscle, bone, and body fat to good use. If you were a polar bear, here's what you'd need to know to survive on the Arctic ice.

1

Walk, Don't Run . . . or Better Yet, Sit Still.

When walking or running, a polar bear expends more than twice the energy used by most other mammals. Want to save energy? Don't move at all. If you do run, make it a short trip. After a five-mile (8-km) run, even young bears in good shape can become overheated.

2

Bearfoot . . . *hmm . . . Bare*foot Is Best.

Ever wonder why your paws are so big? On an adult, they're huge—up to 12 inches (30 cm) across. Working like snowshoes, they spread weight across the snow and ice, keeping you from sinking. That way your paws don't make any crunching noises, which could warn prey that "Bigfoot" is on the way.

3

Don't Let Cubs Become Polar Bear Snacks.

It's a harsh fact of Arctic life that adult males sometimes kill and eat polar bear cubs, so mother bears are very protective. Most will chase away male polar bears much bigger than they are. Male bears are not the only threats from which moms defend their cubs. Some brave mothers will rear up on their hind legs to leap at hovering helicopters!

Bear Should Know

Fat's Where It's At.

Since you live in the cold Arctic climate, having a layer of fat is a good thing. That fat, called blubber, works like a fleece vest—it insulates your body from the frosty air and near-freezing water. When food is scarce, your four-inch (10-cm)-thick blubber gives you energy and helps keep you afloat when you swim because fat weighs less than water.

5

4

Neatness Counts. So Does Drying Off.

A clean bear is a warm bear. That's because dirty, matted fur doesn't hold body heat like clean fur does. After eating, spend up to 15 minutes cleaning yourself—licking your chest, paws, and muzzle with your long tongue. In summertime, take baths right after you eat. Then dry yourself by shaking off excess moisture or using snow like a thick, fluffy towel to rub the water away.

6

Always Wear White.

You may have noticed that the hairs in your thick fur coat aren't really white. Each is transparent with a hollow core that reflects light. This helps you to blend with your surroundings—a neat trick, especially while you're hunting wary seals. Good thing wearing white is always stylish for polar bears.

ROCK-A-BYE
MONKEY

INTAN ENJOYS ACROBATICS.

INTAN CUDDLES WITH HER MOM WHEN SHE'S READY TO REST.

Gleefully vaulting from branch to branch, Intan, a six-week-old monkey, is so daring—and so uncoordinated. She slips, then screams for help while dangling from 60 feet (18 m) up a tree. Mom and other females in the troop rush to her rescue.

Ebony langurs, a kind of monkey, spend most of their lives high in the forest canopy. There they effortlessly leap from tree to tree. But today is Intan's first day in a real tree in a real forest. The troop was just released from captivity into the forest of Bromo Tengger Semeru National Park on the island of Java in Indonesia.

Monkey Business

Illegally captured from the wild and sold as pets, the monkeys in this troop are survivors. The Indonesian Conservation Department rescued them, bringing them to a center where caregivers prepare them for release back into the wild. Little Intan is born while the troop is at the center.

When the monkeys are released, biologists and photographers hide on an observation platform high in a tree to watch them settle in. But the monkeys easily find the observers.

Nice Trip. See You Next Fall!

Intan's mother becomes exasperated as she rescues her baby from climbing predicaments. After a few falls, she carries Intan to the not-so-secret blind, and puts her in photographer Djuna Ivereigh's lap.

Before Ivereigh can move the baby from her lap, Intan leaps up to play with a stick. Chasing it across the platform, Intan accidentally topples over the edge. The humans watch in horror as the baby tumbles 25 feet (8 m) to the ground!

Shrieking langurs rush toward the motionless monkey. Scooping up Intan, Mom gently rocks her baby. Very soon, Intan peeks out, unharmed. She bounds away for more monkey mischief.

The dirty looks the troop give Ivereigh suggest their opinion of her babysitting skills. The near-disastrous result may achieve one goal, though: No troop member will ever trust a human with one of its own again.

Will the RED PANDA Survive?

A mask marks one of the cutest faces in the forest. The red panda looks a little like a raccoon, a bit like a fox, and somewhat like a puppy. Soft, cuddly, reddish fur blankets its body, which is a tad larger than a big house cat's. These harmless creatures live in the high mountain forests of the Himalaya in southeastern Asia. But their numbers in the wild are dwindling.

As loggers and firewood collectors chop down trees, and ranchers allow overgrazing by domestic livestock, the fragile mountain habitat of the red panda erodes.

SPECIALIZED DIET

The diet of the red panda also makes it vulnerable, because it is one of just a few mammal species in the world that eat mainly bamboo. It's not the most nutritious stuff. This giant grass has tough stems and leaves that make it difficult to chew and digest. A bamboo diet doesn't give red pandas much energy, so they have to conserve as much as possible.

SLOW-MOVING SLEEPYHEADS

Red pandas save energy simply by keeping activity to a minimum. They spend six to eight hours a day moving around and eating. The rest of their time is spent resting and sleeping. Their bodies are built to conserve energy. When the weather is cold, the pandas curl into a tight ball on a tree branch and go into a very deep sleep. This reduces their metabolism, or the amount of energy they use. When red pandas wake up, their metabolism returns to normal. But as soon as they go back to sleep their metabolism drops again, saving energy.

Saving the BLUE IGUANA

Found only on the Caribbean island of Grand Cayman, in the Cayman Islands, the blue iguana is one of the most endangered species of lizards in the world. It can't protect itself against threats such as the construction of houses and roads, or predators such as snakes, cats, and dogs. When the number of these wild, dragonlike creatures dropped to fewer than 25 several years ago, experts took action. They began breeding them in captivity. The program has been so successful that some 750 blue iguanas now live wild on the island. Luckily, it may be blue skies ahead for these living "dragons."

COOL CLICK

Test your knowledge of endangered animals at animals.nationalgeographic.com/animals/endangered-animals-quiz/

5 COOL THINGS ABOUT HARP SEALS

With their irresistible faces and fluffy fur, harp seals are some of the cutest animals around. But their snow-white pelts and icy habitat make harp seals especially vulnerable to hunters, global warming, and other environmental threats. Here's more about harp seals—and why it's extra-important to protect these adorable animals.

1 6,000-MILE JOURNEY

Each year, harp seals migrate more than 6,000 miles (9,600 km), spending summers feeding in northern Arctic coastal waters and heading back south in the fall to breed. They migrate in small groups of up to 20 individuals. By late February, harp seals gather in large herds. As many as one million form an enormous herd found on the floating mass of pack ice in the Gulf of St. Lawrence in Canada. Once breeding season is over, the seals travel back north for the summer.

2 SEE-THROUGH COAT

When a harp seal pup is born, its coat has a yellow tint. But it turns completely white within a couple of days. The fine, silky fur is almost transparent. This allows the pup's skin to absorb the sun's rays, which helps it stay warm. The whitecoats, as they are called, look like this only for about two weeks. Then they molt, or shed, their white fur. Their new coats are gray.

DID YOU KNOW?
Harp seals are known as "earless" seals because they don't have external earflaps.

3 HEART TRICK

When a young harp seal sees a polar bear, instinct takes over. The pup can't escape the predator by running away, so it hides—in plain sight. The ball of white fur plays possum. The seal lies motionless with its head tucked into its chubby neck, looking like a heap of snow (below). The pup's heart rate slows from about 80 to 90 beats a minute to only 20 to 30 beats. If the trick works, the bear doesn't see the harp seal and moves on. Then the seal can stretch out and relax. Whew!

4 DEEP DIVERS

It's not unusual for a harp seal to hold its breath for five minutes. But when it needs to, the seal can stay underwater for as long as 20 minutes and dive more than 800 feet (244 m) down. That's six times deeper than a scuba diver can go safely. Harp seals can get places fast, too—100 feet (30 m) down in 15 seconds. As the seals zip through the water hunting for fish, they also stay alert for orcas and sharks that might eat *them*.

5 QUICK-CHANGE ARTISTS

By the time a harp seal is 14 months old, it has changed coats—and nicknames—five times. A whitecoat at first, it then becomes a graycoat, a ragged jacket, a beater, and finally a bedlamer. At four years old a harp seal has a silvery gray coat with a few spots—and it's called a spotted harp. Some females look like that the rest of their lives. Males, as well as many females, develop a distinctive black pattern that is shaped like a harp, which explains the name of the species.

PANDA SHAKE-UP

BEFORE THE EARTHQUAKE, PANDAS PLAY AT THE CENTER.

Giant Panda Home Gets Extreme Makeover

An earthquake rocks China, shaking the ground around the giant pandas and their caregivers at the Wolong Giant Panda Breeding Center in Sichuan Province. Two minutes of terror destroys schools and bamboo forests, and leaves the center in shambles. The pandas are taken to temporary quarters.

China Conservation and Research Center for the Giant Panda, which operates the Wolong center, is the world's largest giant panda breeding and research facility and home to half of the world's captive pandas. Fewer than 2,000 giant pandas are left in the wild. Rebuilding of the Wolong is crucial to the giant panda's survival as a species, so construction began at the end of 2010.

MOVING UP

The new breeding center will be bigger and better than the one destroyed in the 2008 earthquake. In the nursery section, panda mothers and human caregivers will take care of newborns. When a cub is a year old and ready to leave its mother, it will move into the panda kindergarten. That's where it will learn how to find food and explore new environments. Wolong will also have a program to release some captive-born pandas into the wild.

The new captive panda center is planting trees and bamboo in the enormous panda enclosures. In the reintroduction program, pandas will be able to experience a wild setting while scientists monitor their health and safety.

Scientists at Wolong have also worked to restore habitats where human activities have left groups of wild pandas isolated. The goal is to restore wildlife corridors between habitats so that smaller panda populations do not become permanently isolated and unable to reproduce.

AFTER THE EARTHQUAKE, MUCH WAS DESTROYED.

THIS 37-DAY-OLD GIANT PANDA CUB RESTS IN AN INCUBATOR.

ASIA

CHINA

Earthquake epicenter

SICHUAN PROVINCE

Giant panda breeding center

Animal

BEFORE

AFTER

Horse

The exhausted horse can barely walk, but the drug smugglers force it farther into the desert. After overloading the animal with drugs, they're sneaking across the border from Mexico into a remote part of Arizona, U.S.A. Nearly 400 pounds (181 kg) of drugs are carelessly roped onto the horse without any padding. The ropes lashed across his bare back rub through his hair and cut into his skin.

TO THE RESCUE

Then U.S. Border Patrol officers arrive. The smugglers leave the horse as they run and hide. The officers cut the bloody ropes and free the horse from his burden. They call Karen Pomroy, who rehabilitates injured and unwanted horses. She takes him to her sanctuary, feeds him, and names him Sundance.

A NEW HORSE

After five months, Sundance's back is almost healed and he's gained 300 pounds (136 kg). He finally responds to human kindness. "He looks like a million bucks now," says Pomroy.

Harbor Seal

A stranded harbor seal pup cries for his mother, who has disappeared into the cold ocean surf, probably scared off by tourists visiting the Washington State, U.S.A., shore. A vacationing couple hears the spotted pup, and, hoping to help, they carry him to their motel room and crank up the heat. Insulated with blubber, a thick layer of fat, the seal pup overheats.

CRY FOR HELP

The next morning, the couple calls Cascadia Research, a marine mammal protection organization. The pup is dehydrated, overheated, and stressed. The rescuers take the pup to a rehabilitation center so he can be treated and returned to the ocean.

There, rehabilitators feed the pup a formula that closely matches his mother's milk. As the weeks go by, he learns to eat fish. Within two months, he has grown into a sleek, powerful animal who weighs more than 50 pounds (23 kg) and has a full set of teeth. The pup is ready to go back to the sea.

PREPARING FOR RELEASE

Rescues

Serval

Park rangers in Africa's Masai Mara National Reserve are conducting a controlled burn to help the health of the park's vegetation. The fire reaches the home of a family of servals, who have a den hidden inside the brush. One of the babies in the den wanders off alone into the smoke. His mother cannot find him.

MOTO AS A KITTEN

RUNNING FREE

HELP SHOWS UP

Later, tourists spot the orphaned serval kitten in the middle of a dirt road. Their guide delivers it to park rangers, who contact Suzi Eszterhas, a wildlife photographer who has worked with servals. She agrees to raise him and names him "Moto," the local word for "fire." Eszterhas's goal is to someday return Moto to the wild.

BACK TO THE WILD

Eszterhas feeds Moto special milk by bottle and eventually gives him dead rats, since servals eat rodents in the wild. Eszterhas also lets the nocturnal Moto explore the savanna at night. Eventually, Moto wanders off for good. A couple of weeks later, a park ranger who helped care for Moto visits Eszterhas with exciting news. While on a dirt trail, he recognized the cat. Eszterhas is ecstatic that Moto is safe.

BACK HOME

The release site is not far from where the pup was found. When the seal slips into the water, his big, dark eyes take in the scene. His silver whiskers quiver with anticipation. The seal dives underwater, then pops back up, then dives back into the wild where he belongs.

SWIMMING FREE

BIG CATS

A young male jaguar

The world's big cats are disappearing. Find out more and discover ways you can help at http://animals.nationalgeographic .com/animals/big-cats/

What are big cats? To wildlife experts, they are the four living members of the genus *Panthera:* tigers, lions, leopards, and jaguars. They can all unleash a mighty roar and, as carnivores, they survive solely on the flesh of other animals. Thanks to powerful jaws; long, sharp claws; and daggerlike teeth, big cats are excellent hunters.

WHO'S WHO?

FUR

BIG CATS MAY HAVE a lot of features in common, but if you know what to look for, you'll be able to tell who's who in no time.

Most tigers are orange-colored with vertical black stripes on their bodies. This coloring helps the cats blend in with tall grasses as they sneak up on prey. These markings are like fingerprints: No two stripe patterns are alike.

TIGERS

JAGUARS

A jaguar's coat pattern looks similar to that of a leopard, as both have dark spots called rosettes. The difference? The rosettes on a jaguar's torso have irregularly shaped borders and at least one black dot in the center.

LEOPARDS

A leopard's yellowy coat has dark spots called rosettes on its back and sides. In leopards, the rosettes' edges are smooth and circular. This color combo helps leopards blend into their surroundings.

LIONS

Lions have a light brown, or tawny, coat and a tuft of black hair at the end of their tails. When they reach their prime, most male lions have shaggy manes that help them look larger and more intimidating.

JAGUAR
100 to 250 pounds
(45 TO 113 KG)

5 to 6 feet long
(1.5 TO 1.8 M)

LEOPARD
66 to 176 pounds
(30 TO 80 KG)

4.25 to 6.25 feet long
(1.3 TO 1.9 M)

BENGAL TIGER
240 to 500 pounds
(109 TO 227 KG)

5 to 6 feet long
(1.5 TO 1.8 M)

AFRICAN LION
265 to 420 pounds
(120 TO 191 KG)

4.5 to 6.5 feet long
(1.4 TO 2 M)

CHEETAHS: *Built for* SPEED

This wild cat's body makes it an incredible predator.

Breathing deeply, the cheetah prepares her body for the chase. Head low, eyes focused on an impala, she slowly inches forward. In three seconds this streamlined, superfast cat is sprinting at 60 miles an hour (96 kph), eyes locked, laserlike, on the fleeing impala.

> **Long, muscular tail for balance in tight turns**

The legendary Jamaican runner Usain Bolt is the world's fastest human. Bolt ran 200 meters in 19.19 seconds, about 23 miles an hour (37 kph), but that's slow compared with the cheetah. Cheetahs can run about three times faster than Bolt. At top speed a sprinting cheetah can reach 70 miles an hour (113 kph). Next time you're in a car on the highway, imagine a cheetah racing alongside you. That will give you an idea of how fast this speedy cat can run.

Several adaptations help cheetahs run so fast. A cheetah has longer legs than other cats. It also has a

> **Small, short face with enlarged nostrils to take in lots of air**

long, extremely flexible spine. These features work together so a running cheetah can cover up to 23 feet (7 m) in one stride—about the length of five ten-year-olds lying head to feet in a row.

Most other cats can retract their claws when they're not using them. Cheetahs' claws stick out all the time, like dogs' claws. Cheetahs use these strong, blunt claws like an athlete uses cleats on track shoes—to help push off and quickly build up speed. The large center pad on the cheetah's foot is covered with long ridges that act like the treads on a car tire. A sprinting cheetah needs to be able to stop fast, too. It is able to spread its toes wide, and its toe pads are hard and pointed. This helps a cheetah turn quickly

> **Strong, blunt claws and ridged footpads to grip the ground**

and brake suddenly. It can stop in a single stride from a speed of more than 20 miles an hour (32 kph).

All these body adaptations add up to extraordinary hunting abilities. A cheetah stalks up close to a herd of impalas, then streaks forward with lightning speed. As the herd bolts, the cat singles out one individual and follows its twists and turns precisely. As it closes in on its prey the cheetah strikes out with a forepaw, knocks the animal off its feet, and clamps its jaws over the prey's throat.

Snow Leopard SECRETS

High-tech tools help scientists understand how to save these big cats.

On a cool summer night, a snow leopard curiously sniffs an overhanging boulder for a strong scent sprayed by other cats. He rubs his cheeks on the boulder, scrapes the ground with his hind paws, and then urinates.

This act—called scraping—is how snow leopards communicate with one another. A scrape tells other snow leopards what they're doing and may reveal whether a snow leopard is male or female, has cubs, or is looking for a mate.

Recently, researchers studying the 4,000 to 7,000 snow leopards in the wild have set up motion-activated cameras at scraping sites. This is in an effort to gather more information on these elusive cats and expose many new details about how many snow leopards there are, how long they live, and how we can protect them.

Even though snow leopards live in some of the most rugged mountain terrain on Earth, people pose the biggest threat to their survival. Poachers can sell a snow leopard's hide and bones for thousands of dollars. Herders often kill any snow leopard that attacks their livestock. Hunters target ibex, wild sheep, and other animals for food and trophies—removing important snow leopard prey.

Like a snow leopard reality show, the cameras expose everything that happens. The images also help researchers count the number of snow leopards in an area and reveal whether prey animals, livestock, or poachers are nearby.

Other researchers will gently trap the wild cats to put on satellite radio collars to track where the cats roam, and to learn new things about how and where they live. Technology like this is essential to help researchers protect snow leopards in the wild and protect their habitat.

Despite their name, snow leopards are not snow-colored. Their spotted gray or beige fur actually stands out against a snowy background—but blends in with rocks.

MARKING TERRITORY

TWO CUBS

CHASING DOWN PREY

THINK LIKE A *Tiger*

Getting inside a tiger's mind could help save a species.

A TIGER CAN TELL IT'S IN ANOTHER'S TERRITORY BY SNIFFING TREES MARKED WITH URINE.

TIGERS LIVE IN BOTH COLD AND HOT CLIMATES.

TIGERS ARE SO RARE that fewer than 4,000 remain in the wild. The problem is not so much that the forests tigers live in are disappearing, says Ullas Karanth, a senior conservation scientist with the New York–based Wildlife Conservation Society. "Worldwide, there is habitat enough to support 50,000 tigers."

The problem is that the forests are empty. Local human hunters have wiped out the deer, wild pigs, and wild cattle that tigers prey on. Without food—at least the equivalent of one elk-size deer a week—tigers can't survive and multiply. "They vanish," says Karanth.

Karanth believes tigers need their own space. This can be done by finding a potential tiger habitat and paying the people who live there to move to new settlements. But first scientists must know how many tigers there are and where they live.

To find that out, Karanth has developed a way to count tigers. He places hundreds of motion-activated cameras in a forest in India. These cameras sense animals passing by and snap their picture. To figure out where to place the cameras to catch the elusive tigers, Karanth tries to think like a tiger.

TIGER SECRETS

Where can you find a tiger? Water holes are always a good bet. Tigers go there to drink to cool off, and to ambush prey. A hungry tiger might also visit a salt lick, where soil is naturally salty. Deer often gather there.

TIGERS ARE STEALTH HUNTERS, EVEN IN WATER!

How do tigers get there? To reach their destinations, tigers usually opt for the easiest route. They follow old logging trails, dry riverbeds, and dirt roads. Paw prints are easy to spot in soft soil, and a tiger marking its territory might scratch the ground and drop waste three times each mile (1.6 km). However, distinguishing tiger droppings from those of a leopard or wild dog takes some experience, as does smelling urine spray on bushes or trees. Karanth can pick up the scent of tiger urine in the air. It smells strong—musky and sweet.

SMILE, PLEASE

After lazing about all afternoon, a tiger yawns and rises to his feet. He's getting hungry. He goes on the hunt. Spying him from a grassy hillside, a herd of deer suddenly raise their tails and scream an alarm call. No matter. Even if it takes him 30 tries to make a kill, his belly will soon be full. Before long, the wild cat ambles past a motion sensor and click! A camera snaps a portrait of one well-fed tiger that gives Karanth a reason to smile.

ALMOST ANY ANIMAL A TIGER CAN CATCH IS ON ITS MENU.

Nature's SUPERCATS LEOPARDS

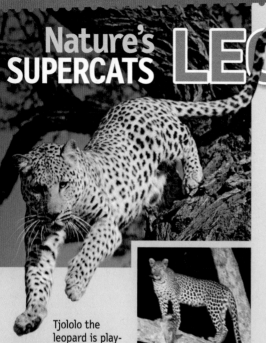

POWERFUL PROWLERS

No big cat is more at home in a tree than a leopard. It's in the trees that leopards often reveal their trademark strength. Thanks to muscular necks and stocky legs, these cats are made for pouncing and climbing. Plus, their massive heads pack powerful jaws that let leopards haul prey that's twice their weight up the trunks of trees two stories high. That would be like climbing a ladder while carrying your dad or big brother—with your teeth! The cats scramble skyward not only to hide prey from scavengers or escape from lions, but also to mount attacks from tree limbs, pouncing on unsuspecting prey below.

A LEOPARD TAKES HER PREY UP A TREE.

Tjololo the leopard is playing tug-of-war in a tree, and he's in no mood to lose. His opponents: two hyenas that had darted out of the night to swipe Tjololo's freshly killed impala. Not about to let the hyenas steal his meal, Tjololo (pronounced cha-LO-lo) does what leopards do best: He grasps the impala in his powerful jaws and carries it straight up the tree.

ADAPTABLE FELINES

Not all leopards spend their lives in trees, though. The cats are also perfectly happy hiding their dinners in the brush. This ability to adapt has helped the leopard become the most widespread member of the cat species. Leopards also adapt their diet to whatever prey is plentiful. They'll go after crocodiles, zebras, and other big animals. But they also snack on smaller prey, like rodents, lizards, and hares—no meal is too tiny for this wild cat.

NAT GEO EXPLORER

Dereck and Beverly Joubert: Award-Winning Wildlife Filmmakers From Botswana

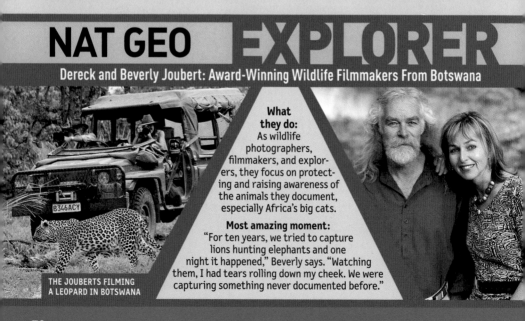

What they do: As wildlife photographers, filmmakers, and explorers, they focus on protecting and raising awareness of the animals they document, especially Africa's big cats.

Most amazing moment: "For ten years, we tried to capture lions hunting elephants and one night it happened," Beverly says. "Watching them, I had tears rolling down my cheek. We were capturing something never documented before."

THE JOUBERTS FILMING A LEOPARD IN BOTSWANA

LIONS OF THE KALAHARI DESERT

Eyes half-closed against the wind-blasted sand, a sleek, black-and-gold-maned lion (above) strides along a dry riverbed in the Kalahari Desert. He is one of the lions that roam the desolate sand dunes of southern Africa's Kalahari and Namib Deserts. These lions thrive in an intensely hot landscape. They have learned how to go without water for weeks.

Life for a desert lion is very different from life for a lion in the grassy plains of Africa, such as in the Serengeti of Kenya and Tanzania. There, large prides of up to 20 lions spend most of their time together. A pride is very much like a human family.

Fritz Eloff, a scientist who spent 40 years studying the desert lions of the Kalahari, found that desert lions live, on average, in small groups of fewer than six. Family ties are just as strong, but relationships are long-distance. Desert lions often break up into even smaller groups.

BUSY NIGHTS

Life for Kalahari lions is a constant battle against thirst and high temperatures. In summer during the day, the surface temperature of the sand can be 150°F (66°C). That's hot enough to cook an egg.

Not surprisingly, Kalahari lions hunt mostly after the sun has gone down. The big cats usually rest until the middle of the night, waiting for a cool desert wind. Then they spend the rest of the night walking—looking for food.

In the Serengeti, food is very plentiful. Lions rarely have to walk more than a couple of miles before they find a meal. But life in the desert is not so easy. With only a few scattered animals such as porcupines and gemsboks—horse-size antelopes—for prey, desert lions have to walk farther and work harder to catch dinner.

DANGEROUS DINNER

When Kalahari lions do find something to eat, it is usually spiky or dangerous. One out of every three animals they catch is a porcupine. The desert lion's main prey is the gemsbok, which can provide ten times as much meat as a porcupine. But gemsboks are difficult to bring down; they've been known to kill lions by skewering them on their three-foot (0.9 m)-long, saberlike horns.

Water is scarce in the Kalahari, so the desert lions have to be as resourceful at finding a drink as they are at finding a meal. One hot day, just as a light rain began to fall, Eloff watched two lionesses. Side by side, they licked the raindrops off each other.

These lean, strong lions have amazingly learned to survive, and by cooperating they manage to thrive in an inhospitable, almost waterless world.

5 COOL THINGS ABOUT Butterflies

MONARCH PUPA

2

1

Butterflies are nature's magicians.
Butterflies begin life as caterpillars. Once grown, the caterpillar becomes a pupa. Protected by a cocoon, the pupa transforms into a butterfly, a process called metamorphosis.

Some butterflies start out smelly.
Not all butterflies stink, but the caterpillar of the zebra swallowtail butterfly sure does! Its nasty odor helps keep it safe from hungry animals.

ZEBRA SWALLOWTAIL

3

Butterflies taste WITH THEIR "FEET."
Butterflies have chemical receptors on their legs, similar to taste buds, that allow them to taste the sweetness of a peach just by standing on it.

4

MANY butterflies ARE poisonous.
The monarch, for example, eats only poisonous milkweed plants, making both the caterpillar and the adult butterfly a dangerous snack for predators.

5

Some are winged tricksters.
Owl butterflies startle predators with huge "eyes" on their wings. The false eyes divert an attacker's attention, giving the butterfly time for a hasty escape.

OWL BUTTERFLY

Bet you didn't know

8 surprising facts about spiders

1 **Golden silk** orb-weaver spiders vibrate their webs to **distract** predators.

2 Black widow spiders are more **venomous** than **rattlesnakes.**

3 After a **large meal,** a **tarantula** may not **eat** for a **month.**

4 Crab spiders **change color** to **blend in** with their surroundings.

5 There are more than **37,000 species** of **spiders.**

6 A spider **eats** about **2,000 insects** a year.

7 The **oldest** known **spider fossils** are more than **300 million** years old.

8 A pound (0.45 kg) of **spider silk** could **stretch** around the Equator.

BIZARRE Insects

Check out some of the strangest bugs on Earth!

The bright-colored head of the puss moth caterpillar warns predators to stay away. This species, one of the most toxic caterpillars in North America, can spray acid from its head when it is attacked.

puss moth caterpillar

walking leaf

The flat, green insect is a master of disguise: It's often hard to tell between this bug and an actual leaf, thanks to its large, feathery wings. This clever camouflage provides protection from potential predators.

giraffe-necked weevil

No surprise, this bug gets its name from its extra-long neck. The males have longer necks than females do, which they use to fight other males for mating rights.

thorn bugs

One tiny thorn bug may not be a match for a bigger predator, but when grouped together on a branch, these spiky bugs create a prickly pack no bird wants a bite of!

spiny katydid

This katydid is covered in sharper-than-knives spikes. If a predator attacks, this species springs into action, defending itself by jabbing an enemy with its spiny legs and arms.

cockshafer beetle

The wild, feathery antennae on the male cockshafer may be cool to look at, but they're also helpful tools. They enable the bug to sniff for food and feel out its surrounding environment.

acorn weevil

The acorn weevil's hollow nose is longer than its body, and perfect for drilling through the shells of acorns. A female will feast on the nut by sucking up its rich, fatty liquid, and then lay her eggs in the acorn.

crab spider

Is it a spider—or a crab? With its red-and-white coloring and pointy spines sticking out from its flat body, this arachnid looks a lot like a crustacean. But crab spiders stay on dry land, usually in the woods or in gardens.

man-faced stinkbug

There are more than 4,500 species of stinkbugs world-wide, including this brilliant yellow species, whose shield-shaped body displays a unique pattern resembling a tribal mask. Like all stinkbugs, this species secretes a foul-smelling liquid from scent glands between its legs when it feels threatened.

rhinoceros beetle

Ounce for ounce, this insect, which gets its name from the horn-like structure on a male's head, is considered one of the world's strongest creatures. It is capable of carrying up to 850 times its own body weight.

5 SiLLY Pet Tricks

1 PIG TACKLES TEETER-TOTTER

Nelliebelle the pig's short legs make it tough for her to balance, but she still trots up and down a teeter-totter without hesitation and has never fallen. It probably helps that she's rewarded with her favorite food: vegetarian pizza. Talk about being hungry for success!

2 LIZARDS POSE FOR FANS

Larry and Lauri the Chinese water dragons bring new meaning to the term "lounge lizards." The pair poses in a reclining position on matching mini-couches for up to two hours in front of street audiences and even the family dog! The trick to having them hold their pose? "It's all about trust," says owner Henry Lizardlover (yep, that's his real name). "My lizards know they're safe with me."

Zachary the macaw is on a roll—literally. Although this brilliant bird has learned more than 20 tricks, cruising along on a custom-built scooter is one of Zachary's favorites. He holds the handlebars of the scooter with his beak, places one foot on the board, and then gives a big push off the ground with his other foot. It's almost as good as flying.

3 PARROT CRUISES ON SCOOTER

4 DOG PERFORMS HANDSTAND

How does Jesse the Jack Russell terrier burn off extra energy? He does handstands! Owner Heather Brook first taught Jesse this trick by encouraging Jesse to place his back paws on a wall. When Jesse held the handstand there, Brook rewarded him with his favorite squeeze toy and a chicken treat. Eventually, Jesse learned to kick off the ground directly into a handstand. But he doesn't perform just on command: "Jesse will do handstands if he has an audience," Brook says. "Especially if we have some food."

5 CAT PLAYS PIANO

Forget batting yarn and chasing mice—Nora the cat plays the piano! "One day we heard notes coming from downstairs," says owner Betsy Alexander, a piano teacher. "And there was Nora sitting at the piano like one of my students, her paws on the keys." Alexander believes that Nora associated the piano with receiving attention after observing her owner praise students, and started banging away. "To her, the piano is a giant toy," she says.

Lifestyles of the

Celebs and royalty aren't the only ones lapping up luxury. With decked-out doghouses, private jets, and cat crowns, the lifestyles of some pets are totally drool-worthy. In 2012, pet owners spent about $50 billion on their furry companions. "Pets are an important part of the family," says Bob Vetere, associate president of the American Pet Products Association. "Some owners like to shower their animals with nice things."

Loving your pet doesn't have to cost an arm and a paw. Hugs, kisses, snacks, and attention are all your furry friend needs to feel like royalty.

COCO'S LOOKIN' GOOD WITH HER FLASHY LOCKS.

KITTY GLITTER

Like many pampered pets, Coco the cat has all the must-have fashion accessories. When this kitty wants to show off her rock-star style, she slips on a hot-pink wig. For a more elegant look, the feline fashionista dons a faux fur coat and tiara. This kitty is sitting pretty!

CANINE CASTLES

Coco Puff the Yorkshire terrier and Rio the Doberman pinscher love to kick back in their two-bedroom doghouse. Many people are buying custom-made homes like this one for their pets. "Owners want an area where their dogs feel relaxed," says Michelle Pollak of La Petite Maison, which builds luxury pet homes. Fancy doggie digs can have wood floors, bay windows, and balconies. Some are big enough to hold six people!

THIS DOG FEELS RIGHT AT HOME IN HIS POOCH PALACE.

RICH and FURRY

BASED ON A WORK BY THOMAS GAINSBOROUGH CALLED "THE BLUE BOY," THIS PAINTING FEATURES A SERIOUSLY DAPPER-LOOKING KITTY!

▼ JOIN THE CLUB

Frank the bulldog's favorite hangout isn't a dog park—it's a country club! The Club Beverly Hills is an ultra-fancy resort that caters to canines. "Dogs are so excited when they arrive here, they leap out of the car," owner Marjorie Lewis says. Members start their visits by running around a specially made fitness course. To relax, posh pets can soak in a hot tub, get massages, or do yoga with a human instructor.

CATS ON CANVAS ▲

Tiger the tabby's owners wanted more than just photographs of their beloved feline. So they asked an artist to paint a portrait. "Pet paintings are a tribute to the bond people share with their animals," says Rebecca Collins of Art Paw portrait studio. Collins and her team create pet paintings (starting at $135) based on snapshots. They'll even re-create famous works of art and add your pet to the scene.

DOG DOES YOGA!

RICOCHET THE GOLDEN RETRIEVER LIVES THE HIGH LIFE WITH A GOURMET MEAL ON A PLANE.

◄ JET-SET PETS

Beijit the golden retriever travels in style. When she flies on private jets with her owners, they hire a pet flight attendant to care for her. "Our animal customers get majorly pampered," says Carol Martin, owner of Sit 'n Stay Global. The company's pet flight attendants serve fresh-cooked entrées on fine china and give thirsty critters chilled spring water in crystal bowls. After the plane lands, pet flight attendants become pet nannies, caring for their animal clients while the owners go sightseeing. *Bone* voyage!

BEIJIT ENJOYS THE VIEW.

20 Cutest Animals of 2014

From monkeys to meerkats, baby animals easily qualify as some of the cutest creatures on Earth. Here's NG Kids' roundup of cuddly critters that are sure to make you say *awww*.

1

GET UP, STAND UP

A group of meerkats stands at attention by its burrow. Extremely family-oriented, meerkat "mobs" spend a lot of time playing together in a tight-knit group. The furry family may look sweet, but if confronted, they will stand together, arching their backs, raising their hair, and hissing.

2

SNOW ADORABLE!

Siku the polar bear frolics in the snow near his home in Denmark's Scandinavian Wildlife Park. Siku—whose name is an Inuit word for "sea ice"—has become a symbol of how important it is to protect polar bears from losing their habitat due to global warming.

3

SWEET SIBLINGS

Two Amur tiger cubs get ready for a snooze at their home in the Columbus Zoo and Aquarium in Ohio, U.S.A. Critically endangered, this pair is being raised together by humans after one of the cubs struggled to nurse after birth. They are just 2 of 150 Amur tigers living in accredited North American zoos.

4

WATER BABY

Not much beats being rocked to sleep in the water. This baby sea otter spends most of its time on its mother's belly while she floats around. Sea otters are built for aquatic life from birth, with water-repellent fur, webbed back feet, and nostrils and ears that close when they're underwater.

5

STARTING SMALL

Coyote pups may be tiny at first, but they eventually grow to be the size of medium dogs. They're cared for from birth by both parents, who give their offspring an early start on hunting by bringing live mice to their den for stalking practice.

6

BEAR-Y HUNGRY

In the fall, this brown bear cub will start packing on about three pounds (1.4 kg) a day to prepare for its deep winter sleep. Those pounds of fat are what the bear will live on while snoozing. Luckily, Mom is an expert at sniffing out a meal in their northwestern U.S. habitat and can detect food from 18 miles (29 km) away.

7

HANGING OUT

This young raccoon might be an expert climber—many raccoons spend their first few months living in a nest in a tree hole. As adults, raccoons rely more on their sense of touch than on their senses of sight and smell to find meals such as frogs, bird eggs, insects, and even snakes.

8

UP A TREE

This baby orangutan may have figured out the best part of life in the trees: just hanging out! Orangutans spend up to 95 percent of their time high up in trees on the Indonesian islands of Borneo and Sumatra. They sleep, eat, and play in nests that are big enough for a ten-year-old kid to stretch out in.

9

CHOW TIME!

Yum! A group of Alpine marmots emerge from their burrow to munch on feeding biscuits in Austria. Though marmots typically stick to a diet of grass, grain, plants, insects, and worms, they seem to enjoy this crunchy snack—one that won't make them sick—that some visitors offered them.

10

SNEAK A PEEK

Peek-a-boo! Just like human kids, young pandas are very playful. Here, a baby panda named Fu Hu peeks out from behind a tree during his first time out in the snow. The size of a stick of butter when they're born, pandas eventually grow to weigh as much as a large adult human. But even as grown-ups, they still love to have a good time!

11

THE EYES HAVE IT

The peepers on these adorable amphibians aren't just for show. If a hungry snake approaches, a sleeping red-eyed tree frog can flash its bright red eyes and hopefully startle the predator. Then the frog, which lives in rain forests of southern Mexico and Central and South America, can hop away.

13

BLENDING IN

Hares, beware! This critter may look adorable, but it could be your enemy. Silent and sneaky, the ermine can pounce on prey that's larger than it is, such as an arctic hare. The stealthy stalker gets help from its changing coat, which is white during winter and brown in spring and summer—perfect camouflage.

12

SPOT ON

This cuddly looking bobcat may have one of the finest fur coats in the animal world, but it's not all about looking good. The spotted fur helps North America's most common wild cat blend in with many habitats. Those ear tufts? Bobcats may twitch them to communicate with other bobcats.

14

WHAT A HOOT!

Why, hello there! A Eurasian Pygmy owl peers out of a tree in a forest in Sweden. These tiny owls—which grow to be about the size of a robin—are small enough to squeeze into tree holes made by woodpeckers, where they build their nests.

15

HOT DOG

Think you have the world's cutest dog? Well, meet Boo the Pomeranian, a canine fuzzball who has captured the hearts of people around the world. This precious pup has more than 5.8 million fans on Facebook and a book featuring photos of Boo dressed up in costumes and just being...you guessed it...cute!

16

SMILEY SQUID

Say cheese? It may look like this piglet squid is smiling, but in reality this deepwater dweller isn't quite hamming for the camera. Rather, the squid's friendly "face" is the result of tentacles and unusual skin patterns, which form the shape of an adorable mug topped by a mop of curly hair.

18

TALL TALE

Talk about a grand entrance: Baby giraffes fall about six feet (1.8 m) from their moms during birth before hitting the ground. But the bumpy landing doesn't stop the little guys from getting a jump start on life—they're usually up on their hooves and walking at just an hour old.

17

JUST LION AROUND

A mother Galápagos sea lion lounges around with her pup. These species share a tight bond: Although baby sea lions usually learn to swim by the time they're two weeks old, they stick to their mothers' sides for a few years before venturing out on their own.

19

BADGE OF HONOR

What's black and white and striped all over? An American badger, of course! These species are easily recognized by the telltale white stripe, which runs from the tip of their noses all the way to the back of their heads. But it's the badgers' black cheek patches—called "badges"—that give them their name.

20

FAST FRIENDS

When Sobe the iguana first met Johann the cat, the reptile seemed unsure of what to make of the pointy-eared fur ball. Instead of scampering away, the cat nuzzled the iguana. Johann began to visit Sobe's enclosure to nap, and Sobe protected the cat when he was recovering from surgery. Sounds like these two were the ultimate dream team!

Prehistoric
TIME LINE

HUMANS HAVE WALKED on Earth for some 200,000 years, a mere blip in Earth's 4.5-billion-year history. A lot has happened during that time. Earth formed, and oxygen levels rose in the millions of years of the Precambrian time. The productive Paleozoic era gave rise to hard-shelled organisms, vertebrates, amphibians, and reptiles.

Dinosaurs ruled the Earth in the mighty Mesozoic. And 64 million years after dinosaurs became extinct, modern humans emerged in the Cenozoic era. From the first tiny mollusks to the dinosaur giants of the Jurassic and beyond, Earth has seen a lot of transformation.

THE PRECAMBRIAN TIME
4.5 billion to 542 million years ago

- The Earth (and other planets) formed from gas and dust left over from a giant cloud that collapsed to form the sun. The giant cloud's collapse was triggered when nearby stars exploded.
- Low levels of oxygen made Earth a suffocating place.
- Early life-forms appeared.

THE PALEOZOIC ERA
542 million to 251 million years ago

- The first insects and other animals appeared on land.
- 450 million years ago (m.y.a.), the ancestors of sharks began to swim in the oceans.
- 430 m.y.a., plants began to take root on land.
- More than 360 m.y.a., amphibians emerged from the water.
- Slowly the major landmasses began to come together, creating Pangaea, a single supercontinent.
- By 300 m.y.a., reptiles had begun to dominate the land.

What Killed the Dinosaurs?

WAS IT AN ASTEROID OR A VOLCANO? These two common theories have been used by scientists to explain the disappearance of dinosaurs 65 million years ago. Researchers believe that a huge impact, such as from an asteroid or comet, or a massive bout of volcanic activity might have choked the sky with debris that starved Earth of the sun's energy. The resulting greenhouse gases may have caused the temperature to soar, causing half of the world's species—including the dinosaurs—to die in a mass extinction.

DINO TIMES

THE MESOZOIC ERA

251 million to 65 million years ago

The Mesozoic era, or the age of the reptiles, consisted of three consecutive time periods (shown below). This is when the first dinosaurs began to appear. They would reign supreme for more than 150 million years.

TRIASSIC PERIOD

251 million to 199 million years ago

- Appearance of the first mammals. They were rodent-size.
- The first dinosaur appeared.
- Ferns were the dominant plants on land.
- The giant supercontinent of Pangaea began breaking up toward the end of the Triassic.

JURASSIC PERIOD

199 million to 145 million years ago

- Giant dinosaurs dominated the land.
- Pangaea continued its breakup, and oceans formed in the spaces between the drifting landmasses, allowing sea life, including sharks and marine crocodiles, to thrive.
- Conifer trees spread across the land.

CRETACEOUS PERIOD

145 million to 65 million years ago

- The modern continents developed.
- The largest dinosaurs developed.
- Flowering plants spread across the landscape.
- Mammals flourished, and giant pterosaurs ruled the skies over the small birds.
- Temperatures grew more extreme. Dinosaurs lived in deserts, swamps, and forests from the Antarctic to the Arctic.

THE CENOZOIC ERA—TERTIARY PERIOD

65 million to 2.6 million years ago

- Following the dinosaur extinction, mammals rose as the dominant species.
- Birds continued to flourish.
- Volcanic activity was widespread.
- Temperatures began to cool, eventually ending in an ice age.
- The period ended with land bridges forming, which allowed plants and animals to spread to new areas.

Who Ate What?

Herbivores
- Primarily plant-eaters
- Weighed up to 100 tons (91 t)—the largest animals ever to walk on Earth
- Up to 1,000 blunt or flat teeth to grind vegetation
- Many had cheek pouches to store food.
- Examples: *Styracosaurus, Mamenchisaurus*

Carnivores
- Meat-eaters
- Long, strong legs to run faster than plant-eaters; ran up to 30 miles an hour (48 kph)
- Most had good eyesight, strong jaws, and sharp teeth.
- Scavengers and hunters; often hunted in packs
- Grew to 45 feet (14 m) long
- Examples: *Velociraptor, Gigantoraptor, Tyrannosaurus rex*

TYRANNOSAURUS REX

Ancient dinosaur in color

What color were dinosaurs?

For decades, scientists could only take educated guesses about the color of dinosaurs. Now, we're closer to figuring out their color patterns. Thanks to pigment in dino fuzz—tiny, featherlike hairs found on some fossils—scientists have been able to determine the coloring of a 155-million-year-old prehistoric dinosaur the size of a chicken, with black-and-white spangled wings and a red feathered mohawk crown. So will dino fuzz determine the color of every species? Probably not. But these new findings do shed a bright light onto the dino's otherwise dark and mysterious past.

GIGANTORAPTOR

DID YOU KNOW?

The *Camarasaurus* dinosaur may have been as big as a bus, but that didn't stop this species from walking up to 200 miles (322 km) in search of food and water. Like modern-day birds and elephants, these long-necked plant-eaters may have endured marathon migrations during the dry season, only to return to their natural habitat during the wetter winters.

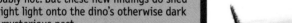

VELOCIRAPTOR   **SINOSAUROPTERYX**

MAMENCHISAURUS

PARASAUROLOPHUS

ERKETU

Dinosaur fossil

Fossils preserved in plaster

Paleontologists learn about dinosaurs by studying fossils—plant and animal remains that have been preserved in rock.

Bet you didn't know

Some **DINOSAUR SKULLS** were about as long as **an adult human is tall.**

TUOJIANGOSAURUS

STYRACOSAURUS

MONONYKUS

93

DINO Classification

Classifying dinosaurs and all other living things can be a complicated matter, so scientists have devised a system to help with the process. Dinosaurs are put into groups based on a very large range of characteristics.

Scientists put dinosaurs into two major groups: the bird-hipped ornithischians and the reptile-hipped saurischians.

Dinosaur Superlatives

Heaviest
Argentinosaurus is believed to have weighed 220,000 lbs. (99,790 kg)—more than 15 elephants!

Longest
The *Seismosaurus* was longer than three school buses.

Thickest skull
The *Pachycephalosaurus's* huge head and nine-inch (23 cm)-thick skull may have been used for head-butting.

Biggest claws
With hooklike claws almost a foot (20–30 cm) long, the *Deinocheirus* was probably one of the most deadly dinosaurs.

Longest-lived
Sauropods are believed to have had a lifespan of about 100 years.

Longest name
Micropachycephalosaurus (23 letters)

First to be named
Megalosaurus was named in 1822 by Reverend William Buckland, an English geologist.

Ornithischian

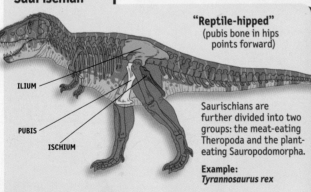

ILIUM
PUBIS
ISCHIUM

"Bird-hipped"
(pubis bone in hips points backward)

Ornithischians have the same-shaped pubis as birds of today, but today's birds are actually more closely related to the saurischians.

Example: *Styracosaurus*

Saurischian

ILIUM
PUBIS
ISCHIUM

"Reptile-hipped"
(pubis bone in hips points forward)

Saurischians are further divided into two groups: the meat-eating Theropoda and the plant-eating Sauropodomorpha.

Example: *Tyrannosaurus rex*

Within these two main divisions, dinosaurs are then separated into orders and then families, such as Stegosauria. Like other members of the Stegosauria, *Stegosaurus* had spines and plates along the back, neck, and tail.

10 DINOS YOU SHOULD KNOW

Dinosaur (Group) *Example*
What the name means
Length: XX feet (XX m)
Time Range: When they lived
Where: Where their fossils were found
COOL FACT: An amazing fact about this particular dinosaur.

A *Megalosaurus* was a frightening sight. The fierce meat-eater's prey probably included the slow-moving stegosaurs of its time.

2 *Argentinosaurus* **(Saurischian)**
Argentina lizard
Length: 130 to 140 feet (40 to 43 m)
Time Range: Late Cretaceous
Where: Argentina
COOL FACT: *Argentinosaurus* was one of the heaviest dinosaurs.

1 *Megalosaurus* **(Saurischian)**
Great reptile
Length: 27 feet (8.2 m)
Time Range: Middle Jurassic
Where: England, France, Portugal
COOL FACT: *Megalosaurus* bones were first discovered in England in 1677.

3 *Buitreraptor* **(Saurischian)**
Vulture thief
Length: 4 feet (1.2 m)
Time Range: Late Cretaceous
Where: Argentina
COOL FACT: With teeth too small to hunt big animals, *Buitreraptor* ate insects.

4 *Camarasaurus* (Saurischian)

Chambered lizard

Length: 59 feet (18 m)

Time Range: Late Jurassic

Where: U.S. (Colorado, Utah)

COOL FACT: *Camarasaurus* grew new teeth about every five months.

5 *Cryolophosaurus* (Saurischian)

Frozen-crested reptile

Length: 20 feet (6.1 m)

Time Range: Early Jurassic

Where: Antarctica

COOL FACT: *Cryolophosaurus* is the first dino found in Antarctica.

6 *Diplodocus* (Saurischian)

Double beamed

Length: 90 feet (27 m)

Time Range: Late Jurassic

Where: U.S. (Colorado, Montana, Utah, Wyoming)

COOL FACT: *Didplodocus* had the longest tail of any dinosaur.

7 *Edmontosaurus* (Ornithiscian)

Edmonton lizard

Length: 42 feet (13 m)

Time Range: Late Cretaceous

Where: U.S. (Alaska, Montana); Canada (Alberta)

COOL FACT: *Edmontosaurus* herds traveled great distances to find food.

8 *Therizinosaurus* (Saurischian)

Cut off reptile

Length: 36 feet (11 m)

Time Range: Late Cretaceous

Where: Mongolia, China

COOL FACT: *Therizinosaurus* had huge claws that measured 3 feet (0.9 m).

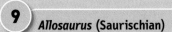

9 *Allosaurus* (Saurischian)

Strange reptile

Length: 28 feet (8.5 m)

Time Range: Early Cretaceous

Where: U.S. (Colorado, Montana, Utah, Wyoming)

COOL FACT: *Allosaurus*'s powerful jaws held 70 sharp teeth.

10 *Stegosaurus* (Ornithischian)

Roofed reptile

Length: 30 feet (9 m)

Time Range: Late Jurassic

Where: U.S. (Colorado, Utah, Wyoming)

COOL FACT: *Stegosaurus* probably used its spiked tail as a weapon.

A pair of *Allosaurus* close in on a fleeing *Camarasaurus*.

6 NEWLY DISCOVERED DINOS

Humans have been searching for—and discovering—dinosaur remains for hundreds of years. In that time, at least 1,000 species of dinos have been found all over the world, and thousands more may still be out there waiting to be unearthed. Recent discoveries include the dog-size, 230-million-year-old *Eodromaeus*, found in Argentina and believed to be one of the world's earliest predators. For more exciting dino discoveries, read on.

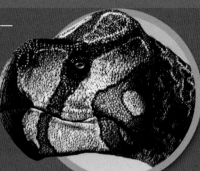

1 *Bicentenaria argentina* (Saurischian)
Argentine Bicentenary
Length: 8 feet (2.4 m)
Time Range: Cretaceous
Where: Argentina

4 *Unescoceratops koppelhusae* (Saurischian)
UNESCO's ceratopsian
Length: About 3 feet (1 m)
Time Range: Late Cretaceous
Where: Alberta, Canada

5 *Yutyrannus huali* (Saurischian)
Beautiful feathered tyrant
Length: 30 feet (9 m)
Time Range: Cretaceous
Where: China

2 *Spinops sternbergorum* (Ornithiscian)
Sternbergs' spine face
Length: 20 feet (6 m)
Time Range: Late Cretaceous
Where: Canada

3 *Talos sampsoni* (Saurischian)
In Greek mythology, Talos is the protector of Crete. "Sampsoni" honors paleontologist Dr. Scott D. Sampson.
Length: 7 feet (2 m)
Time Range: Late Cretaceous
Where: U.S. (Utah)

6 *Zhuchengtyrannus magnus* (Saurischian)
Tyrant from Zhucheng
Length: 36 feet (11 m)
Time Range: Cretaceous
Where: China

FLYING MONSTERS

Imagine a time when huge, flying creatures—some the size of small airplanes!—ruled the skies. That's what life was like 231 million to 65 million years ago, when agile predators, called pterosaurs, cruised around like birds do today. Here's more about how three pterosaur species lived—before they went extinct.

DIMORPHODON
(213 MILLION TO 194 MILLION YEARS AGO)

With a big head and four-and-a-half-foot (1.4-m) wingspan, the *Dimorphodon* was quite clumsy. It also had a four-foot (1.2-m)-long tail that interfered with walking. Mammals didn't fear this flier: Its small, sharp choppers were perfect for crunching insects, scaly fish, and reptiles, but not much else. Because they couldn't chew, it was crunch, gulp, and go!

QUETZALCOATLUS
(70 MILLION TO 66 MILLION YEARS AGO)

The size of a very small airplane, *Quetzalcoatlus* was the biggest creature ever to fly. Some scientists think it could cruise up to 80 miles an hour (129 kph) for about 10,000 miles (16,000 km). That's close to halfway around the world! This creature may have been big, but with a long, unbending neck and no teeth, it looked more funny than fearsome.

Scientists think there were about **160** species of pterosaurs.

TAPEJARA
(108 MILLION TO 90 MILLION YEARS AGO)

With a 10- to 20-foot (3- to 6-m) wingspan, *Tapejara* was built to cruise the skies. A larger palm bone supported its longer narrow wings and helped it change direction at top speeds and roll like a fighter plane. A three-foot (0.9-m)-tall crest on its head may have worked like a sail to help it turn in midair. *Tapejara* was completely toothless and used its hooked beak and its pointy chin to rip through a fishy meal or fruit buffets.

WATCH THESE GUYS FLY—NOW!
Go online to watch pterosaurs in action:
flyingmonsters-movie.com

99

STUMP YOUR PARENTS

AMAZING ANIMALS QUIZ

What's your parents' animal IQ? Quiz them on this chapter's content to see how their wildlife wisdom stacks up. ANSWERS BELOW

1 **True or false?** Galápagos penguins need to protect themselves from sunburn.

2 How many tigers remain in the wild?
a. 50,000
b. fewer than 4,000
c. about 1,500
d. 75

3 Bigfoot might be a fitting nickname for which animal?
a. polar bear
b. giraffe
c. serval
d. hummingbird

4 A pig's snout helps it _____.
a. dig
b. smell food from a great distance
c. snort loudly
d. fling dirt at other pigs

5 What does *Megalosaurus* mean?
a. double beamed
b. strange reptile
c. great reptile
d. supersmart

6 What have wild dolphins not used as a toy?
a. coconuts
b. seaweed
c. rocks
d. Nintendo

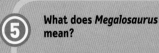

Wildly Good Animal Reports

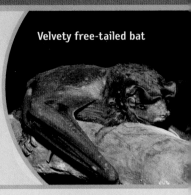

Velvety free-tailed bat

Your teacher wants a written report on the velvety free-tailed bat. Not to worry. Use these organizational tools, so writing a report won't drive you batty.

STEPS TO SUCCESS: Your report will follow the format of a descriptive or expository essay (see p. 35 for "How to Write a Perfect Essay") and should consist of a main idea, followed by supporting details and a conclusion. Use this basic structure for each paragraph as well as the whole report, and you'll be on the right track.

1. Introduction
State your **main idea.**
> *The velvety free-tailed bat is a common and important species of bat.*

2. Body
Provide **supporting points** for your main idea.
> *The velvety free-tailed bat eats insects and can have a large impact on insect populations.*
> *It ranges from Mexico to Florida and South America.*
> *As with other bats, its wings are built for fast, efficient flight.*

Then **expand** on those points with further description, explanation, or discussion.
> *The velvety free-tailed bat eats insects and can have a large impact on insect populations.*
> *Its diet consists primarily of mosquitoes and other airborne insects.*
> *It ranges from Mexico to Florida and South America.*
> *It sometimes takes refuge in people's attics.*
> *As with other bats, its wings are built for fast, efficient flight.*
> *It has trouble, however, taking off from low or flat surfaces and must drop from a place high enough to gain speed to start flying.*

3. Conclusion
Wrap it up with a summary of your whole paper.
> *Because of its large numbers, the velvety free-tailed bat holds an important position in the food chain.*

KEY INFORMATION

Here are some things you should consider including in your report:

> **What does your animal look like?**
> **To what other species is it related?**
> **How does it move?**
> **Where does it live?**
> **What does it eat?**
> **What are its predators?**
> **How long does it live?**
> **Is it endangered?**
> **Why do you find it interesting?**

SEPARATE FACT FROM FICTION: Your animal may have been featured in a movie or in myths and legends. Compare and contrast how the animal has been portrayed with how it behaves in reality. For example, penguins can't dance the way they do in *Happy Feet*.

PROOFREAD AND REVISE: As with any great essay, when you're finished, check for misspellings, grammatical mistakes, and punctuation errors. It often helps to have someone else proofread your work, too, as he or she may catch things you have missed. Also, look for ways to make your sentences and paragraphs even better. Add more descriptive language, choosing just the right verbs, adverbs, and adjectives to make your writing come alive.

BE CREATIVE: Use visual aids to make your report come to life. Include an animal photo file with interesting images found in magazines or printed from websites. Or draw your own! You can also build a miniature animal habitat diorama. Use creativity to help communicate your passion for the subject.

THE FINAL RESULT: Put it all together in one final, polished draft. Make it neat and clean, and remember to cite your references.

Wonders of Nature

An aurora borealis glows brightly over Iceland. This natural light show, also known as the northern lights, happens when the solar wind interacts with the Earth's magnetic field.

Weather and Climate

Weather is the condition of the atmosphere—temperature, precipitation, humidity, and wind—at a given place at a given time. Climate, however, is the average weather for a particular place over a long period of time. Different places on Earth have different climates, but climate is not a random occurrence. It is a pattern that is controlled by factors such as latitude, elevation, prevailing winds, the temperature of ocean currents, and location on land relative to water. Climate is generally constant, but evidence indicates that human activity is causing a change in the patterns of climate.

WEATHER EXTREMES

MOST SNOW RECORDED IN ONE SEASON: 1,140 inches (29 m) in Mount Baker, Washington, U.S.A.

FASTEST TEMPERATURE RISE: 49°F (27.2°C) in 15 minutes, in Rapid City, South Dakota, U.S.A.

MOST DAYS IN A ROW ABOVE 100°F (37.8°C): 160 days in Marble Bar, Western Australia

GLOBAL CLIMATE ZONES

Climatologists, people who study climate, have created different systems for classifying climates. One often-used system is called the Köppen system, which classifies climate zones according to precipitation, temperature, and vegetation. It has five major categories—Tropical, Dry, Temperate, Cold, and Polar—with a sixth category for locations where high elevations override other factors.

ARCTIC OCEAN

ARCTIC CIRCLE

TROPIC OF CANCER

ATLANTIC OCEAN

PACIFIC OCEAN

EQUATOR

PACIFIC OCEAN

INDIAN OCEAN

TROPIC OF CAPRICORN

ANTARCTIC CIRCLE

Climate

Tropical   Dry   Temperate   Cold   Polar

WEATHER COMPARISONS

Weather events can be so big and widespread that it's sometimes hard to comprehend them. For example, a single hurricane can cover hundreds of miles; its eye alone can be up to 200 miles (320 km) wide. That's about as far as Paris, France, is from London, England, U.K. But weather is also a part of daily life. Let's think about weather in terms of some everyday objects and events.

Is It Hot Enough to Fry an Egg on a Sidewalk?

It's possible for sidewalks to get hot enough (158°F/70°C), but once an egg hits the surface, the sidewalk cools. The sun alone can't cook the egg thoroughly.

How Fast Is a Hurricane?

A powerful hurricane can reach wind speeds of more than 155 miles per hour (249 kph). That's about as fast as some Indy cars speed around the track.

How Much Rain Is in a Snowfall?

Snowflakes come in many different shapes and sizes, so each snowfall contains a different amount of moisture. Rule of thumb: 10 inches (25 cm) of snow is equal to an inch (2.5 cm) of rain.

Freaky Weather

Nature can be unbelievably powerful. A major earthquake can topple huge buildings and bring down entire mountainsides. Hurricanes, blizzards, and tornadoes can paralyze major cities. But as powerful as these natural disasters are, here are five other episodes of wacky weather that will really *blow* you away!

1 FIRE RAINBOW

Can clouds catch fire? No, but it may look like it when you spot a circumhorizontal arc, also known as a "fire rainbow." This rare sight occurs when the sun travels through wispy, high-altitude cirrus clouds—and only when the sun is very high in the sky. The result? The entire cloud lights up in an amazing spectrum of colors, sometimes extending for hundreds of miles (km) in the sky.

You head outside after a snowstorm and see dozens of log- or drum-shaped snowballs. These rare creations are called snow rollers, formed when wet snow falls on icy ground, so snow can't stick to it. Pushed by strong winds, the snow rolls into logs. Maybe this is nature's way of saying it's time for a snowball fight.

SNOWBALL FACTORY 2

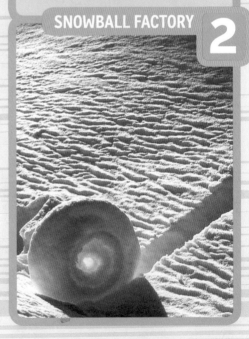

3 MYSTERY WAVES

Imagine you're on an ocean liner when a wall of water ten stories tall races toward you like an unstoppable freight train. It's a rogue wave, also called a freak wave, which can appear without warning at any time in the open sea. These waves were once considered myths, but scientists now know they are very real—and very dangerous to even the largest ships.

HOLE PUNCH CLOUDS 4

Nope, that's not a UFO—it's a rare formation in the sky called a Hole Punch cloud. This wild sight usually occurs when patches of high clouds freeze and fall away as ice crystals, eventually leaving a huge hole. Once unable to solve the mystery, researchers now believe that airplanes taking off or landing are the likely cause of these cloud holes.

5 THE MOTHER OF ALL TORNADOES

The fastest wind speed ever recorded—318 miles an hour (512 kph)—occurred during a tornado near Oklahoma City, Oklahoma, U.S.A., in 1999. Scientists classify tornadoes by the damage they can do. With wind speeds of 70 miles an hour (113 kph), a tornado can tear branches from trees. A tornado with wind speeds of more than 300 miles an hour (483 kph) has the power to derail train cars, tear grass from the ground, and even rip pavement from the street.

Natural Disasters

Every world region has its share of natural disasters—the mix just varies from place to place. The Ring of Fire—grinding tectonic plate boundaries that follow the coasts of the Pacific Ocean—shakes with volcanic eruptions and earthquakes. Lives and livelihoods here and along other oceans can be swept away by tsunamis. North America's heartland endures blizzards in winter and tornadoes that can strike in spring, summer, or fall. Tropical cyclones batter many coastal areas in Asia and Australia with ripping winds, torrents of rain, and huge storm surges along their deadly paths.

HURRICANE!

A monster storm with 150-mile-an-hour (241-kph) winds churns west across the Atlantic Ocean. Scientists at the National Hurricane Center in Miami have tracked it for days using satellite images. Now they're worried it may threaten the United States.

It's time for the "hurricane hunters" to go to work! All ships and airplanes have been warned away from this monster. But two four-engine airplanes head toward the storm. Their mission? To collect data inside the hurricane that will tell meteorologists where the storm is going, when it will get there, and how violent it will be.

The word "hurricane" comes from Huracan, the god of big winds and evil spirits once worshipped by the Maya people of Central America. These superstrong storms—which usually last about nine days—are the most destructive during their first 12 hours onshore, when high winds can topple homes and cause major flooding.

To help people prepare for a hurricane that's hustling to shore, the U.S. National Oceanic and Atmospheric Administration (NOAA) sends out the hurricane hunters, who fly straight into the storm to determine characteristics such as temperature, air pressure, wind speed, and wind direction. It's a dangerous job, but by mission's end, the hunters' work will help to keep everyone in the hurricane's path safe.

HURRICANES IN 2014

HELLO, MY NAME IS . . .

Hurricane names come from six official international lists. The names alternate between male and female.

When a storm becomes a hurricane, a name from the list is used, in alphabetical order. Each list is reused every six years. A name "retires" if that hurricane caused a lot of damage or many deaths.

Arthur
Bertha
Cristobal
Dolly
Edouard
Fay
Gonzalo
Hanna
Isaias
Josephine
Kyle
Laura
Marco
Nana
Omar
Paulette
Rene
Sally
Teddy
Vicky
Wilfred

Scale of Hurricane Intensity

CATEGORY	ONE	TWO	THREE	FOUR	FIVE
DAMAGE	Minimal	Moderate	Extensive	Extreme	Catastrophic
WINDS	74–95 mph (119–153 kph)	96–110 mph (154–177 kph)	111–130 mph (178–209 kph)	131–155 mph (210–249 kph)	Over 155 mph (249+ kph)
(DAMAGE refers to wind and water damage combined.)					

Tornado!

TIM SAMARAS

Most people take shelter when a tornado's coming. Not Tim Samaras. The former National Geographic Emerging Explorer chases the deadly storms, spending every May and June driving across the United States' Tornado Alley in search of the next twister. His mission? To find out why tornadoes form so he can predict them and give people earlier warnings to take shelter before a storm hits.

Samaras and other tornado chasers and meteorologists typically use weather measurement probes to collect data from the twisters. When placed directly in the twister's violent path, the probes record factors like humidity,

TORNADO ALLEY
More tornadoes occur on the Great Plains of the United States—an area called Tornado Alley—than on any other place on Earth.

pressure, temperature, wind speed, and direction. This information is crucial for determining how violent a twister may become—and how it may impact the people and places in its path.

Samaras's job is full of thrills and scary moments. When a tornado with more than 200-mile-an-hour (322-kph) winds swept through Manchester, South Dakota, U.S.A., Samaras recalls "debris flying overhead, telephone poles were snapped and flung 300 yards [274 m] through the air, roads ripped from the ground, and the town of Manchester literally sucked into the clouds."

Tornado Safety Tips

GO DEEP
Ride out the storm in your basement. If you don't have a basement, go to a closet, bathroom, or small room in the center of your house.

TAKE COVER
If you're outside, run into the closest house or building. Once indoors, get under heavy furniture or a mattress and protect your head.

GET LOW
If you're stuck outside, lie flat in a ditch or low spot, or crouch near a building.

BE ALERT
Don't go outside if there is a tornado watch or warning.

Wildfire!

During the summer of 2012, a fire erupted in the hills above Colorado Springs, Colorado, U.S.A. What was first thought to be a contained blaze soon spread, becoming an uncontrollable wildfire that grew to 2,000 acres (800 ha) wide in less than 24 hours. With hundreds of homes—and thousands of people—in danger, firefighters, assisted by helicopters, air tankers, and military planes, worked tirelessly to extinguish the blaze. But with high winds, record heat, and unseasonable dryness, it took more than two weeks before what became known as the Waldo Canyon Fire was completely contained. The blaze destroyed 18,247 acres (7,384 ha) and is considered the most destructive wildfire on record in Colorado.

How do wildfires start? Most often, they're sparked by a careless act by a human, such as leaving a campfire unattended or irresponsibly disposing of a cigarette. Some are deliberately set. Some are ignited by lightning strikes or fallen power lines. However they begin, wildfires can quickly rage out of control, as they did in Colorado.

Highly trained forest firefighters are equipped and experienced to fight huge forest fires. Some, called smokejumpers, actually parachute into a remote area to battle the blaze. But no matter how many firefighters and gallons of water are doused on the flames, it usually takes a break in the weather to finally beat a wildfire. The Colorado fires continued to rage until heavy rain offered relief. About two weeks after the fires ignited, the flames were finally extinguished.

NAT GEO EXPLORER

Mark Thiessen: Wildfire Photographer

THIESSEN'S PHOTO OF A FIRE-FIGHTER DRIVING THROUGH FLAMES THAT JUMPED THE ROAD IN MONTANA, U.S.A.

What he does:
Takes photographs from the front lines of wildfires every summer.

Most amazing moment:
Photographing a wildfire in Idaho, U.S.A. "To our left is a huge wall of flame that's coming in our direction. The flames start to twirl together and you get this 30-foot [9-m]-tall fire tornado. It's so fascinating, but also so dangerous."

Tsunami Heroes

RESCUED OR REUNITED, ANIMALS AND PEOPLE PULL TOGETHER AFTER A HUGE NATURAL DISASTER.

When a 9.0-magnitude earthquake struck off the coast of Honshu, Japan, in 2011, it knocked people off their feet and made tall buildings sway. Then things got even worse. Miles offshore, the massive movement created a series of huge waves called a tsunami, which rushed toward the island nation. Walls of water as tall as 30 feet (9 m) crashed into the coast and wiped out everything in the way—and separated humans from their pets. Many animal lovers went out of their way to help animals in need after the tsunami. Here are two stories of survival and hope.

DOG AT SEA

SAFE ON LAND

PUP RESCUED FROM ROOF

Three weeks after the disaster, a helicopter crew spots a dog pacing across the roof of a wrecked house floating more than a mile (1.6 km) off-shore. A rescue team reaches the canine by canoe, carrying her aboard a larger boat on a stretcher. A woman from a nearby town sees the rescue on the local news and instantly recognizes her missing pet, a two-year-old mixed breed named Ban. Dog and owner are happily reunited—safe and on dry land.

RESCUED

PORPOISE SURVIVES STRANDING

A tiny porpoise is spotted in a flooded rice field, more than a mile (1.6 km) away from the shore. Pet shop owner Ryo Taira wades into the water, grabs the three-foot (1-m)-long animal and cradles it in his arms. He then wraps the exhausted porpoise in wet towels and drives it to a nearby beach. As soon as it's placed into the sea, the porpoise springs back to life and energetically swims away.

THE WATER CYCLE

RISING UP

Some of the water and spray from the waterfall in this picture will **evaporate** into the air. In other bodies of water, heat from the sun causes some water to evaporate, or turn into water vapor, or gas. This water vapor rises from the stream, river, or lake and goes into the air.

HANGING OUT

Water covers more than 70 percent of Earth's surface in the form of oceans, lakes, and rivers. When water ends up on land from rain, snow, or hail, it may soak into the earth, becoming part of the ground-water and leaving the water cycle for a while.

Scientists think that the water we drink, bathe in, and use to grow crops today has been here on Earth since long before the time of the dinosaurs. It has just been moving around and around in the atmosphere in a nearly endless cycle. But there's not much water in the air. In fact, if all of the atmosphere's water rained down at once, it would only cover the globe to a depth of one inch (2.5 cm). It's a good thing, then, that we have the water cycle—Earth's original recycling project. Here's how it works:

CHILLING OUT

As water vapor cools in the air, it **condenses.** This means that it changes back into liquid form. You will notice the same kind of thing happening if you pour a cold glass of water on a hot day. Water forms on the outside of the glass. The water vapor in the warm air touches the cold glass and turns to liquid.

FALLING DOWN

After so much water has condensed that the air can't hold it anymore, it falls as **precipitation**—rain, hail, sleet, or snow—into Earth's oceans, lakes, and rivers.

RUNNING OFF

Melted snow and rain that run downhill eventually end up in large bodies of water. The transfer of land water to the ocean is called **runoff.**

LOCATED AT THE BORDER OF CHINA AND VIETNAM, THE DETIAN WATERFALL IS ONE OF THE LARGEST WATERFALLS IN ASIA. ITS NAME MEANS "VIRTUOUS HEAVEN."

THE OC

PACIFIC OCEAN

STATS

Surface area
65,436,200 sq mi (169,479,000 sq km)

Portion of Earth's water area
47 percent

Greatest depth
Challenger Deep
(in the Mariana Trench)
-36,070 ft (-10,994 m)

Surface temperatures
Summer high: 90°F (32°C)
Winter low: 28°F (-2°C)

Tides
Highest: 30 ft (9 m) near Korean peninsula
Lowest: 1 ft (0.3 m) near Midway Islands

Cool creatures: giant Pacific octopus, bottlenose whale, clownfish, great white shark

ATLANTIC OCEAN

STATS

Surface area
35,338,500 sq mi (91,526,300 sq km)

Portion of Earth's water area
25 percent

Greatest depth
Puerto Rico Trench
-28,232 ft (-8,605 m)

Surface temperatures
Summer high: 90°F (32°C)
Winter low: 28°F (-2°C)

Tides
Highest: 52 ft (16 m)
Bay of Fundy, Canada
Lowest: 1.5 ft (0.5 m)
Gulf of Mexico and Mediterranean Sea

Cool creatures: blue whale, Atlantic spotted dolphin, sea turtle

GREAT WHITE SHARK

GREEN SEA TURTLE

EANS

INDIAN OCEAN

STATS

Surface area
28,839,800 sq mi (74,694,800 sq km)

Portion of Earth's water area
21 percent

Greatest depth
Java Trench
-23,376 ft (-7,125 m)

Surface temperatures
Summer high: 93°F (34°C)
Winter low: 28°F (-2°C)

Tides
Highest: 36 ft (11 m)
Lowest: 2 ft (0.6 m)
Both along Australia's west coast

Cool creatures: humpback whale, Portuguese man-of-war, dugong (sea cow)

DUGONG

ARCTIC OCEAN

STATS

Surface area
5,390,000 sq mi (13,960,100 sq km)

Portion of Earth's water area
4 percent

Greatest depth
Molloy Deep
-18,599 ft (-5,669 m)

Surface temperatures
Summer high: 41°F (5°C)
Winter low: 28°F (-2°C)

Tides
Less than 1 ft (0.3 m) variation throughout the ocean

Cool creatures: beluga whale, orca, harp seal, narwhal

ORCA

To see the major oceans and bays in relation to landmasses, look at the map on pages 262 and 263.

Coral Reefs

Just below the surface of the Caribbean Sea's crystal-clear water, miles (km) of vivid corals grow in fantastic shapes that shelter tropical fish of every color. Coral reefs account for a quarter of all life in the ocean and are often called the rain forests of the sea. Like big apartment complexes for sea creatures, coral reefs provide a tough limestone skeleton for fish, clams, and other organisms to live in— and plenty of food for them to eat, too.

And how does the coral get its color? It's all about the algae that cling to its limestone polyps. Algae and coral live together in a mutually helpful relationship. The coral provides a home to the algae and helps the algae convert sunlight to food that the corals consume. But as beautiful as coral reefs are, they are also highly sensitive. A jump of even 2°F (1.1°C) in water temperature makes the reef rid itself of the algae, leaving the coral with a sickly, bleached look. Pollution is another threat; it can poison the sensitive corals. Humans pose a threat, too: One clumsy kick from a swimmer can destroy decades of coral growth.

QUEEN ANGELFISH

MANTA RAY

SEA STAR
ON A SPONGE

SOME SEA STARS HAVE MORE THAN 40 ARMS.

GIANT BUMPHEAD
PARROTFISH

MORAY EEL

BY THE NUMBERS

2,900 is the number of coral reefs in Australia's Great Barrier Reef, the world's largest reef.

109 countries have coral reefs.

4 feet (1.2 m) is the length of the giant bumphead parrotfish, one of the largest fish found in coral reefs.

117

HOW DOES Your Garden GROW?

The plant kingdom is more than 300,000 species strong, growing all over the world: on top of mountains, in the sea, in frigid temperatures—everywhere. Without plants, life on Earth would not be able to survive. Plants provide food and oxygen for animals and humans.

Three characteristics make plants distinct:

1 Most have chlorophyll (a green pigment that makes photosynthesis work and turns sunlight into energy), while some are parasitic.

2 They cannot change their location on their own.

3 Their cell walls are made from a stiff material called cellulose.

Photosynthesis

light

oxygen

carbon dioxide

water

Plants are lucky—they don't have to hunt or shop for food. Most use the sun to produce their own food. In a process called photosynthesis, the plant's chloroplast (the part of the plant where the chemical chlorophyll is located) captures the sun's energy and combines it with carbon dioxide from the air and nutrient-rich water from the ground to produce a sugar called glucose. Plants burn the glucose for energy to help them grow. As a waste product, plants emit oxygen, which humans and other animals need to breathe. When we breathe, we exhale carbon dioxide, which the plants then use for more photosynthesis—it's all a big, finely tuned system. So the next time you pass a lonely houseplant, give it thanks for helping you live.

Family Project

Tweet and Eat

Welcome the arrival of spring and attract birds to your yard with this cool bird feeder.

YOU WILL NEED
- HALF-GALLON MILK OR JUICE CARTON
- DOUBLE-SIDED TAPE
- HOLE PUNCH
- 2 TWIGS
- CRAFT GLUE
- WOODEN CRAFT STICKS
- WATERPROOF, NONTOXIC PAINT
- BIRDSEED
- TWINE

WHAT TO DO

GET STARTED Clean the carton and let it dry.

ENTRANCE Draw a three-inch (8-cm) square on the front of the carton, starting two inches (5 cm) from the bottom. Then draw a triangle above the square. The top of the square should form the bottom of the triangle. Cut out the square and triangle in one piece.

AWNING Fold down the triangle, creating a horizontal seam between the triangle and square. Then unfold. Fold the whole cutout in half vertically. Then unfold. Cut along the vertical seam from the top to the bottom of the triangular section only. Attach the "awning" to the carton by taping the cut triangular section inside the opening and bending up the square section of the cutout (right).

PERCHES Punch two parallel holes below the opening in the carton, each an inch (2.5 cm) from the side of the carton. Punch two identical holes in the back of the carton. Make sure they are aligned with the holes in front. Slide a twig through each set of holes from front to back.

DECORATE Glue craft sticks to the outside of the carton until it is completely covered. Cut the sticks to fit as needed. Let dry. Paint the bird feeder. Let dry. Fill the feeder with birdseed. Then punch two holes in the top of the feeder (see picture). String twine through these holes and hang your feeder from a tree.

WANT FEATHERED FRIENDS TO CHOW DOWN AT YOUR FEEDER? TRY ADDING A BIRDBATH NEARBY.

Biomes

A BIOME, OFTEN CALLED A MAJOR LIFE ZONE, is one of the natural world's major communities where plants and animals adapt to their specific surroundings. Biomes are classified depending on the predominant vegetation, climate, and geography of a region. They can be divided into six major types: forest, fresh water, marine, desert, grassland, and tundra. Each biome consists of many ecosystems.

Biomes are extremely important. Balanced ecological relationships among biomes help to maintain the environment and life on Earth as we know it. For example, an increase in one species of plant, such as an invasive one, can cause a ripple effect throughout the whole biome.

Because biomes can be fragile in this way, it is important to protect them from negative human activity, such as deforestation and pollution. We must work to conserve these biomes and the unique organisms that live within them.

FOREST

The forest biomes have been evolving for about 420 million years. Today, forests occupy about one-third of Earth's land area. There are three major types of forests: tropical, temperate, and boreal (taiga). Forests are home to a diversity of plants, some of which may hold medicinal qualities for humans, as well as thousands of animal species, some still undiscovered. Forests can also absorb carbon dioxide, a greenhouse gas, and give off oxygen.

FRESH WATER

Most water on Earth is salty, but freshwater ecosystems—including lakes, ponds, wetlands, rivers, and streams—usually contain water with less than one percent salt concentration. The countless animal and plant species that live in a freshwater biome vary from continent to continent, but include algae, frogs, turtles, fish, and the larvae of many insects. Throughout the world, people use food, medicine, and other resources from this biome.

MARINE

The marine biome covers almost three-fourths of Earth's surface, making it the largest habitat on our planet. The four oceans make up the majority of the salt-water marine biome. Coral reefs are considered to be the most biodiverse of any of the biome habitats. The marine biome is home to more than one million plant and animal species. Some of the largest animals on Earth, such as the blue whale, live in the marine biome.

DESERT

Covering about one-fifth of Earth's surface, deserts are places where precipitation is less than 10 inches (25 cm) per year. Although most deserts are hot, there are other kinds as well. The four major kinds of deserts in the world are hot, semiarid, coastal, and cold. Far from being barren wastelands, deserts are biologically rich habitats with a vast array of animals and plants that have adapted to the harsh conditions there.

GRASSLAND

Biomes called grasslands are characterized by having grasses instead of large shrubs or trees. Grasslands generally have precipitation for only about half to three-fourths of the year. If it were more, they would become forests. Widespread around the world, grasslands can be divided into two types: tropical (savannas) and temperate. Grasslands are home to some of the largest land animals on Earth, such as elephants, hippopotamuses, rhinoceroses, and lions.

TUNDRA

The coldest of all biomes, a tundra is characterized by an extremely cold climate, simple vegetation, little precipitation, poor nutrients, and a short growing season. There are two types of tundra: arctic and alpine. A very fragile environment, a tundra is home to few kinds of vegetation. Surprisingly, though, there are quite a few animal species that can survive the tundra's extremes, such as wolves, caribou, and even mosquitoes.

STUMP YOUR PARENTS

WONDERS OF NATURE QUIZ

Are your parents in tune with the great outdoors? If they can't answer these questions from the chapter, maybe they should take a hike!

ANSWERS BELOW

1 Which country is home to the world's largest coral reef?

a. Mexico
b. Indonesia
c. Philippines
d. Australia

2 **True or false?** The fastest wind speed ever recorded was 318 miles an hour (512 kph).

3 Which is not a hurricane name in 2014?

a. Nana
b. Teddy
c. Marco
d. Ruthie

4 Which of these weather phenomena is not real?

a. fire rainbow
b. snow tires
c. freak wave
d. Hole Punch cloud

5 Where would you find the highest tide?

a. King Sound, Australia
b. Severn Estuary, U.K.
c. Bay of Fundy, Canada
d. An underground river on Mars

6 Where would you find a dugong?

a. Indian Ocean
b. Sahara desert
c. Tornado Alley
d. Nowhere, dugongs aren't real animals.

ANSWERS:
1. d; 2. True. Recorded near a tornado in Oklahoma, U.S.A., in 1999; 3. d; 4. b; 5. c; 6. a

SPEAK NATURALLY

Oral Reports Made Easy

Does the thought of public speaking start your stomach churning like a tornado? Would you rather get caught in an avalanche than give a speech?

Giving an oral report does not have to be a natural disaster. The basic format is very similar to a written essay. There are two main elements that make up a good oral report—the writing and the presentation. As you write your oral report, remember that your audience will be hearing the information as opposed to reading it. Follow the guidelines below, and there will be clear skies ahead.

TIP:
Make sure you practice your presentation a few times. Stand in front of a mirror or have a parent record you so you can see if you need to work on anything, such as eye contact.

Writing Your Material

Follow the steps in the "How to Write a Perfect Essay" section on p. 35, but prepare your report to be spoken rather than written. Try to keep your sentences short and simple. Long, complex sentences are harder to follow. Limit yourself to just a few key points. You don't want to overwhelm your audience with too much information. To be most effective, hit your key points in the introduction, elaborate on them in the body, and then repeat them once again in your conclusion.

An oral report has three basic parts:

- **Introduction**—This is your chance to engage your audience and really capture their interest in the subject you are presenting. Use a funny personal experience or a dramatic story, or start with an intriguing question.

- **Body**—This is the longest part of your report. Here you elaborate on the facts and ideas you want to convey. Give information that supports your main idea and expand on it with specific examples or details. In other words, structure your oral report in the same way you would a written essay so that your thoughts are presented in a clear and organized manner.

- **Conclusion**—This is the time to summarize the information and emphasize your most important points to the audience one last time.

Preparing Your Delivery

1 Practice makes perfect.
Practice! Practice! Practice! Confidence, enthusiasm, and energy are key to delivering an effective oral report, and they can best be achieved through rehearsal. Ask family and friends to be your practice audience and give you feedback when you're done. Were they able to follow your ideas? Did you seem knowledgeable and confident? Did you speak too slowly or too fast, too softly or too loudly? The more times you practice giving your report, the more you'll master the material. Then you won't have to rely so heavily on your notes or papers and will be able to give your report in a relaxed and confident manner.

2 Present with everything you've got.
Be as creative as you can. Incorporate videos, sound clips, slide presentations, charts, diagrams, and photos. Visual aids help stimulate your audience's senses and keep them intrigued and engaged. They can also help to reinforce your key points. And remember that when you're giving an oral report, you're a performer. Take charge of the spotlight and be as animated and entertaining as you can. Have fun with it.

3 Keep your nerves under control.
Everyone gets a little nervous when speaking in front of a group. That's normal. But the more preparation you've done—meaning plenty of researching, organizing, and rehearsing—the more confident you'll be. Preparation is the key. And if you make a mistake or stumble over your words, just regroup and keep going. Nobody's perfect, and nobody expects you to be.

123

A young man paddle surfs in Hawaii, U.S.A. Stand-up paddling originated in Hawaii in the 1920s and 1930s.

Culture
Connection

20 CELEBRATIONS

1 CHINESE NEW YEAR
January 31
Also called Lunar New Year, this holiday marks the new year according to the lunar calendar. Families celebrate with parades, feasts, and fireworks. Young people may receive gifts of money in red envelopes.

2 SETSUBUN
February 3
In Japan, people celebrate the start of spring by throwing roasted soybeans out their door and in temples and shrines as a symbolic gesture to drive out demons and welcome good luck to the season.

3 NYEPI
March 31
A national day of silence, this holiday marks Lunar New Year in Bali, Indonesia, and encourages meditation and reflection. Those who follow traditional customs do not talk, use electricity, travel, or eat for 24 hours.

4 EASTER
April 20
A Christian holiday that celebrates the resurrection of Jesus Christ, Easter is celebrated by giving baskets filled with gifts, decorated eggs, or candy to children.

5 FREEDOM DAY
April 27
Established to mark the first national election held in South Africa after the end of a policy of racial segregation called apartheid, this holiday now highlights freedoms for all South African citizens. It's celebrated throughout the country with festivals, performances, and parties.

6 BERMUDA DAY
May 26
The first day of the year that Bermudians take a dip in the ocean.

7 RAMADAN AND EID AL-FITR
June 29–July 29*
A Muslim religious holiday, Ramadan is a month long, ending in the Eid Al-Fitr celebration. Observers fast during this month—eating only after sunset. Muslims pray for forgiveness and hope to purify themselves through observance.

8 BASTILLE DAY
July 14
The French call this day *La Fête Nationale,* or the celebration of the start of the French Revolution in 1789. In Paris, fireworks light up the night skies while dance parties spill into the streets.

9 NAG PANCHAMI
August 1
In Nepal and India, Hindus worship snakes—and keep evil spirits out of their homes—by sticking images of serpents on their doors and making offerings to the revered reptiles.

10 PICNIC DAY
August 4
In Australia's Northern Territory, people dine alfresco to celebrate Picnic Day.

*Dates may vary slightly by location.

Around the World

11 MELON DAY
August 10

Since 1994, people in the Asian nation Turkmenistan have taken a day—aptly named Melon Day—to celebrate the country's sweet muskmelons.

12 LA TOMATINA
August 27

Close to 250,000 pounds (113,000 kg) of tomatoes are hurled during this annual event in the Spanish town of Buñol. The festivities involve more than 45,000 people, making this one of the world's largest food fights.

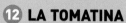

13 OKTOBERFEST
September 20–October 5

Originally celebrating the marriage of Bavarian royalty back in 1810, Oktoberfest is now a mega-festival celebrated all over the world. People enjoy food, drink, music, and merriment.

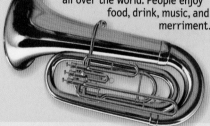

14 ROSH HASHANAH
September 25–26

A Jewish religious holiday marking the beginning of a new year on the Hebrew calendar. Celebrations include prayer, ritual foods, and a day of rest.

15 DIWALI
October 23–27

India's largest and most important holiday. People light their homes with clay lamps to symbolize the inner light that protects against spiritual darkness.

16 MASSKARA
October

Celebrated in Bacolod, Philippines, this relatively young holiday was established in 1980 to promote happiness. People dance in the streets wearing colorful costumes and smiley-face masks.

17 GUY FAWKES DAY
November 5

Over 400 years ago, a man named Guy Fawkes plotted with other conspirators to blow up the British Parliament. He failed, and Brits still celebrate his demise by lighting bonfires and setting off fireworks.

18 HANUKKAH
December 17–December 24

This Jewish holiday is eight days long. It commemorates the rededication of the Temple in Jerusalem. Hanukkah celebrations include the lighting of menorah candles for eight days and the exchange of gifts.

19 CHRISTMAS DAY
December 25

A Christian holiday marking the birth of Jesus Christ, Christmas is usually celebrated by decorating trees, exchanging presents, and having festive gatherings.

20 BOXING DAY
December 26

Some people think this national holiday in Great Britain, Australia, Canada, and New Zealand was initially designated as a day to box up donations for the poor. Today? It's all about shopping, parties, and playing soccer.

What's Your Chinese Horoscope?
Locate your birth year to find out.

In Chinese astrology the zodiac runs on a 12-year cycle, based on the lunar calendar. Each year corresponds to one of 12 animals, each representing one of 12 personality types. Read on to find out which animal year you were born in and what that might say about you.

RAT
1972, '84, '96, 2008
Say cheese! You're attractive, charming, and creative. When you get mad, you can have really sharp teeth!

HORSE
1966, '78, '90, 2002, '14
Being happy is your "mane" goal. And while you're smart and hardworking, your teacher may ride you for talking too much.

OX
1973, '85, '97, 2009
You're smart, patient, and as strong as an ... well, you know what. Though you're a leader, you never brag.

SHEEP
1967, '79, '91, 2003
Gentle as a lamb, you're also artistic, compassionate, and wise. You're often shy.

TIGER
1974, '86, '98, 2010
You may be a nice person, but no one should ever enter your room without asking—you might attack!

MONKEY
1968, '80, '92, 2004
No "monkey see, monkey do" for you. You're a clever problem-solver with an excellent memory.

RABBIT
1975, '87, '99, 2011
Your ambition and talent make you jump at opportunity. You also keep your ears open for gossip.

ROOSTER
1969, '81, '93, 2005
You crow about your adventures, but inside you're really shy. You're thoughtful, capable, brave, and talented.

DRAGON
1976, '88, 2000, '12
You're on fire! Health, energy, honesty, and bravery make you a living legend.

DOG
1970, '82, '94, 2006
Often the leader of the pack, you're loyal and honest. You can also keep a secret.

SNAKE
1977, '89, 2001, '13
You may not speak often, but you're very smart. You always seem to have a stash of cash.

PIG
1971, '83, '95, 2007
Even though you're courageous, honest, and kind, you never hog all the attention.

ANNIVERSARIES

Annual . . . . 1 year
Biennial . . . . 2 years
Triennial . . . . 3 years
Quadrennial . . . . 4 years
Quinquennial . . . . 5 years
Sexennial . . . . 6 years
Septennial . . . . 7 years
Octennial . . . . 8 years
Novennial . . . . 9 years
Decennial . . . . 10 years
Undecennial . . . . 11 years
Duodecennial . . . . 12 years
Tredecennial . . . . 13 years
Quattuordecennial . . . . 14 years
Quindecennial . . . . 15 years
Vigintennial or vicennial . . . 20 years
Semicentennial or
  quinquagenary . . . . 50 years
Semisesquicentennial . . . . . . 75 years
Centennial . . . . 100 years
Quasquicentennial . . . . 125 years
Sesquicentennial . . . . 150 years
Demisemiseptcentennial or
  quartoseptcentennial . . . . 175 years
Bicentennial . . . . 200 years
Semiquincentennial . . . . . . 250 years
Tercentennial or
  tricentennial . . . . 300 years
Semiseptcentennial . . . . . . 350 years
Quadricentennial or
  quatercentenary . . . . 400 years
Quincentennial . . . . 500 years
Sexcentennial . . . . 600 years
Septicentennial or
  septuacentennial . . . . 700 years
Octocentennial . . . . 800 years
Nonacentennial . . . . 900 years
Millennial . . . . 1,000 years
Bimillennial . . . . 2,000 years

2014 CALENDAR

JANUARY
S	M	T	W	T	F	S
			1	2	3	4
5	6	7	8	9	10	11
12	13	14	15	16	17	18
19	20	21	22	23	24	25
26	27	28	29	30	31	

JULY
S	M	T	W	T	F	S
		1	2	3	4	5
6	7	8	9	10	11	12
13	14	15	16	17	18	19
20	21	22	23	24	25	26
27	28	29	30	31		

FEBRUARY
S	M	T	W	T	F	S
						1
2	3	4	5	6	7	8
9	10	11	12	13	14	15
16	17	18	19	20	21	22
23	24	25	26	27	28	

AUGUST
S	M	T	W	T	F	S
					1	2
3	4	5	6	7	8	9
10	11	12	13	14	15	16
17	18	19	20	21	22	23
24	25	26	27	28	29	30
31						

MARCH
S	M	T	W	T	F	S
						1
2	3	4	5	6	7	8
9	10	11	12	13	14	15
16	17	18	19	20	21	22
23	24	25	26	27	28	29
30	31					

SEPTEMBER
S	M	T	W	T	F	S
	1	2	3	4	5	6
7	8	9	10	11	12	13
14	15	16	17	18	19	20
21	22	23	24	25	26	27
28	29	30				

APRIL
S	M	T	W	T	F	S
		1	2	3	4	5
6	7	8	9	10	11	12
13	14	15	16	17	18	19
20	21	22	23	24	25	26
27	28	29	30			

OCTOBER
S	M	T	W	T	F	S
			1	2	3	4
5	6	7	8	9	10	11
12	13	14	15	16	17	18
19	20	21	22	23	24	25
26	27	28	29	30	31	

MAY
S	M	T	W	T	F	S
				1	2	3
4	5	6	7	8	9	10
11	12	13	14	15	16	17
18	19	20	21	22	23	24
25	26	27	28	29	30	31

NOVEMBER
S	M	T	W	T	F	S
						1
2	3	4	5	6	7	8
9	10	11	12	13	14	15
16	17	18	19	20	21	22
23	24	25	26	27	28	29
30						

JUNE
S	M	T	W	T	F	S
1	2	3	4	5	6	7
8	9	10	11	12	13	14
15	16	17	18	19	20	21
22	23	24	25	26	27	28
29	30					

DECEMBER
S	M	T	W	T	F	S
	1	2	3	4	5	6
7	8	9	10	11	12	13
14	15	16	17	18	19	20
21	22	23	24	25	26	27
28	29	30	31			

HALLOWEEN
PET PARADE

There's no sugar in these Halloween treats—just tons of fur. Millions of pets will be dressed up for the holiday, and NG KIDS found the craziest costumes. Some of these guys are so funny, it's scary.

These pets like wearing costumes, but yours may not. Never force your pet to do something it does not want to do.

IT'S KINDA WEIRD GOING FROM PAWS TO CLAWS.

YUP, I'M LOOKIN' GOOD!

ELSITIA THE MINIATURE CHIHUAHUA SPORTS A COOL HAIRDO AND SHADES.

TESLA THE POMERANIAN LOOKS SNAPPY IN HIS LOBSTER COSTUME.

MY SWIMMING SKILLS GO WAY BEYOND THE DOG PADDLE.

MONDEX THE CHIHUAHUA DIVES INTO HALLOWEEN WITH HIS SCUBA DISGUISE.

FETCHING COSTUMES

Which pet outfits are all the rage for Halloween? Check out these popular costume choices.

1. pumpkin
2. devil
3. witch
4. hot dog
5. bee
6. cat
7. superhero
8. ghost
9. pirate
10. accessories: bow ties, fancy collars, and bandanas

Make Your Own BIG CAT COSTUME

Cause an **UPROAR** this Halloween by making one of these cool costumes and raising awareness about **BIG CATS.**

YOU WILL NEED
- YELLOW HOODED SWEAT SUIT
- THICK, FUZZY YELLOW AND BROWN YARN
- YELLOW FELT
- GLUE
- SAFETY PINS
- BROWN FACE PAINT

WHAT TO DO
For the lion's mane, cut a piece of yarn long enough to tie around your head with the hood up. Tie three-inch (8-cm)-long pieces of yellow and brown yarn all around the long piece of yarn. Make fur cuffs for your wrists the same way. For the tail, cut a long strip of felt and glue yarn to the end. Cut two ears out of the felt. Tie the lion's mane around your hood and secure it with safety pins. Pin the ears and tail in place and tie on the fur cuffs. Paint on a brown nose and whiskers and practice your roar.

Lion

Lions, tigers, cheetahs, leopards, jaguars, and other big cats are in danger of extinction. **YOU CAN MAKE A DIFFERENCE.**

causeanuproar.org/kids

Cheetah

YOU WILL NEED
- YELLOW HOODED SWEAT SUIT
- BLACK FABRIC PAINT
- SPONGE
- YELLOW FELT
- SAFETY PINS
- CARDBOARD
- BLACK FACE PAINT

WHAT TO DO
Turn the sweat suit fuzzy side out. Dip the sponge into fabric paint, then dot the front with spots. Allow the paint to dry. Turn the outfit over and add spots to the back. Cut ears out of felt. Pin them to the hood of the sweatshirt. Ask a parent to help you cut cardboard into the shape of a television screen. Paint the cardboard black. Paint on a black nose and facial markings and get ready for your close-up—you've just been spotted on the Nat Geo WILD channel.

GINGERBREAD HOUSES

YOU WILL NEED

- VANILLA FROSTING
- CREAM OF TARTAR
- CARDBOARD
- GRAHAM CRACKERS (OR GINGERBREAD)
- SERRATED KNIFE (ASK FOR A PARENT'S HELP)
- ASSORTED CANDY, PRETZELS, AND COOKIES, INCLUDING SQUARE CARAMELS (NOT SHOWN)
- SHREDDED COCONUT

WHAT TO DO

MIX THE "GLUE" Frosting will hold each graham cracker building together. Combine a can of ready-made vanilla frosting with one-quarter teaspoon of cream of tartar. To apply the frosting, squeeze it out of a sealed freezer bag with a hole cut in one corner.

BUILD THE HOUSE

BASE Cut a piece of cardboard that's big enough to hold the scene.

WALLS The front and back walls are each made of a whole graham cracker turned horizontally. Ask a parent to create the two remaining sides. For each, use a serrated knife to gently saw the top of a whole graham cracker into a peak (inset, above). Run a bead of icing along the bottom edge and sides of the crackers. "Glue" them together in a rectangle on top of the cardboard. Prop up the walls while you work.

PEAKED ROOF Run icing along the tops of the walls. Place two whole graham crackers—turned horizontally—on top of the sides, using icing to hold them in place. Let the icing set overnight.

WAGON USE QUARTER CRACKERS FOR THE BOTTOM AND SIDES. USE HALF OF A QUARTER CRACKER FOR THE BACK. "GLUE" THE PIECES IN PLACE. ADD PRETZEL WHEELS AND A CARAMEL UNDER THE WAGON FOR SUPPORT.

SILO CUT OFF THE TOPS OF TWO CAKE CONES, THEN FROST THE OPEN ENDS TOGETHER. STICK ON COLORFUL LICORICE AND TOP WITH A FOIL BAKING CUP.

SNOWMAN SKEWER TWO MARSHMALLOWS ONTO A PRETZEL STICK. USE GUM-DROPS FOR THE HAT, EYES, AND NOSE; PRETZELS FOR THE ARMS; AND STRING LICORICE FOR A SCARF.

Fun Winter Gift Idea

Snow Globes

YOU WILL NEED
- SMALL JAR (A BABY FOOD JAR WORKS WELL)
- SANDPAPER
- INSTANT-BONDING GLUE (FOLLOW DIRECTIONS ON THE TUBE AND USE WITH ADULT SUPERVISION)
- PLASTIC ANIMAL OR FIGURINE THAT FITS IN THE JAR
- NAIL POLISH REMOVER
- BABY OIL
- 1/2 TEASPOON WHITE GLITTER

WHAT TO DO

Turn the jar's lid upside down. Use sandpaper to scuff the inside of the lid. Glue the bottom of the figurine to the center of the lid. (Nail polish remover cleans glue off skin and surfaces.) Dry for four hours. Fill the jar with baby oil. Add glitter. To seal, put glue around the rim of the jar. Close the lid tightly and dry for four hours. Turn the jar over, and let it snow!

DOGHOUSE Follow the steps at left, but use quarter crackers for all sides and the roof.

BARN Use graham cracker halves for the barn's roof and sides. For the front and back, cut a peak in a whole graham cracker (inset, above left).

DECORATIONS "Glue" on your favorite treats to create doors, rooftops, trees, and anything else you can imagine. Let everything set overnight. Cover the cardboard base with shredded coconut to finish your snowy scene.

DOG "GLUE" TWO GUMDROPS TOGETHER TO FORM THE BODY. STICK ON PIECES OF GUMDROPS FOR THE EARS, NOSE, AND TAIL.

133

CHEETAH

WHISKERS CAN BE TRICKY.

The most useful tools? "A fine paintbrush and a steady hand," Daniele says. "My favorite is a cheetah because it was my first and brought me luck."

THE REAL ANIMAL : CHEETAHS NEED TO DRINK ONLY ONCE EVERY THREE TO FOUR DAYS.

HANDIMALS

MACAW

"THE MOST IMPORTANT THING IS TO PAINT THE EYE

with the shape and expression of each animal," Daniele says. "It gives character and life to the art."

THE REAL ANIMAL

TO OPEN NUTS, A MACAW USES ITS BEAK, WHICH IS STRONG ENOUGH TO BREAK THROUGH A BROOMSTICK.

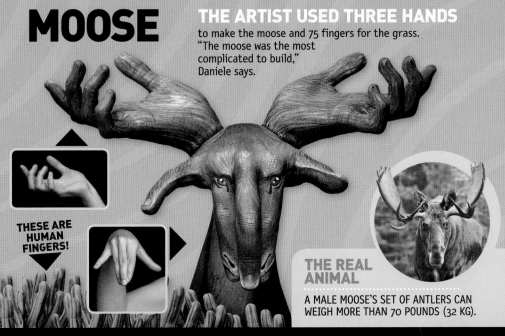

MOOSE

THE ARTIST USED THREE HANDS

to make the moose and 75 fingers for the grass. "The moose was the most complicated to build," Daniele says.

THESE ARE HUMAN FINGERS!

THE REAL ANIMAL

A MALE MOOSE'S SET OF ANTLERS CAN WEIGH MORE THAN 70 POUNDS (32 KG).

CHECK OUT THESE **WILD HANDMADE** CREATIONS.

What do you get when you cross a human hand with an animal? A "handimal"! Artist Guido Daniele positions people's hands into animal shapes, and then paints them to create realistic works of art. "I study my hand in front of a mirror and imagine the forms it can take," says Daniele, who lives in Milan, Italy. Working from photos and his own memory, Daniele paints the animals onto the hands of models—usually his son or daughter. Check out these "handimals" and some of the secrets to Daniele's art. In this case, it's OK to "handle" the animals!

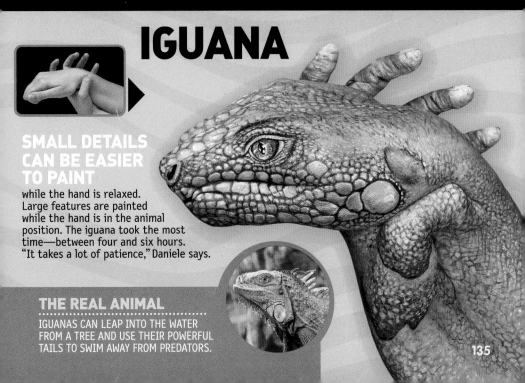

IGUANA

SMALL DETAILS CAN BE EASIER TO PAINT

while the hand is relaxed. Large features are painted while the hand is in the animal position. The iguana took the most time—between four and six hours. "It takes a lot of patience," Daniele says.

THE REAL ANIMAL

IGUANAS CAN LEAP INTO THE WATER FROM A TREE AND USE THEIR POWERFUL TAILS TO SWIM AWAY FROM PREDATORS.

WE ARE ACTUALLY WAX!

JUSTIN BIEBER
Around the time the singer's wax figure was made, he cut his iconic hair. Artists in New York haven't restyled Bieber's 'do just yet—they're waiting to see if the new cut sticks.

Here, Justin Bieber gets a lot of kisses from fans. So do Selena Gomez and Johnny Depp. But they don't mind—they're made of wax!

At the 12 Madame Tussauds attractions around the world, visitors can interact with lifelike wax figures representing celebs and historical figures—even Madame Tussaud herself. The real Tussaud was an art tutor in France in the late 1700s. During the French Revolution, she was forced to make wax masks of executed royals such as Marie Antoinette. After she moved to Great Britain, she began an exhibit in 1835 of wax figures and artifacts from the revolution.

Today the process to create a wax figure is much the same as it was more than 200 years ago.

SELENA GOMEZ
Popular wax figures such as singer and actress Selena Gomez get a lot of hands-on attention from visitors. That's why many hairstyles and faces are washed and restyled regularly.

BARACK AND MICHELLE OBAMA

The First Couple's heads—like all wax heads at Madame Tussauds exhibits—are actually made 2 percent larger than normal head sizes, since wax shrinks over time.

NEIL ARMSTRONG

His wax figure is wearing boots, but the first man to walk on the moon collected so many space rocks that he actually had to leave his boots behind so he wouldn't weigh down the space-craft. Armstrong died in 2012.

TAYLOR SWIFT

Like many celebrities, the singer donated her clothes—and her guitar—for the wax figure.

STEP BY STEP

Artists spend about four months producing each wax figure using the following steps. "It's really bringing the people to life," says Bret Pidgeon, general manager of Madame Tussauds New York.

❶ Some 250 measurements are taken of the subject, everything from the length of a finger to the distance from ear to nose. Artists even try to take a mold of the subject's teeth!

❷ A life-size body model is made of clay. A mold is made for the head.

❸ About ten pounds (4.5 kg) of hot beeswax is poured into the mold to create the head. Another four pounds (1.8 kg) are used for the hands.

❹ Eyeballs are hand painted, and red silk thread is carefully tweaked to look like veins.

❺ Hair is added one strand at a time. It takes about 140 hours.

❻ Some ten coats of oil paint are applied to make the head look like a real person. (This represents former President Jimmy Carter.)

❼ A plastic fiberglass cast is made for the body. Then the figure is dressed and topped with the wax head, ready for display.

Piece of Cake

Some artists are making treats that look just too real to eat! Designer cakes are popping up everywhere, and this cake artist has some sneaky tricks for baking realistic creations. Want to learn more? Read on!

The word "cake" comes from the Viking word *kaka*.

NECK IN NECK

To create this 18-inch-tall, 25-pound (46-cm, 11-kg) giraffe cake, artist Debbie Goard used a plastic pipe in its neck to hold up the head—and the head is the only part not made of cake. A cake head would have been too heavy and fallen over. Her solution? Make it out of rice cereal treats. "People usually feel funny about eating the head, anyway," says Goard, of Debbie Does Cakes in Oakland, California, U.S.A.

CHI-WOW-WA

To create this doggone delicious cake, Goard molded cake around smooth wooden sticks called dowels, and a board was tucked into the belly to support the body. "I've been known to use a saw and drill," she says.

I'M A CAKE!

Ancient Egyptians baked cakes, but they were more like honey-sweetened bread.

EAT THE BEAT

You'd need to lick off your drumsticks if you played this drum. Goard used an airbrush to spray-paint on food coloring to create the blue body and silver rims. Then she brushed on edible glitter to give the drum its realistic sparkle. For the drum's logo, she hooked up her computer to a special printer that uses food coloring for ink and sheets of icing for paper.

PASTA-*LICIOUS*

The spaghetti noodles are fondant—thick icing that's easy to mold. The meatballs are walnut chocolate truffles, and it's all covered in raspberry jam for red sauce. (In case you're wondering, the actual cake is under the noodles.) The hardest part? Goard hand-rolled some 600 strings of spaghetti, one strand at a time.

139

1

THE LARGEST U.S. BILL PRODUCED TODAY IS THE **$100 BILL.** BUT LESS THAN 45 YEARS AGO, YOU COULD PAY FOR STUFF WITH A **$10,000 BILL!**

2

Nearly two dozen countries—from Australia to Nigeria to Mexico—print money on SHEETS OF PLASTIC instead of paper. These brightly colored bills are so tough they can be WASHED WITH SOAP AND WATER.

MONEY AND LUCK

COOL FACTS THAT WILL MAKE YOU SAY, "KA-¢HING!"

3

COINS IN ANCIENT CHINA WERE MINTED WITH HOLES IN THE CENTER SO THEY COULD BE STRUNG AND CARRIED MORE EASILY. A FEW COUNTRIES STILL USE COINS WITH HOLES, INCLUDING DENMARK, JAPAN, PAPUA NEW GUINEA, AND THE PHILIPPINES.

4

A BRITISH COUNTERFEITING GANG PRINTED 50 MILLION POUNDS (U.S. $80 MILLION) IN FAKE BILLS BEFORE THEIR ARREST IN 1998.

5

Until the early 1900s, **A WHOLE COCONUT** was the accepted form of currency in the **NICOBAR ISLANDS,** west of Thailand in the **INDIAN OCEAN.**

6

LOONIE is the nickname for the Canadian one-dollar coin, which features the image of a bird called a loon, commonly found in Canada.

7

IN 2007, MONGOLIA ISSUED A COMMEMORATIVE COIN WITH A PORTRAIT OF **U.S. PRESIDENT JOHN F. KENNEDY.** IF YOU PUSH A TINY BUTTON, THE COIN PLAYS A SOUND BITE FROM A SPEECH.

JOHN F. KENNEDY (1917-1963)

HOW TO FENG SHUI YOUR ROOM

IF FENG SHUI DOESN'T WORK FOR YOU, THAT'S OK. THIS STORY IS JUST FOR FUN!

Want to make more friends? Get better grades? Feng shui may help! Feng shui (FUNG SHWAY) is the ancient art of placement. Though it's not a science, people have been swearing by feng shui "cures" for thousands of years to bring them good luck. How? By placing or rearranging items in your home, positive chi—or energy—can flow freely and change your luck for the better. Try a few of these feng shui cures in your bedroom and see what happens!

1
Hanging a mobile keeps positive chi moving.

2
Hang a soft-ringing bell on each side of your door to give you positive thoughts, which inspire good luck and happiness.

3
Hang three pictures of family and friends in a triangle pattern to get along better with your loved ones. In feng shui, the number three stimulates good chi.

4
Draw a picture of what you want and put it under your mattress. Your dreams just may come true.

5
Move your desk or a book-case to the left of the door to get better grades.

6
Put a quartz crystal on your desk to improve your con-centration. Girls should place theirs on the left; boys on the right.

7
Hang a bulletin board of your achievements on the wall opposite your door for inspiration and motivation.

8
Put a stuffed version of your birth-year animal (see p. 128) on your bed for extra luck.

9
Three pillows on your bed may help you to be a better friend—and find new ones.

10
Keep a plant in your room if you crave more time with family and friends.

11
Place a light-green or purple bowl in your room, and add a coin when you enter or leave to help save money.

12
Place your bed along a wall so you have a clear view of your door. This will help you sleep better.

12 Ways to Say Happy Birthday

1 **ARABIC** Eid milaad sa'eed

2 **FRENCH (CANADA)** Bonne Fête

3 **GERMAN** Alles Gute zum Geburtstag

4 **GREEK** Hronia polla

5 **HAWAIIAN** Hau'oli La Hanau

6 **HEBREW** Yom Huledet Sameakh

7 **HINDI** Janmadin mubarak ho

8 **MANDARIN** Shengrì kuàilè

9 **RUSSIAN** S dniom rojdeniya

10 **SPANISH** ¡Feliz cumpleaños!

11 **SWAHILI** Nakutakia mema kwa siku yako ya kuzaliwa!

12 **TURKISH** Dogum günün kutlu olsun

LANGUAGES IN PERIL

TODAY, there are more than 7,000 languages spoken on Earth. But by 2100, more than half of those may disappear. In fact, experts say one language dies every two weeks, due to the increasing dominance of larger languages, such as English, Spanish, and Mandarin. So what can be done to keep dialects from disappearing? Efforts like National Geographic's Enduring Voices Project are now tracking down and documenting the world's most threatened indigenous languages, such as Tofa, spoken by only 30 people in Siberia, and Magati Ke, from Aboriginal Australia. The hope is to preserve these languages—and the cultures they belong to.

10 LEADING LANGUAGES

Approximate population of first-language speakers (in millions)

1. Chinese*	1,213
2. Spanish	329
3. English	328
4. Arabic	221
5. Hindi	182
6. Bengali	181
7. Portuguese	178
8. Russian	144
9. Japanese	122
10. German	90

Some languages have only a few hundred speakers, while Chinese has some 1,213 million native speakers worldwide. That's more than triple the next largest group of language speakers. Colonial expansion, trade, and migration account for the spread of the other most widely spoken languages. With growing use of the Internet, English is becoming the language of the technology age.

*Includes all forms of the language.

Bet you didn't know

6 FUN language facts

1 The **most commonly** used letters in the English language are **E, T, A,** and **O.**

2 The Russian word for **"RED"** also means **"beautiful."**

3 The **longest** word in English is pneumonoultramicroscopicsilicovolcanoconiosis, a lung disease.

4 **Babies' cries** can sound **different** in various **languages.**

5 People in **Papua New Guinea** speak a total of **820 languages.**

6 **The word taxi** means the same thing in English, German, French, Swedish, Spanish, and Portuguese.

World Religions

Around the world, religion takes many forms. Some belief systems, such as Christianity, Islam, and Judaism, are monotheistic, meaning that followers believe in just one supreme being. Others, like Hinduism, Shintoism, and most native belief systems, are polytheistic, meaning that many of their followers believe in multiple gods.

All of the major religions have their origins in Asia, but they have spread around the world. Christianity, with the largest number of followers, has three divisions—Roman Catholic, Eastern Orthodox, and Protestant. Islam, with about one-fifth of all believers, has two main divisions—Sunni and Shiite. Hinduism and Buddhism account for almost another one-fifth of believers. Judaism, dating back some 4,000 years, has more than 13 million followers, less than one percent of all believers.

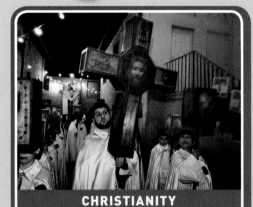

CHRISTIANITY

Based on the teachings of Jesus Christ, a Jew born some 2,000 years ago in the area of modern-day Israel, Christianity has spread worldwide and actively seeks converts. Followers in Switzerland (above) participate in an Easter season procession with lanterns and crosses.

BUDDHISM

Founded about 2,400 years ago in northern India by the Hindu prince Gautama Buddha, Buddhism spread throughout East and Southeast Asia. Buddhist temples have statues, such as the Mihintale Buddha (above) in Sri Lanka.

HINDUISM

Dating back more than 4,000 years, Hinduism is practiced mainly in India. Hindus follow sacred texts known as the Vedas and believe in reincarnation. During the festival of Navratri, which honors the goddess Durga, the Garba dance is performed (above).

CLOSE-UP

Now that's a BIG crowd!

I t has been 1,200 years since the bishop of Rome became known as the pope. Today, the pope is still the head of the Roman Catholic Church. Every Easter Sunday about 100,000 people gather in St. Peter's Square in Vatican City to receive his blessing.

ISLAM

Muslims believe that the Koran, Islam's sacred book, records the words of Allah (God) as revealed to the Prophet Muhammad beginning around A.D. 610. Believers (above) circle the Kaaba in the Haram Mosque in Mecca, Saudi Arabia, the spiritual center of the faith.

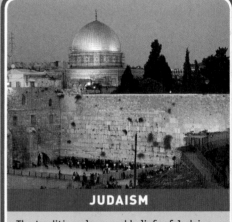

JUDAISM

The traditions, laws, and beliefs of Judaism date back to Abraham (the Patriarch) and the Torah (the first five books of the Old Testament). Followers pray before the Western Wall (above), which stands below Islam's Dome of the Rock in Jerusalem.

145

STUMP YOUR PARENTS

CULTURE CONNECTION QUIZ

How much do your parents know about different cultures? Quiz them on this chapter's content to measure their worldly knowledge. ANSWERS BELOW

1 Where is Melon Day celebrated?
a. Thailand
b. Turkmenistan
c. Indonesia
d. Cantaloupe Island

2 **True or false?** Feng shui is the ancient art of making dumplings.

3 According to the Chinese Horoscope, 2014 is the year of the _____?

a. horse b. rat c. snake d. tiger

Justin Bieber wax figure

4 Before Madame Tussaud made wax figures, what was her profession?
a. a Russian circus performer
b. a Swiss nurse
c. a French art tutor
d. a fairytale princess

5 If your school is celebrating its semisesquicentennial, how old is it?
a. 50 years old
b. 75 years old
c. 125 years old
d. 150 years old

6 Which of the following has not been used as currency?
a. coconuts
b. whale teeth
c. printed sheets of plastic
d. gummy bears

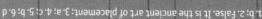

ANSWERS:
1. b; 2. False. It is the ancient art of placement; 3. a; 4. c; 5. b; 6. d

HOMEWORK HELP

Explore a New Culture

INDIAN STAMP

5 RUPEE COIN

INDIAN FLAG

You're a student, but you're also a citizen of the world. Writing a report on a foreign nation or your own country is a great way to better understand and appreciate how people in other parts of the world live. Pick the country of your ancestors, one that's been in the news, or one that you'd like to visit someday.

Passport to Success

A country report follows the format of an expository essay because you're "exposing" information about the country you choose.

Simple Steps

1. RESEARCH Gathering information is the most important step in writing a good country report. Look to Internet sources, encyclopedias, books, magazine and newspaper articles, and other sources to find important and interesting details about your subject.

2. ORGANIZE YOUR NOTES Put the information you gathered into a rough outline. For example, sort everything you found about the country's system of government, climate, etc.

3. WRITE IT UP Follow the basic structure of good writing: introduction, body, and conclusion. Remember that each paragraph should have a topic sentence that is then supported by facts and details. Incorporate the information from your notes, but make sure it's in your own words. And make your writing flow with good transitions and descriptive language.

4. ADD VISUALS Include maps, diagrams, photos, and other visual aids.

5. PROOFREAD AND REVISE Correct any mistakes, and polish your language. Do your best!

6. CITE YOUR SOURCES Be sure to keep a record of your sources.

FUN and GAMES

MISSION TO MARS

WHEEL IN THE SKY

ANIMAL PARK

WRECK 'N' RAC

ROCK 'N' ROLL

These eight snapshots were taken at this theme park. Find the scene that appears in each snapshot. ANSWERS ON PAGE 338

Treasure Hunt

The Animal Jam characters found an old treasure map, but a maze stands between them and their riches. Help them find their way through Jamaa to the treasure.

BONUS: Find ten gems hidden in the maze's paths. ANSWERS ON PAGE 338

NATIONAL GEOGRAPHIC

ANIMAL JAM

START

FINISH

EXPLORE!

NATIONAL GEOGRAPHIC KIDS' virtual world online: AnimalJam.com

Enter the special code **NGEXPLORER** for a bonus!

Boettger's chameleon

Just Joking

KNOCK, KNOCK.

Who's there?
Hawaii.
Hawaii who?
I'm great.
Hawaii you?

KATHRYN: You said this cat was good for mice, but he doesn't go near them.

EVA: Well, isn't that good for the mice?

TONGUE TWISTER!

Say this fast three times:

I love unique New York.

Q Where do **pirates** go to have **fun?**

A The arrr-cade.

You've **got** to be joking...

Q What do **apes** like to eat with **milk?**

A Chocolate chimp cookies.

155

Funny FILL-IN
The Mad Inventor

Ask a friend to give you words to fill in the blanks in this story without showing it to him or her. Then read it out loud for a laugh.

I was going to be rich! I had just invented the first electric _____ (noun). Using a(n) _____ (tool) from _____ (relative's name)'s toolbox, I built it out of old _____ (noun, plural) and rubber _____ (noun, plural). The first time I turned it on, the machine worked _____ (adverb ending in -ly). I couldn't believe it! "_____ (exclamation)!" I quickly invited a(n) _____ (adjective) billionaire to check out my invention. I couldn't wait to sell it for _____ (large number) million dollars and live like _____ (name of a celebrity). But when I turned it on, something went terribly wrong. The machine started _____ (verb ending in -ing) and _____ (verb ending in -ing). Suddenly it spewed _____ (something slimy) and shot slices of _____ (food) in all directions. The billionaire started screaming at the top of his _____ (body part, plural) and ran out of my lab. Good thing I still get my weekly allowance.

We Gave It a Swirl

Use the clues below to figure out which animals appear in these swirled pictures. ANSWERS ON PAGE 338

1

HINT: If one of these "ladies" lands on you, it might bring good luck.

2

HINT: Don't go bananas trying to figure out what's in this picture.

3

4

HINT: This hoofed mammal likes to stick its neck out.

5

HINT: This predator has no manners. It swallows its food whole.

HINT: Now a winged beauty, this highflier used to get around on six legs.

157

Find the HIDDEN ANIMALS

Animals often blend into their environments for protection. Find the animals listed below in the photographs. Match the letter to the correct photo.

ANSWERS ON PAGE 338

1. hare
2. snake
3. eel
4. deer
5. owl
6. shrimp
7. tiger
8. praying mantis
9. fish
10. lemur
11. bat

A

B

C

D

E

159

Lion

Just Joking

KNOCK, KNOCK.

Who's there?
Amos.
Amos who?
A mosquito bit me!

Q What part of **the fish** weighs the most?

A The scales.

WAITER: Why do you laugh while cooking breakfast?

CHEF: Because the egg always cracks a yolk.

TONGUE TWISTER!

Say this fast three times:

Three free-thinking frogs think friendly thoughts.

You've **got** to be joking...

Q Why did the **colt** have a sore throat?

A He was a little horse.

ANSWERS ON PAGE 338

CHANGE YOUR STRIPES

These photographs show close-up views of stripes in the animal kingdom. Unscramble the letters to identify what's in each picture.

RGIET

_____

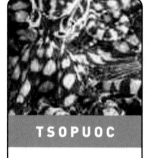

TSOPUOC

_____

ETBTYRULF

_____

HFJLYISEL

_____

LASIN

_____

NHAEELCOM

_____

RUETLT

_____

TMERIH ARBC

_____

ERZSAB

_____

161

Laugh Out Loud

"I HAD THE HARDEST TIME GETTING OUT OF BED THIS MORNING."

"AW, MOM.
DO I REALLY HAVE TO GO
TO SCHOOL TODAY?"

"HOW MANY TIMES DO I HAVE TO TELL YOU...KEEP YOUR EXOSKELETONS OFF THE FLOOR!"

WHEee!

TURTLE RIDES

"I'M SORRY, BUT YOU KNOW THE RULES.
PENGUINS CAN'T FLY."

"OPEN WIDE
AND SAY 'PEEP.'"

Movie Matches

THEATER 12

Thirteen pairs of best friends are meeting in the lobby before the movie starts. Match them up by spotting the one thing each pair has in common—and find the kid whose friend is in line at the restroom!

ANSWERS ON PAGE 338

SIGNS
OF THE TIMES

Seeing isn't always believing. One of these funny signs is not real. Can you figure out which one is fake?

ANSWER ON PAGE 338

3. WHOA

1. SKY

4. Nowhere ↓ Somewhere ↓

5. Leprechaun crossing

2. NO DISSING ZONE

6. KILLER MANGOS

Funny FILL-IN
Crash Course

Ask a friend to give you words to fill in the blanks in this story without showing it to him or her. Then read it out loud for a laugh.

My family decided to go mini-golfing this past weekend. We grabbed the long metal

_____ and walked up to the first hole. I took a big swing. "_____!"
    noun, plural   silly word

I yelled. The ball bounced off a yellow dinosaur and went _____
                                                                      verb ending in -ing

through the air. My family scrambled to hide behind the _____ as the
                                                                            noun

ball zipped past them. It hit _____ on the top of the _____,
                                  relative's name   body part

_____ against a giant plastic _____ , and smacked into a
    past-tense verb   food

fake _____ . Finally, the ball landed with a(n) _____ in
          animal   funny noise

the _____ pond. As the ball sank to the bottom, everyone
              type of liquid

started to _____ . _____ joked that I needed putting
                 verb   another relative's name

lessons from a professional _____ before we got to the next hole.
                                      noun

165

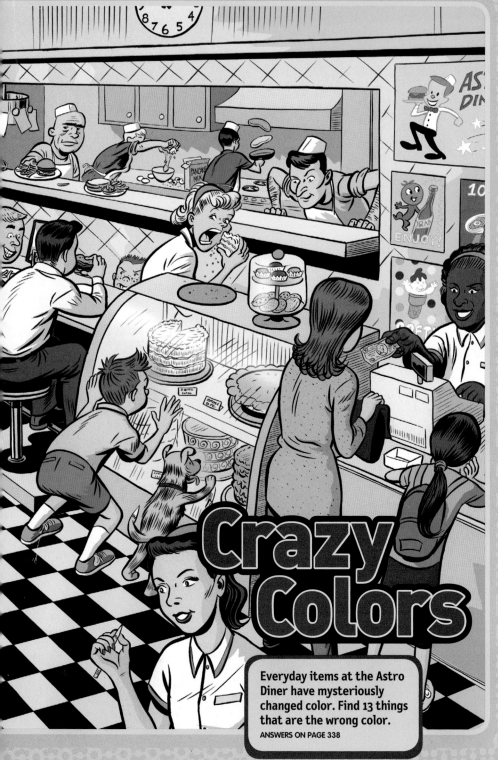

Crazy Colors

Everyday items at the Astro Diner have mysteriously changed color. Find 13 things that are the wrong color.

ANSWERS ON PAGE 338

Bark Park

Have you ever seen a dog that resembles its owner? Look for clues in the dog park to figure out which canine belongs to which owner. ANSWERS ON PAGE 338

Just Joking

Sea otter

KNOCK, KNOCK.
Who's there?
Ewan.
Ewan who?
It's just me.

Q How are **two banana peels** like shoes?

A They're a pair of slippers.

TONGUE TWISTER!

Say this fast three times:

Rolling red wagons race wildly down roads.

Q What do you call a **grizzly bear** with **no teeth?**

A A gummy bear.

You've **got** to be joking...

TWO SNAKES ARE TALKING.

SNAKE 1:
"Are we venomous?"

SNAKE 2:
"Yes, why?"

SNAKE 1:
"I just bit my lip."

169

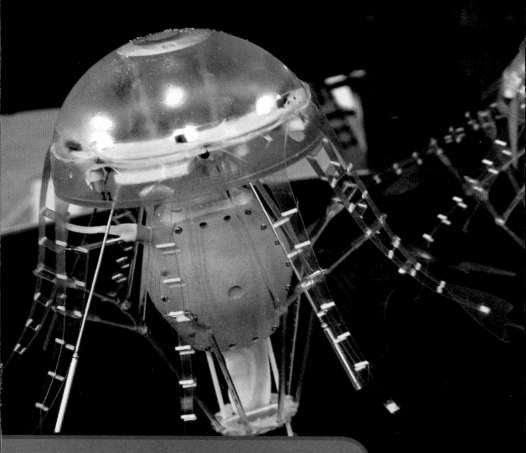

Super Science

Jellyfish-like robots called AquaJellies can communicate with one another to avoid underwater collisions. They demonstrate how robots may interact in the future.

THE UNIVERSE BEGAN WITH A BIG BANG

Clear your mind for a minute and try to imagine this: All the things you see in the universe today—all the stars, galaxies, and planets—are not yet out there. Everything that now exists is concentrated in a single, incredibly hot, dense state that scientists call a singularity. Then, suddenly, the basic elements that make up the universe flash into existence. Scientists say that actually happened about 13.7 billion years ago, in the moment we call the big bang.

For centuries scientists, religious scholars, poets, and philosophers have wondered how the universe came to be. Was it always there? Will it always be the same, or will it change? If it had a beginning, will it someday end, or will it go on forever?

These are huge questions. But today, because of recent observations of space and what it's made of, we think we may have some of the answers. Everything we can see or detect around us in the universe began with the big bang. We know the big bang created not only matter but also space itself. And scientists think that in the very distant future, stars will run out of fuel and burn out. Once again the universe will become dark.

POWERFUL PARTICLE

It's just one tiny particle, but without it the world as we know it would not exist. That's what scientists are saying after the recent discovery of the Higgs boson particle, a subatomic speck related to the Higgs field, which is thought to give mass to everything around us. Without the Higgs boson, all the atoms created in the big bang would have zipped around the cosmos too quickly to collect into stars and planets. So you can think of it as a building block of the universe —and of us!

EARLY LIFE ON EARTH

About 3.5 billion years ago Earth was covered by one gigantic reddish ocean. The color came from hydrocarbons.

The first life-forms on Earth were Archaea that were able to live without oxygen. They released large amounts of methane gas into an atmosphere that would have been poisonous to us.

About 3 billion years ago erupting volcanoes linked together to form larger landmasses. And a new form of life appeared—cyanobacteria, the first living things that used energy from the sun.

Some 2 billion years ago the cyanobacteria algae filled the air with oxygen, killing off the methane-producing Archaea. Colored pools of greenish-brown plant life floated on the oceans. The oxygen revolution that would someday make human life possible was now under way.

About 530 million years ago the Cambrian explosion occurred. It's called an explosion because it's the time when most major animal groups first appeared in our fossil records. Back then, Earth was made up of swamps, seas, a few active volcanoes, and oceans teeming with strange life.

More than 450 million years ago life began moving from the oceans onto dry land. About 200 million years later dinosaurs began to appear. They would dominate life on Earth for more than 150 million years.

WHAT IS LIFE?

This seems like such an easy question to answer. Everybody knows that singing birds are alive and rocks are not. But when we start studying bacteria and other microscopic creatures, things get more complicated.

SO WHAT EXACTLY IS LIFE?

Most scientists agree that something is alive if it can do the following: reproduce; grow in size to become more complex in structure; take in nutrients to survive; give off waste products; and respond to external stimuli, such as increased sunlight or changes in temperature.

KINDS OF LIFE

Biologists classify living organisms by how they get their energy. Organisms such as algae, green plants, and some bacteria use sunlight as an energy source. Animals (like humans), fungi, and some Archaea use chemicals to provide energy. When we eat food, chemical reactions within our digestive system turn our food into fuel.

Living things inhabit land, sea, and air. In fact, life also thrives deep beneath the oceans, embedded in rocks miles below the Earth's crust, in ice, and in other extreme environments. The life-forms that thrive in these challenging environments are called extremophiles. Some of these draw directly upon the chemicals surrounding them for energy. Since these are very different forms of life than what we're used to, we may not think of them as alive, but they are.

HOW IT ALL WORKS

To try and understand how a living organism works, it helps to look at one example of its simplest form—the single-celled bacterium called *Streptococcus*. There are many kinds of these tiny organisms, and some are responsible for human illnesses. What makes us sick or uncomfortable are the toxins the bacteria give off in our bodies.

A single *Streptococcus* bacterium is so small that at least 500 of them could fit on the dot above the letter *i*. These bacteria are some of the simplest forms of life we know. They have no moving parts, no lungs, no brain, no heart, no liver, and no leaves or fruit. Yet this life-form reproduces. It grows in size by producing long chain structures, takes in nutrients, and gives off waste products. This tiny life-form is alive, just as you are alive.

What makes something alive is a question scientists grapple with when they study viruses, such as the ones that cause the common cold and smallpox. They can grow and reproduce within host cells, such as those that make up your body. Because viruses lack cells and cannot metabolize nutrients for energy or reproduce without a host, scientists ask if they are indeed alive. And don't go looking for them without a strong microscope—viruses are a hundred times smaller than bacteria.

Scientists think life began on Earth some 3.9 to 4.1 billion years ago, but no fossils exist from that time. The earliest fossils ever found are from the primitive life that existed 3.6 billion years ago. Other life-forms, some of which are shown below, soon followed. Scientists continue to study how life evolved on Earth and whether it is possible that life exists on other planets.

MICROSCOPIC ORGANISMS*

Common soil *Bacillus*

Flu virus

Recently discovered primitive virus

Cyanobacteria

Diatom

Paramecium

E. coli bacteria

Streptococcus bacteria

*Organisms are not drawn to scale.

The Three Domains of Life

Biologists divide all living organisms into three domains: Bacteria, Archaea, and Eukarya. Archaean and Bacterial cells do not have nuclei; they are so different from each other that they belong to different domains. Since human cells have a nucleus, humans belong to the Eukarya domain.

1 BACTERIA

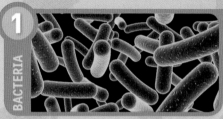

Domain Bacteria: These single-celled microorganisms are found almost everywhere in the world. Bacteria are small and do not have nuclei. They can be shaped like rods, spirals, or spheres. Some of them are helpful to humans, and some are harmful.

2 ARCHAEA

Domain Archaea: These single-celled micro-organisms are often found in extremely hostile environments. Like Bacteria, Archaea do not have nuclei, but they have some genes in com-mon with Eukarya. For this reason, scientists think the Archaea living today most closely resemble the earliest forms of life on Earth.

3 EUKARYA

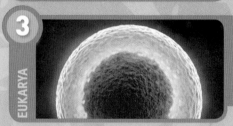

Domain Eukarya: This diverse group of life-forms is more complicated than Bacteria and Archaea, as Eukarya have one or more cells with nuclei. These are the tiny cells that make up your whole body. Eukarya are divided into four groups: fungi, protists, plants, and animals.

FYI

What is a domain? Scientifically speaking, a domain is a major taxonomic division into which natural objects are classified (see p. 38 for "What Is Taxonomy?").

FUNGI

Kingdom Fungi (about 100,000 species): Mainly multicellular organisms, fungi cannot make their own food. Mushrooms and yeast are fungi.

PROTISTS

Protists (about 250,000 species): Once considered a kingdom, this group is a "grab bag" that includes unicellular and multicellular organisms of great variety.

PLANTS

Kingdom Plantae (about 300,000 spe-cies): Plants are multicellular, and many can make their own food using photosyn-thesis (see p. 118 for "Photosynthesis").

ANIMALS

Kingdom Animalia (about a million species): Most animals, which are multi-cellular, have their own organ systems. Animals do not make their own food.

 **Bet you didn't know**

 **10** **facts** about

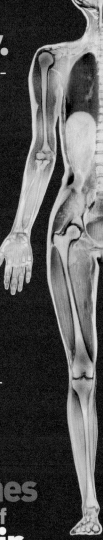

1
Brain cells live **longer** than all of the other cells in your **body.**

2
The **more** you concentrate, the less you **blink.**

3
Your **teeth** are **harder** than your **bones.**

4
Some **people** can **hear** their **eyeballs moving.**

5
It is **not** possible to **tickle** yourself.

6
You can buy **fake eyebrows** and **eyelashes** made out of **real hair.**

the human body

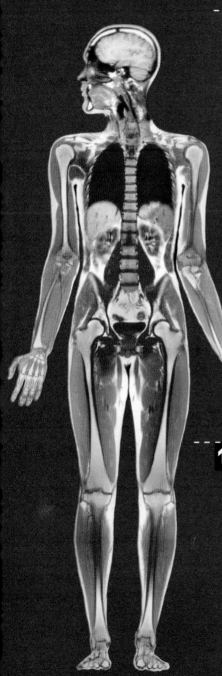

7 Fingernails grow faster than toenails.

8 Your heart beats about **100,000** times each day.

9 Your foot is about the same length as the distance between your elbow and wrist.

10 The saliva you produce in your lifetime could fill nearly **30,000** water bottles.

Your Amazing
brain

Inside your body's supercomputer

You carry around a three-pound (1.4-kg) mass of wrinkly material in your head that controls every single thing you will ever do. From enabling you to think, learn, create, and feel emotions to controlling every blink, breath, and heartbeat—this fantastic control center is your brain. It is a structure so amazing that a famous scientist once called it the "most complex thing we have yet discovered in our universe."

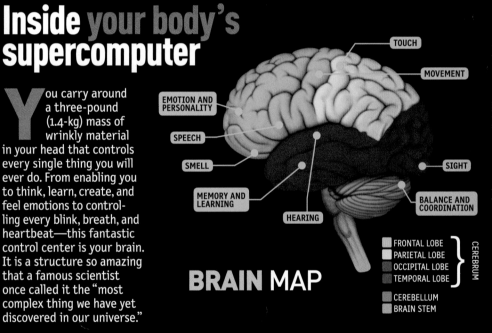

BRAIN MAP

TOUCH
MOVEMENT
EMOTION AND PERSONALITY
SPEECH
SMELL
SIGHT
MEMORY AND LEARNING
BALANCE AND COORDINATION
HEARING

FRONTAL LOBE
PARIETAL LOBE
OCCIPITAL LOBE
TEMPORAL LOBE

CEREBRUM

CEREBELLUM
BRAIN STEM

THE BIG QUESTION

WHAT TAKES UP TWO-THIRDS OF YOUR BRAIN'S WEIGHT AND ALLOWS YOU TO SWIM, EAT, AND SPEAK?

Answer: The huge hunk of your brain called the cerebrum. It's definitely the biggest part of the brain. The four lobes of the cerebrum house the centers for memory, the senses, movement, and emotion, among other things.

The cerebrum is made up of two hemispheres—the right and the left. Each side controls the muscles of the opposite side of the body.

Your Amazing
eyes

Discover the magic of your body's built-in cameras.

You carry around a pair of cameras in your head so incredible they can work in bright sunshine or at night. Only about an inch (2.5 cm) in diameter, they can bring you the image of a tiny ant or a twinkling star trillions of miles (km) away. They can change focus almost instantly and stay focused even when you're shaking your head or jumping up and down. These cameras are your eyes.

A CRUCIAL PART OF YOUR EYE IS AS FLIMSY AS A WET TISSUE.

A dragonfly darts toward your head! Light bounces off the insect, enters your eye, passes through your pupil (the black circle in the middle of your iris), and goes to the lens. The lens focuses the light onto your retina—a thin lining on the back of your eye that is vital but is as flimsy as a wet tissue. Your retina acts like film in a camera, capturing the picture of this dragonfly. The picture is sent to your brain, which instantly sends you a single command—*duck!*

YOU BLINK MORE THAN 10,000 TIMES A DAY.

Your body has many ways to protect and care for your eyes. Each eye sits on a cushion of fat, almost completely surrounded by protective bone. Your eyebrows help prevent sweat from dripping into your eyes. Your eyelashes help keep dust and other small particles out. Your eyelids act as built-in windshield wipers, spreading tear fluid with every blink to keep your eyes moist and wash away bacteria and other particles. And if anything ever gets too close to your eyes, your eyelids slam shut with incredible speed—in two-fifths of a second—to protect them!

YOUR EYES SEE EVERYTHING UPSIDE DOWN AND BACKWARD!

As amazing as your eyes are, the images they send your brain are a little quirky: They're upside down, backward, and two-dimensional! Your brain automatically flips the images from your retinas right side up and combines the images from each eye into a three-dimensional picture. There is a small area of each retina, called a blind spot, that can't record what you're seeing. Luckily your brain makes adjustments for this, too.

YOUR PUPILS CHANGE SIZE WHENEVER THE LIGHT CHANGES.

Your black pupils may be small, but they have an important job—they grow or shrink to let just the right amount of light enter your eyes to let you see.

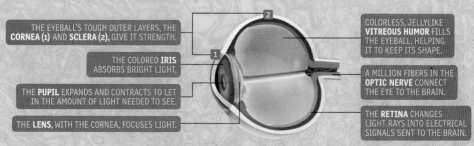

THE EYEBALL'S TOUGH OUTER LAYERS, THE **CORNEA (1)** AND **SCLERA (2)**, GIVE IT STRENGTH.

THE COLORED **IRIS** ABSORBS BRIGHT LIGHT.

THE **PUPIL** EXPANDS AND CONTRACTS TO LET IN THE AMOUNT OF LIGHT NEEDED TO SEE.

THE **LENS**, WITH THE CORNEA, FOCUSES LIGHT.

COLORLESS, JELLYLIKE **VITREOUS HUMOR** FILLS THE EYEBALL, HELPING IT TO KEEP ITS SHAPE.

A MILLION FIBERS IN THE **OPTIC NERVE** CONNECT THE EYE TO THE BRAIN.

THE **RETINA** CHANGES LIGHT RAYS INTO ELECTRICAL SIGNALS SENT TO THE BRAIN.

179

All about YOU

What Your BIRTH ORDER Says About YOU

Whether you're the oldest, the youngest, or an only child, your birth order can shape your personality. "Your position in the family line makes a big impact on the person you are now—and who you'll grow up to be," says psychologist Kevin Leman, author of *The Birth Order Book.* Here's what your sibling status may say about you.

IF YOU'RE THE OLDEST, YOU...

are well organized and reliable, excel in school, and have a knack for computers. You're a natural-born leader and like to be in charge of projects, although you don't like big changes. Many firstborns go on to become entertainers.

Celeb matches:
Taylor Swift, Justin Bieber

IF YOU'RE A MULTIPLE...

the same birth-order rules apply. If you're a twin or triplet and were born first, your personality is probably like an oldest child's. If you were born last, your personality is probably like a youngest child's. This is usually true even if you have siblings other than your twin or triplets.

Celeb matches: Dylan and Cole Sprouse (Dylan's older by 15 minutes.)

IF THESE PERSONALITY PROFILES DON'T MATCH YOU, THAT'S OK. THESE ARE JUST FOR FUN!

IF YOU'RE THE YOUNGEST, YOU...

are good at reading people's emotions and understanding how to act accordingly. You aren't scared to say what you think and therefore often get what you want. You love attention and may be the class clown—you could grow up to be a famous comedian.

Celeb matches:
Jack Black, Jim Carrey

IF YOU'RE IN THE MIDDLE, YOU...

have a lot of friends and try to resolve fights rather than start them. Always thinking of better ways to do things, you're likely to start a business, such as a lawn-mowing service or lemonade stand. Middle children often become successful business leaders.

Celeb matches:
Donald Trump,
Jennifer Lopez

IF YOU'RE AN ONLY CHILD, YOU...

rely on your imagination to keep things interesting. An independent person, you're comfortable talking to new people. You're hardworking and goal oriented, and you like doing things right the first time around. You may become a professional athlete or government leader.

Celeb matches:
Maria Sharapova,
Selena Gomez

BODY MYTHS BUSTED!

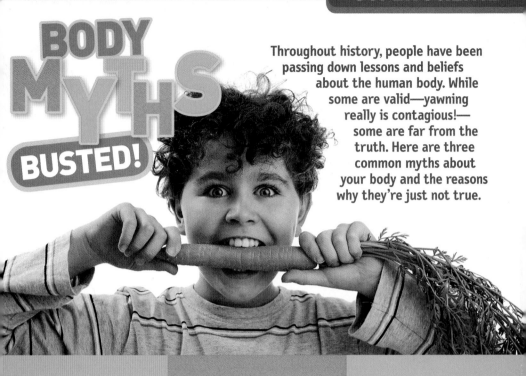

Throughout history, people have been passing down lessons and beliefs about the human body. While some are valid—yawning really is contagious!—some are far from the truth. Here are three common myths about your body and the reasons why they're just not true.

MYTH 1
Eating carrots improves your eyesight.

HOW IT STARTED
Legend has it that during World War II, British soldiers claimed to have excellent night vision because they consumed carrots. It was actually because of radar—the carrot bit was just used to confuse the Germans.

WHY IT'S NOT TRUE
Carrots do offer a high dose of vitamin A, which helps you maintain healthy eyesight. But eating more of the orange veggies won't make you see better—only glasses can do that.

MYTH 2
Humans use only 10 percent of their brain.

10%?

HOW IT STARTED
In 1907, psychologist William James suggested that we only use a small part of our "mental and physical resources," which may have led to the 10 percent figure.

WHY IT'S NOT TRUE
Whether you're aware of it or not, your brain is firing on four cylinders almost all of the time—otherwise, you would stop breathing. Your brain activity slows when you're in a deep sleep or under anesthesia.

MYTH 3
If your ears are burning, someone is talking about you.

HOW IT STARTED
Ancient Romans believed that certain physical signs—including ringing or burning ears—were signs that someone outside of earshot was chatting about you.

WHY IT'S NOT TRUE
Outside of having a sixth sense or bionic hearing, it's impossible to know when your name is coming up in someone else's conversation when you can't actually hear or see them talking. Besides, burning ears are usually a sign of sickness, sunburn, or overheating.

183

PLANETS

CERES

MARS

EARTH

VENUS

JUPITER

MERCURY

SUN

MERCURY
Average distance from the sun:
   35,980,000 miles (57,900,000 km)
Position from the sun in orbit: first
Equatorial diameter: 3,030 miles (4,878 km)
Length of day: 58 Earth days
Length of year: 88 Earth days
Surface temperatures: -300°F (-184°C)
   to 800°F (427°C)
Known moons: 0
**Fun fact: Mercury travels around the sun
   faster than any other planet.**

VENUS
Average distance from the sun:
   67,230,000 miles (108,200,000 km)
Position from the sun in orbit: second
Equatorial diameter: 7,520 miles (12,100 km)
Length of day: 243 Earth days
Length of year: 225 Earth days
Average surface temperature: 864°F (462°C)
Known moons: 0
Fun fact: Venus spins backward.

EARTH
Average distance from the sun:
   93,000,000 miles (149,600,000 km)
Position from the sun in orbit: third
Equatorial diameter: 7,900 miles (12,750 km)
Length of day: 24 hours
Length of year: 365 days
Surface temperatures: -126°F (-88°C)
   to 136°F (58°C)
Known moons: 1
**Fun fact: Earth rotates 1.5 milliseconds
   slower every century.**

MARS
Average distance from the sun:
   141,633,000 miles (227,936,000 km)
Position from the sun in orbit: fourth
Equatorial diameter: 4,221 miles (6,794 km)
Length of day: 25 Earth hours
Length of year: 1.88 Earth years
Surface temperatures: -270°F (-168°C)
   to 80°F (27°C)
Known moons: 2
**Fun fact: A 100-pound (45-kg) person would
   weigh 38 pounds (17 kg) on Mars.**

THERE IS
NO GRAVITY
AT THE CENTER
OF THE

SATURN

URANUS

NEPTUNE

PLUTO

HAUMEA

MAKEMAKE

ERIS

This artwork shows the 13 planets and dwarf planets that astronomers now recognize in our solar system. The relative sizes and positions of the planets are shown but not the relative distances between them. Many of the planets closest to Earth can be seen without a telescope in the night sky.

FOR INFORMATION ABOUT DWARF PLANETS—CERES, PLUTO, HAUMEA, MAKEMAKE, AND ERIS — SEE P. 186.

JUPITER
Average distance from the sun:
   483,682,000 miles (778,412,000 km)
Position from the sun in orbit: sixth
Equatorial diameter: 88,840 miles (142,980 km)
Length of day: 9.9 Earth hours
Length of year: 11.9 Earth years
Average surface temperature: -235°F (-148°C)
Known moons: 66*
Fun fact: Jupiter weighs twice as much as all the other planets in the solar system combined.

SATURN
Average distance from the sun:
   890,800,000 miles (1,433,500,000 km)
Position from the sun in orbit: seventh
Equatorial diameter: 74,900 miles (120,540 km)
Length of day: 10 Earth hours
Length of year: 29.46 Earth years
Average surface temperature: -218°F (-139°C)
Known moons: at least 62*
Fun fact: Saturn's rings are made of ice and rocks.

URANUS
Average distance from the sun:
   1,784,000,000 miles (2,870,970,000 km)
Position from the sun in orbit: eighth
Equatorial diameter: 31,760 miles (51,120 km)
Length of day: 17.9 Earth hours
Length of year: 84 Earth years
Average surface temperature: -323°F (-197°C)
Known moons: 27
Fun fact: Some of Uranus's 27 moons are named for characters from William Shakespeare's plays.

NEPTUNE
Average distance from the sun:
   2,795,000,000 miles (4,498,250,000 km)
Position from the sun in orbit: ninth
Equatorial diameter: 30,775 miles (49,528 km)
Length of day: 16 Earth hours
Length of year: 164.8 Earth years
Average surface temperature: -353°F (-214°C)
Known moons: 13
Fun fact: On Neptune the wind blows up to 1,243 miles an hour (2,000 kph).

*Includes provisional moons, which await confirmation and naming from the International Astronomical Union.

DWARF PLANETS

Haumea

Eris

Thanks to advanced technology, **astronomers have been spotting many never-before-seen celestial bodies with their telescopes. One new discovery? A population of icy objects orbiting the Sun beyond Pluto. The largest, like Pluto itself, are classified as dwarf planets. Smaller than the moon but still massive enough to pull themselves into a ball, dwarf planets neverthe-less lack the gravitational "oomph" to clear their neighborhood of other sizable objects. So, while larger, more massive planets pretty much have their orbits to themselves, dwarf planets orbit the sun in swarms that include other dwarf planets as well as smaller chunks of rock or ice.**

So far, astronomers have identified five dwarf planets: Ceres (which circles the Sun in the asteroid belt between Mars and Jupiter), Pluto, Haumea, Makemake, and Eris. Astronomers are studying hundreds of newly found objects in the frigid outer solar system, trying to figure out just how big they are. As time and technology advance, the family of known dwarf planets will surely continue to grow.

CERES
Position from the sun in orbit: fifth
Length of day: 9.1 Earth hours
Length of year: 4.6 Earth years
Known moons: 0

PLUTO
Position from the sun in orbit: tenth
Length of day: 6.4 Earth days
Length of year: 248 Earth years
Known moons: 5*

HAUMEA
Position from the sun in orbit:
  eleventh
Length of day: 4 Earth hours
Length of year: 282 Earth years
Known moons: 2

MAKEMAKE
Position from the sun in orbit: twelfth
Length of day: 22.5 Earth hours
Length of year: 305 Earth years
Known moons: 0

ERIS
Position from the sun in orbit:
  thirteenth
Length of day: 25.9 Earth hours
Length of year: 561 Earth years
Known moons: 1

*Includes provisional moons.

SUPER SUN!

THE SUN IS 400 TIMES LARGER THAN THE MOON.

The **SUN'S** surface is **9,932°F!** (5,500°C)

THERE IS real gold in the SUN.

Even from 93 million miles (150 million km) away, the sun's rays are powerful enough to provide the energy needed for life to flourish on Earth. This 4.6-billion-year-old star is the anchor of our universe and accounts for 99 percent of the matter in the solar system. What else makes the sun so special? For starters, it's larger than one million Earths and is the biggest object in our solar system. The sun also converts about four million tons (3,628,739 t) of matter to energy every second, helping to make life possible here on Earth. Now that's *sun*-sational!

Storms on the Sun!

Solar flares are ten million times more powerful than a volcanic eruption on Earth.

With the help of specialized equipment, scientists have observed solar flares—or bursts of magnetic energy that explode from the sun's surface as a result of storms on the sun. Solar storms occur on a cycle of about 11 years, with 2013 slated to be the most active year for these types of events. And while most solar storms will not impact the Earth, the fiercer the flare, the more we may potentially feel its effects, as it could disrupt power grids or interfere with GPS navigation systems. Solar storms can also trigger stronger-than-usual auroras, light shows that can be seen on Earth.

Some solar storms travel at speeds of **UP TO THREE MILLION MILES AN HOUR** (4.8 million kph).

Solar storm

187

Sky Calendar
2014

Jupiter

Partial solar eclipse

Leonid meteor shower

January 3–4 Quadrantids Meteor Shower Peak. View up to 40 meteors per hour.

January 5 Jupiter at Opposition. The giant planet is at its closest approach to Earth.

April 8 Mars at Opposition. Mars is at its closest approach to Earth.

April 15 Total Lunar Eclipse. Visible in most of North America, South America, and Australia.

May 10 Saturn at Opposition. The best time to view the ringed planet. It makes its closest approach to Earth.

July 28–29 Southern Delta Aquarids Meteor Shower Peak. View up to 20 meteors per hour.

August 12–13 Perseids Meteor Shower Peak. One of the best! Up to 60 meteors per hour.

August 18 Conjunction of Venus and Jupiter. Visible in the east just before sunrise, these two planets will be unusually close together.

August 29 Neptune at Opposition. The blue planet will be at its closest approach to Earth. Because Neptune is so far away, binoculars or a telescope are recommended for viewing. Unless you have a very powerful telescope, Neptune will appear as a small blue dot.

October 7 Uranus at Opposition. Uranus will be at its closest approach to Earth. Because

the planet is so far away, binoculars or a telescope are recommended for viewing. Unless you have a very powerful telescope, Uranus will appear as a small blue-green dot.

October 8 Total Lunar Eclipse. Visible throughout most of North America, South America, eastern Asia, and Australia.

October 21–22 Orionids Meteor Shower Peak. View up to 20 meteors per hour.

October 23 Partial Solar Eclipse. Visible throughout most of North America.

November 17–18 Leonid Meteor Shower Peak. View up to 15 meteors per hour.

December 13–14 Geminids Meteor Shower Peak. A spectacular show! Up to 60 multi-colored meteors per hour.

Dates may vary slightly depending on your location. Check with a local planetarium for the best viewing time in your area.

SOLAR AND LUNAR ECLIPSES

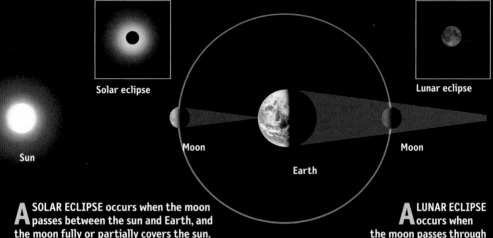

Solar eclipse

Lunar eclipse

Sun

Moon

Earth

Moon

A SOLAR ECLIPSE occurs when the moon passes between the sun and Earth, and the moon fully or partially covers the sun. Sometimes, the moon passes directly in front of the sun without completely covering it, leaving a visible ring of sunlight. This is called an annular eclipse. Solar eclipses occur up to five times each year and may last up to several minutes.

A LUNAR ECLIPSE occurs when the moon passes through Earth's shadow. For a lunar eclipse to take place, the sun, Earth, and moon must line up during a full moon. They happen less frequently than solar eclipses, but last longer—more than an hour and a half.

The Big Dipper, also called the Plough, is part of the constellation commonly known as the Great Bear.

SKY DREAMS

L ONG AGO, people looking at the sky noticed that some stars made shapes and patterns. By playing connect-the-dots, they imagined people and animals in the sky. Their legendary heroes and monsters were pictured in the stars.

Today, we call the star patterns identified by the ancient Greeks and Romans "constellations." There are 88 constellations in all. Some are only visible when you're north of the Equator, and some only when you're south of it.

In the 16th-century age of exploration, European ocean voyagers began visiting southern lands, and they named the constellations that are visible in the Southern Hemisphere, such as the Southern Cross. Astronomers used the star observations of these navigators to fill in the blank spots on their celestial maps.

Constellations aren't fixed in the sky. The star arrangement that makes up each one would look different from another location in the universe. Constellations also change over time because every star we see is moving through space. Over thousands of years, the stars in the Big Dipper, which is part of the larger constellation Ursa Major (the Great Bear), will move so far apart that the dipper pattern will disappear.

CONSTELLATIONS

Nothing to do on a clear night? Look up! There's so much to see in that starry sky. The constellations you can see among the stars vary with the season. As the following maps show, some are more visible in the winter and spring, while others can be spotted in the summer and fall.

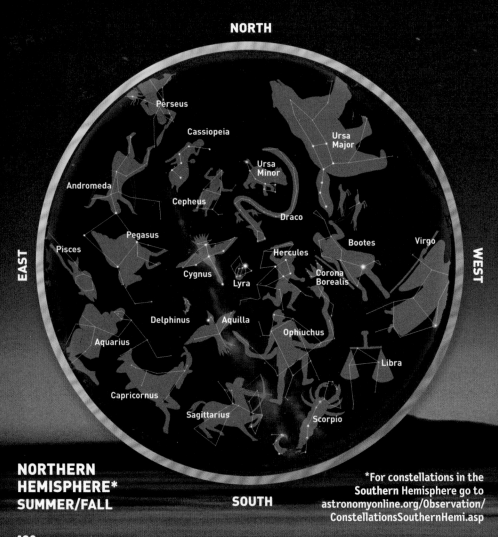

NORTH

EAST

WEST

SOUTH

Perseus
Cassiopeia
Ursa Major
Ursa Minor
Andromeda
Cepheus
Draco
Pegasus
Bootes
Virgo
Pisces
Hercules
Cygnus
Corona Borealis
Lyra
Delphinus
Aquilla
Ophiuchus
Aquarius
Libra
Capricornus
Sagittarius
Scorpio

NORTHERN HEMISPHERE*
SUMMER/FALL

*For constellations in the Southern Hemisphere go to astronomyonline.org/Observation/ConstellationsSouthernHemi.asp

Planet or Star?

On a clear night, you'll see a sky filled with glittering lights. But not every bright spot is a star—you may be peeking at a planet instead. How do you tell a star from a planet? While stars twinkle, planets shine more steadily and tend to be the brightest objects in the sky, other than the moon. Planets also move slowly across the sky from night to night. If you think you've spotted one, keep checking on it as the week goes by. If it has moved closer or farther from the moon, then it's probably a planet.

WANT TO SPOT A SATELLITE? Look for an **OBJECT** that travels quickly and steadily among **THE STARS.**

NORTH

EAST

WEST

SOUTH

Cepheus

Draco

Cassiopea

Ursa Minor

Bootes

Andromeda

Perseus

Ursa Major

Virgo

Auriga

Aries

Gemini

Leo

Cancer

Taurus

Crater

Canis Minor

Orion

Hydra

Canis Major

NORTHERN HEMISPHERE * WINTER/SPRING

Continents on the Move

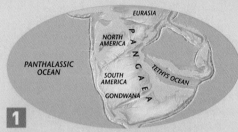

1

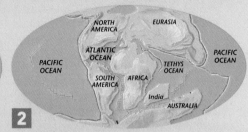

2

PANGAEA About 240 million years ago, Earth's landmasses were joined together in one super-continent that extended from Pole to Pole.

BREAKUP By 94 million years ago, Pangaea had broken apart into landmasses that would become today's continents. Dinosaurs roamed Earth during a period of warmer climates.

3

4

EXTINCTION About 65 million years ago, an asteroid smashed into Earth, creating the Gulf of Mexico. This impact may have resulted in the extinction of half the world's species, including the dinosaurs. This was one of several major mass extinctions.

ICE AGE By 18,000 years ago, the continents had drifted close to their present positions, but most far northern and far southern lands were buried beneath huge glaciers.

A LOOK INSIDE

The distance from Earth's surface to its center is 3,963 miles (6,378 km) at the Equator. There are four layers: a thin, rigid crust; the rocky mantle; the outer core, which is a layer of molten iron; and finally the inner core, which is believed to be solid iron.

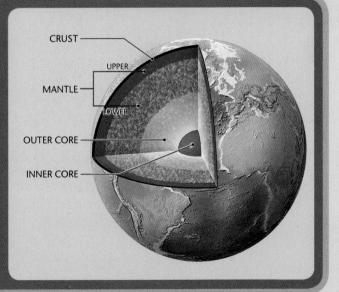

CRUST

UPPER

MANTLE

LOWER

OUTER CORE

INNER CORE

ROCK STARS

The world is full of rocks. Some big, some small, some formed deep beneath the Earth, and some formed at the surface. While they may look similar, not all rocks are created equally. Look closely, and you'll see differences between every boulder, stone, and pebble. Here's more about the three top varieties of rocks.

Igneous

Named for the Greek word meaning "from fire," igneous rocks form when hot, molten liquid called magma cools. Pools of magma form deep underground and slowly work their way to the Earth's surface. If they make it all the way, the liquid rock erupts and is called lava. As the layers of lava build up they form a mountain called a volcano. Typical igneous rocks include obsidian, basalt, and pumice, which is so chock-full of gas bubbles that it actually floats in water.

OBSIDIAN PUMICE

Metamorphic

Metamorphic rocks are the masters of change! These rocks were once igneous or sedimentary, but thanks to intense heat and pressure deep within the Earth, they have undergone a total transformation from their original form. These rocks never truly melt; instead, the heat twists and bends them until their shapes substantially change. Metamorphic rocks include slate as well as marble, which is used for buildings, monuments, and sculptures.

MARBLE SLATE

Sedimentary

When wind, water, and ice constantly wear away and weather rocks, smaller pieces called sediment are left behind. These are sedimentary rocks, also known as gravel, sand, silt, and clay. As water flows downhill it carries the sedimentary grains into lakes and oceans, where they get deposited. As the loose sediment piles up, the grains eventually get compacted or cemented back together again. The result is new sedimentary rock. Sandstone, gypsum, and shale are sedimentary rocks that have formed this way.

SANDSTONE GYPSUM

It's a Rocky World!

ROCKS AND MINERALS CAN BE FOUND

in a wide range of different environments. In addition to being useful materials, they also give scientists clues to how our world has changed over time.

GYPSUM Sedimentary rock that forms from the evaporation of mineral-rich water.

GRANITE Plutonic igneous rock rich in quartz and feldspar. It is a hard rock used as a building stone and for monuments.

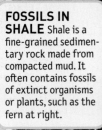

FOSSILS IN SHALE Shale is a fine-grained sedimentary rock made from compacted mud. It often contains fossils of extinct organisms or plants, such as the fern at right.

SANDSTONE Sedimentary rock that forms when sand grains get cemented back together again.

BASALT The most common type of igneous rock, basalts form most of the Earth's crust under the ocean.

OLIVINE This group of greenish minerals is found mainly in dark-colored igneous rocks such as basalt, peridotite, and gabbro.

BERYL Commonly found in pegmatite and schist. Well-formed green beryl crystals are also known as emeralds.

TOURMALINE Commonly found in both igneous and metamorphic rocks.

SULFUR AND SALT CRYSTALS They give the crater of Dallol volcano in Ethiopia its unique color.

FELDSPAR Like quartz, feldspar can be found in all three major rock types.

FLUORITE Most often found in igneous and meta-morphic rocks.

NATIVE COPPER This soft metal forms with basalt in hydrothermal vents near volcanoes.

195

Birthstones

In the past, people believed that certain gems brought good luck to those people born in different months and that these gems stood for special qualities in a person. The chart on the left lists the primary birthstone for each month as well as the unique character trait that it represents in a person.

MONTH	STONE	CHARACTER TRAIT
1 January 	Garnet	Constancy
2 February	Amethyst	Sincerity
3 March	Aquamarine	Courage
4 April	Diamond	Innocence
5 May	Emerald	Love and Success
6 June	Moonstone	Health and Longevity
7 July	Ruby	Contentment
8 August	Peridot	Happily Married
9 September	Sapphire	Clear Thinking
10 October	Pink Tourmaline	Hope
11 November	Citrine	Fidelity
12 December	Blue Topaz	Prosperity

Match Game

How's your eye at spotting a gemstone? Can you tell what your birthstone looks like before it is cut and polished? In the column to the left are the 12 birthstones the way they would look in a jewelry store. Below are the same 12 gems as they appear in nature. See if you can match the finished stone with its natural counterpart. ANSWERS ON PAGE 197.

A

B

G

H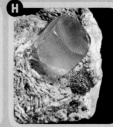

A lapidary uses a polishing wheel to finish a gemstone.

Cutting and Polishing

Gemstones in the field hardly ever look like a gem.
Instead they usually look dull, with rough edges, and often
resemble plain, ordinary rocks. Before a gemstone can be considered
a gem, it usually has to be worked. A lapidary is the person who cuts,
polishes, and engraves stones in order to make them look more attractive.

ANSWERS: 1E, 2K, 3C, 4I, 5A, 6G, 7F, 8L, 9D, 10J, 11B, 12H

COOL inventions

LIGHT-UP MOTORCYCLE

Most sci-fi movie vehicles are created on a computer and exist only on-screen. But after seeing the motorcycle in the movie *TRON: Legacy*, a few inventors decided to turn that futuristic bike into reality with the Light Cycle. The blue lights lining the tires and body are actually sticker-like strips that have a special coating to make them glow. The Light Cycle's most distinctive feature is its hollow, SUV-size wheels. The bike's controls are like a regular motorcycle's, but you lie on your stomach and drive it with your arms and legs stretched out. Marc Parker, one of the bike's creators, says that the funky body position adds to the thrill of the ride. "You feel like Superman—like you're flying."

FISH (TOILET) TANK

The next time you go to the bathroom, don't forget the fish food. The Fish 'n Flush turns a regular toilet into an aquarium. Two see-through tanks attach to the toilet. The inner tank is what flushes the toilet. Surrounding that tank is an aquarium. When you flush, the water level of the inner tank goes down, making it seem as if water is emptying from your aquarium. Don't worry—it's an illusion. The fish tank's water level remains the same, so your fishies are fine.

BUBBLE TENT

CLEAR VIEW

Sleep under the stars without being bitten by bugs or waking up with a backache. You can rent a clear Cristal Bubble tent at certain beaches, in open fields, or in big gardens. They come in several sizes and stay inflated thanks to a turbine that continuously blows air inside. Some even have beds, floors, and electricity. For more privacy, a few models are see-through only on the top. This kind of camping is not exactly roughing it—but what a great way to watch for nocturnal critters or check out a meteor shower.

TOPSY-TURVY RIDE

You'll literally roll on the ground laughing with the Buzzball. Take a seat, strap yourself in, and press the two hand triggers to get rolling. Each trigger is connected to a separate motor that powers the two wheels under your chair. You and the seat remain mostly upright, but as the wheels start to spin, the Buzzball begins to roll. To steer, press one of the triggers. That prompts the wheel on one side to turn, causing the Buzzball to roll in that direction. Depending on how fast you're going, the ball simply turns, or it tumbles around multiple times—like being in a roller coaster, motion simulator, and skateboard bowl all at once.

SPACE Robots

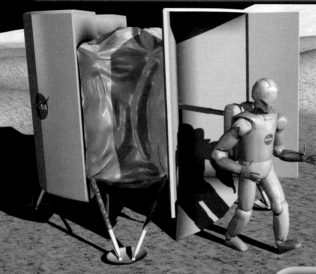

SOMEDAY YOU MIGHT CONTROL AN AVATAR ON THE MOON.

R obot avatars may one day be handy companions to space travelers, whether they're as far away as Mars or as close as a space station or moon base. Though still a concept, robonauts, controlled remotely by humans, are expected to be a huge help to astronauts. "Our goal is for robots to work side by side with humans," says NASA's Matt Ondler. "Robonauts will help our astronauts with the three D's: jobs that are dirty, dull, and dangerous."

TO THE MOON

HEADING FOR THE MOON

Someday, NASA hopes to send a humanoid robot, called R2, to the moon. Sending a robot to the moon will be far less expensive than sending a human. A robot is sturdier, can survive in tighter spaces, and doesn't need air. Even better, robots don't care how long it takes for NASA to return them to Earth.

Once on the moon, the robonaut could perform experiments, send live video back to Earth, and explore the lunar surface. R2 will be able to

COLLECTING ROCK SAMPLES

move using legs, or by attaching its torso to a four-wheeled rover and becoming part of the vehicle like a Transformer. And when R2's battery is low, it can plug into a solar-powered recharging station and get some much-needed juice.

AVATARS IN SPACE

The future R2 would be designed to operate by itself. But for delicate and difficult tasks, a human operator would control it like an avatar in a video game. NASA will need people skilled at operating robonauts to ensure the success of future missions. So the next time your mom complains that you're spending too much time on video games, just tell her you're training for a job with NASA!

EXPLORING THE SURFACE

3 COOL THINGS ABOUT GPS

Thanks to GPS, you may never get lost—or lose anything—again! Short for *global positioning system*, this superhelpful technology relies on satellites in space to collect and plot your position. You can use that info for everything from finding a friend's house to tracking down your dog. Here are some cool ways GPS can help you!

1. Find Your Pets

Forget hanging fliers around your neighborhood: When your pet goes missing, just check your phone! Thanks to GPS tracking devices that attach to your dog or cat's collar, you can find out exactly where your pet is from your phone or computer. Some products even send text messages to you if your pet wanders too far from home.

2. Locate Lost Items

Can't find your smartphone? You may be able to locate it with the help of GPS. Many laptops, mobile phones, and tablets are equipped with a built-in GPS receiver that can send out signals to show you its approximate location on a map.

3. Predict the Weather

Knowing the forecast for tomorrow is one thing. But what about the weather tomorrow exactly at 2:55 p.m.? Meteorologists and geodesists are drawing on data from GPS satellites, including atmospheric temperatures, to help generate more accurate—and up to the minute—weather forecasts. How *cool!*

How GPS Works

A system of about 30 satellites is orbiting 12,550 miles (20,200 km) above the Earth, traveling at speeds of about 8,500 miles (13,800 km) an hour. As they orbit, the satellites transmit signals to GPS receivers on Earth. Once your GPS receiver picks up radio signals from at least four of these satellites, it can calculate their coordinates to pinpoint your exact position on Earth.

GPS units use satellites to determine your location.

ANIMAL KILLERS

BUSTED!

The cool science behind solving wildlife mysteries

Like detectives, scientists at the National Fish and Wildlife Service's (FWS) Forensics Laboratory examine evidence left behind at crime scenes to help solve mysteries. Here's how they use cutting-edge technology to help solve crimes against animals—and catch the crooks!

THE VICTIMS: ELK
THE CRIME SCENE: COLORADO
THE EVIDENCE: FINGERPRINT

CRIME SCENE EVIDENCE

FINGERPRINT

STICKY FINGERS

To passersby, the man was enjoying a campout. But he was really illegally sneaking into reserved hunting grounds to kill elk for their prized antlers. Instead of the permitted bow and arrow, he was using a gun.

The hunter couldn't move the large antler racks home during hunting season, so he wrapped them in duct tape and hid them in tree branches. He'd return for them after hunting season.

But the suspect left something else behind. After wardens found one of the racks, FWS lab technicians discovered a fingerprint on the duct tape. No two people have the same fingerprints. So the scientists searched a database, which matched the print with the suspect. They could confidently point their finger at the hunter, who pleaded guilty and went to jail.

BULLET
CRIME SCENE EVIDENCE

THE VICTIMS: TIGERS
THE CRIME SCENE: ILLINOIS
THE EVIDENCE: BULLET

SMOKING GUN

In an abandoned warehouse, two men shot and killed two endangered tigers that they had bought at a roadside zoo. They hoped to sell the hides, skulls, and meat. But the suspects did a sloppy cleanup job. When an undercover agent from the FWS bought a full-body tiger-skin rug from the ringleader, she found a bullet in the tiger's skull.

A gun leaves a pattern of marks on the bullet it fires, which can match it back to that particular weapon. At a lab, scientists fired a test round of bullets from the ringleader's gun and then used a microscope to compare the marks from the test round to the bullet they found. They matched. Now the ringleader is locked up—instead of the tigers that would have been his next victims.

MICROSCOPE

CRIME SCENE EVIDENCE
MEATBALLS

THE VICTIMS: FOX, COYOTE, BIRDS
THE CRIME SCENE: IDAHO
THE EVIDENCE: DNA

BAD MEAT

The meatball trail stretched two miles (3.2 km) in the snow. What should have been a tasty treat for any animal was actually poisoned with a pesticide. FWS agents found the bodies of a fox, coyote, and three magpies that had died after eating the tainted meat. Based on a tip that someone was using poisoned meat-balls to kill wolves, agents searched a man's garage. They discovered a blood-stained tool and a bottle containing pesticide, which was identified as the same poison in the meatballs. All the agents had to do was prove the man made the meatballs, then they would know he had also tried to kill endangered wolves.

A geneticist gathered DNA samples from a meat-ball and from the tool. Found in the body's cells, DNA determines the traits of all living things. And no two living things have the same DNA. The DNA samples from the meatball and the tool matched, which proved the man had made the poisoned meatballs. The trail of evidence led straight to the killer.

CRIME SCENE EVIDENCE
DNA

STUMP YOUR PARENTS

SUPER SCIENCE QUIZ

When it comes to science, do your parents know their stuff? Test their science smarts with this quiz, based on info provided in this chapter.

ANSWERS BELOW

1 **True or false?** The planet Mercury spins backward.

2 **When did dinosaurs begin to appear?**
a. 3 billion years ago
b. 2 billion years ago
c. 250 million years ago
d. 1492

3 **Your heart beats about _____ times each day.**
a. 100,000
b. 500,000
c. 1,000,000
d. 10,000,000

4 **What does GPS stand for?**
a. geographic puzzle solution
b. global positioning system
c. global pinpoint satellite
d. green pea soup

5 **Which is an example of sedimentary rock?**
a. pumice
b. sandstone
c. marble
d. slate

6 **Which of the following is not a dwarf planet?**
a. Eris
b. Makemake
c. Pluto
d. Sneezy

Research Like a Pro

There is so much information on the Internet. How do you find what you need and make sure it's accurate?

Be Specific

To come up with the most effective keywords, write down what you're looking for in the form of a question, and then circle the most important words in that sentence. Those are the keywords to use in your search. And for best results use words that are specific rather than general.

Research

Research on the Internet involves "looking up" information using a search engine (see list below). Type one or two keywords—words that describe what you want to know more about—and the search engine will provide a list of websites that contain information related to your topic.

Use Trustworthy Sources

When conducting Internet research, be sure the website you use is reliable and the information it provides can be trusted. Sites produced by well-known, established organizations, companies, publications, educational institutions, or the government are your best bets.

Don't Copy

Avoid Internet plagiarism. Take careful notes and cite the websites you use to conduct research.

HELPFUL AND SAFE SEARCH ENGINES FOR KIDS

Google Safe Search	squirrelnet.com/search/Google_SafeSearch.asp
Yahoo! Kids	kids.yahoo.com
SuperKids	super-kids.com
Ask Kids	askkids.com
Kids Click	kidsclick.org
AOL Kids	kids.aol.com

Going Green

A Bornean angle-headed lizard explores
its forest habitat in Danum Valley, Malaysia.

Animal

All around the world, countless animals are being driven out of their habitats as a result of deforestation, or trees being cut down for lumber or logs or to clear land. Some animals are able to safely escape to safer spots. Others are not so lucky. Here are two tales of how wild animals were saved from potential peril.

VICTIM: THREE-TOED SLOTH
HABITAT: BULLDOZED
RESULT: DEHYDRATION, TRAUMA

HIGH IN A TROPICAL RAIN FOREST, a young male three-toed sloth slowly moves along a tree branch. Suddenly the branch begins to fall. People from a nearby village in French Guiana, on the north coast of South America, are bulldozing part of the forest.

THE TREE CRASHES, and the sloth tumbles about 50 feet (15 m) to the forest floor. Alive but dazed, he's unable to walk or climb, and is vulnerable to predators like eagles. Village children discover the terrified animal. They carry him to safety and call Paulette Decrette, head of the Chou-Ai (cherished sloth) Association.

DECRETTE TAKES the sloth to a care center. He is traumatized and dehydrated. Decrette is able to calm the sloth enough that she can hand-feed him healthy rehydrating yogurt from a bottle. She names him Marcel. After Marcel's condition seems stable, he moves to an outdoor enclosure where he can climb on a jungle gym of tree branches.

TWO WEEKS LATER, Marcel is well enough to be released back into the wild. Decrette takes him to a protected forest reserve and holds him up to a branch. He immediately latches on and begins to climb. "He loves to be free," she says.

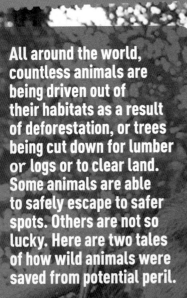

TENDER CARE AND BOTTLE-FEEDING SAVE THIS SLOTH.

ENJOYING FREEDOM

Rescues

BOTTLE-FEEDING HELPED THIS ORPHAN SURVIVE.

FOSTER FAMILY AT PLAY

VICTIM: BOBCAT KITTEN
HABITAT: BULLDOZED
RESULT: ORPHANED

A WEEKS-OLD BOBCAT KITTEN cowers beside a road in Tampa, Florida, U.S.A. The forest nearby has been bulldozed, leaving nowhere to hide. The kitten's mother has disappeared—perhaps hit by a car.

LUCKILY, THE KITTEN IS FOUND and brought to Big Cat Rescue (BCR), a sanctuary that helps abused and abandoned wild cats. Keepers at BCR name the cat Hope and bottle-feed her for a few days. Then, something special happens: A domestic cat living at the sanctuary, already nursing two kittens of her own, accepts Hope into the family. It doesn't take long before Hope is playfully chasing and wrestling her new siblings.

SOON HOPE GRADUATES from nursing to eating ground turkey. Her next treat is a dead chick left in her enclosure. (In the wild, Hope's mother would stalk and kill food and bring it back to her young.) Before long, she's eating dead chicks and mice three times a day. Her wild instincts begin to show.

AS THE PET KITTENS AND HOPE GROW, the entire family moves to a large outdoor enclosure. Hope seems to enjoy the new space, digging in the dirt and scaling up and down the enclosure's wire walls.

AS HOPE turns four months old, it's time to learn to catch food. Her keepers release live rats into her enclosure during the day, and Hope quickly becomes an expert hunter.

NOW NEARLY A YEAR OLD—the age at which young bobcats generally separate from their mothers—Hope is ready for release. Her keepers let her go into an open field surrounded by woods. At the edge of the forest she stops and looks back over her shoulder for a few seconds. Then she turns and runs off, ready for life on her own.

209

GREEN & Inventions

SUN-POWERED PLANE

Soar around the globe on the power of sunshine. A plane called the Solar Impulse doesn't burn a drop of fuel. Solar panels line nearly every inch of the plane's passenger-jet-size wingspan, absorbing energy from the sun and storing it in lightweight batteries that power four electric propellers. The plane completed its first overnight flight in 2010, proving that it could harness enough solar power during the day to keep it flying through the night. The Swiss team of engineers and pilots who developed the plane is now building a more advanced version for an around-the-world flight scheduled for 2014. A one-seater aircraft, the Solar Impulse is built to be as lightweight as possible. Even the pilot has a weight limit!

MUSICAL SHOWER

WET RADIO

You love singing in the shower, but your family doesn't seem to appreciate your, um, talent. Here's a way to quiet the unappreciative booing—and help protect the planet. The H_2O Shower Powered Radio, which runs on energy created by the flow of water, drowns out your shower voice. To set it up, attach the radio to the base of the showerhead. When you turn on the shower, water runs through the radio, rotates a tiny turbine (similar to a waterwheel), and creates energy to power the radio. The device can even store enough juice to keep playing for up to an hour, post-shower. Rock on.

POWER TREE

SOLAR TREE

Charge your iPod in an environmentally friendly way. Inspired by a bonsai tree, the Electree has branches with solar panels for "leaves." Position the tree however you like, creating different shapes and angles by rotating and moving the branches. Then just place it next to a window so the solar panels can soak up some rays. The energy produced by the panels is stored in a battery hidden in the base. When your phone, iPod, or DS starts running low on power, simply plug it into the tree to charge it. Now all you need is sunny weather.

LEAN, GREEN CAR

The Very Light Car (VLC) looks like it's from the far-off future, but in just a few years you might be cruising around town in one. This ultra-green vehicle is capable of getting some 110 miles a gallon (47 km/L)—about four times what today's cars get. Like a race car, the VLC has a long, narrow, diamond-shaped body with wheels that sit on the outside, allowing it to cruise smoothly. At just 830 pounds (376 kg), the VLC is much lighter than regular cars, which typically weigh about 3,500 pounds (1,587 kg). This also contributes to the VLC's efficiency, since lighter objects require less energy to move. (Think of how exhausting it is to walk with a full backpack compared with an empty one.) With sleek looks and an eco-friendly design, this is one carpool ride you'll love showing up to school in.

GREENHOUSES

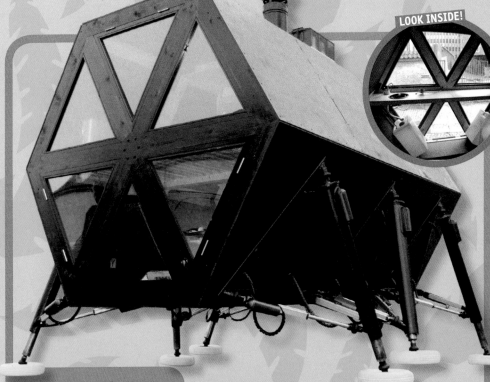

LOOK INSIDE!

What: Moveable House

Why it's cool: The Walking House is an agile abode about the size of a large room, with a bed and a small sitting area. Moving in a buglike fashion at speeds of up to 197 feet (60 m) an hour, it uses its six legs to maneuver in every direction.
Eco-friendly features: Power comes straight from the sun—solar panels on the roof catch the rays needed to keep the house chugging along. A wood-burning stove, rainwater-catching system, and composting toilet keep things eco-friendly.

What: Monte-Silo House

Why it's cool: This home in Woodland, Utah, U.S.A., is constructed of two metal grain silos, linked together to form an 1,800-square-foot (167-sq-m) living space.
Eco-friendly features: The exterior metal is a recyclable material, while solar heat helps warm up the house during the winter.

What: Free Spirit Spheres

Why it's cool: These wood and fiberglass hanging tree houses in Vancouver Island, British Columbia, Canada, are equipped with a working kitchen (but no bathroom!) and sleep four.
Eco-friendly features: What better way to reduce your carbon footprint than living close to nature in one of these 11-foot (3.3-m)-wide spheres?

What: The Hill House

Why it's cool: Built right into the sandy hills of North Norfolk Coast, England, U.K., this house was designed to maximize exposure to sunlight. In summer, when the sun is highest, the home's curved roof serves as a shield from the rays. In the winter, as the sun hangs lower in the sky, it heats the glass and warms up the home.
Eco-friendly features: You won't get cold feet in this house—a huge geothermal pump sucks up the warmth from the Earth and sends it to a heater beneath the home's floors.

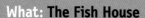

What: The Fish House

Why it's cool: Wide, open spaces allow for natural ventilation, so this house in Singapore stays cool with the ocean breeze. Plus, windows in a basement-level media room offer an underwater glimpse of the pool.
Eco-friendly features: The home's wavy roof—meant to symbolize the ocean—is covered in thin solar panels that provide energy to the house. Additional rooftop is covered in green grass, doubling as an outdoor space.

GLOBAL WARMING

Climate Change, Explained

Fact: The world is getting warmer. The global surface temperature has risen by 1.3°F (.72°C) over the past 100 years. In fact, the summers of 2011 and 2012 were the hottest summers of the past 50 years in the United States and southern Canada. These are the direct effects of climate change, which refers not only to the increase in the Earth's average temperature (also known as global warming), but also to the long-term effects on winds, rain, and ocean currents. Global warming is the reason glaciers and polar ice sheets are melting—resulting in rising sea levels and shrinking habitats. This makes survival for some animals a big challenge. Warming also means more flooding along the coasts and drought for inland areas.

Why are temperatures climbing?

Some of the recent climate changes can be tied to natural causes—such as changes in the sun's intensity, the unusually warm ocean currents of El Niño, and volcanic activity—but human activities are a major factor as well.

Everyday activities that require burning fossil fuels, such as driving gasoline-powered cars, contribute to global warming. These activities produce greenhouse gases, which enter the atmosphere and trap heat. At the current rate, the Earth's global average temperature is projected to rise from 2 to 11.5°F (1 to 6.4°C) by the year 2100, and it will get even warmer after that. And as the climate continues to warm, it will unfortunately continue to affect the environment and our society in many ways.

Polar bear on a piece of melting iceberg

Reduce Your
Carbon Footprint

Everything you buy, use, and throw away affects the Earth. Activities such as driving cars and heating or cooling buildings can release greenhouse gases like carbon dioxide into the air. The amount of greenhouse gases produced by your activities is called your carbon footprint. By reducing your footprint, you can help the planet. Here are three ways to do just that.

RIDE A BIKE! Instead of having your mom or dad drive you to a friend's house in the neighborhood, hop on your bike and ride there instead.

PRINT SMART. When you print from the computer, use both sides of the paper. Talk to your teacher about doing the same for classroom printouts.

GO LOCAL. Talk to your parents about buying local, organic food. Each ingredient in a U.S. meal has traveled an average of 1,500 miles (2,400 km). If everyone ate one meal per week of local, organic food, we'd save 1.1 million barrels of oil every week.

IS THE EARTH
Changing Shape?

YES, according to a recent study, which determined that each year, the planet is getting wider around the Equator and flatter at the Poles. But the shift in size and shape is super-subtle: Experts say that in the past few years or so, the distance from the Equator to the Earth's center (also known as the equatorial radius) has grown about one twenty-fifth of an inch (1 mm) per year.

So what's causing the Earth to get bigger—and flatter? Scientists aren't quite sure, but they think it might have something to do with changes in ocean climate. Climate events like El Niño shift where the mass of water is stored among the oceans, in water vapor in the atmosphere, and in soil on the continents. This can result in slight changes in the Earth's gravity field—which may ultimately shift the shape of the planet.

Pollution
Cleaning Up Our Act

So what's the big deal about a little dirt on the planet? Pollution can affect animals, plants, and people. In fact, some studies show that more people die every year from diseases linked to air pollution than from car accidents. And right now nearly one billion of the world's people don't have access to clean drinking water.

A LITTLE POLLUTION=BIG PROBLEMS

You can probably clean your room in a couple of hours. (At least we hope you can!) But you can't shove air and water pollution under your bed or cram them into the closet. Once released into the environment, pollution—whether it's oil leaking from a boat or chemicals spewing from a factory's smokestack—can have a lasting environmental impact.

KEEP IT CLEAN

It's easy to blame things like big factories for pollution problems. But some of the mess comes from everyday activities. Exhaust fumes from cars and garbage in landfills can seriously trash the Earth's health. We all need to pitch in and do some housecleaning. It may mean bicycling more and riding in cars less. Or not dumping water-polluting oil or household cleaners down the drain. Look at it this way: Just as with your room, it's always better not to let Earth get messed up in the first place.

Bottled Up!

Sure, water is good for you. But before you sip, think about how often you use plastic water bottles—and what you're doing with them when you're done. For every six water bottles we use, only one will wind up in a recycling bin. The rest end up in landfills or as litter on land or in rivers, lakes, and oceans, taking many hundreds of years to disintegrate. So, what can you do? Fill up from the tap and drink out of a refillable steel container. And if you do use a plastic bottle, make sure to recycle it.

Declining Biodiversity
Saving All Creatures Great and Small

Earth is home to a huge mix of plants and animals—perhaps 100 million species—and scientists have officially identified and named only about 1.9 million so far! Scientists call this healthy mix biodiversity.

THE BALANCING ACT

The bad news is that half of the planet's plant and animal species may be on the path to extinction, mainly because of human activity. People cut down trees, build roads and houses, pollute rivers, overfish, and overhunt. The good news is that many people care. Scientists and volunteers race against the clock every day, working to save wildlife before time runs out. By building birdhouses, planting trees, and following the rules for hunting and fishing, you can be a positive force for preserving biodiversity, too. Every time you do something to help a species survive, you help our planet to thrive.

WILDLIFE BIODIVERSITY

Insects, Centipedes, and Millipedes

Other Animals

Mammals

Florida manatee

Habitat Destruction
Living on the Edge

Even though tropical rain forests cover only about 7 percent of the planet's total land surface, they are home to half of all known species of plants and animals. Because people cut down so many trees for lumber and firewood and clear so much land for farms, hundreds of thousands of acres of rain forest disappear every year.

SHARING THE LAND

Wetlands are also important feeding and breeding grounds. People have drained many wetlands, turning them into farm fields or sites for industries. More than half the world's wetlands have disappeared within the past century, squeezing wildlife out. Balancing the needs of humans and animals is the key to lessening habitat destruction.

Toucan

217

World Energy & Minerals

Almost everything people do—from cooking to powering the International Space Station—requires energy. But energy comes in different forms. Traditional energy sources, still used by many people in the developing world, include burning dried animal dung and wood. Industrialized countries and urban centers around the world rely on coal, oil, and natural gas—called fossil fuels because they formed from decayed plant and animal material accumulated from long ago. Fossil fuel deposits, either in the ground or under the ocean floor, are unevenly distributed on Earth, and only some countries can afford to buy them. Fossil fuels are also not renewable, meaning they will run out one day. And unless we find other ways to create energy, we'll be stuck. Without energy we won't be able to drive cars, use lights, or send emails to friends.

TAKING A TOLL

Environmentally speaking, burning fossil fuels isn't necessarily the best choice, either: Carbon dioxide from the burning of fossil fuels, as well as other emissions, are contributing to global warming. Concerned scientists are looking at new ways to harness renewable, alternative sources of energy, such as water, wind, and sun.

DIGGING FOR FOSSIL FUELS

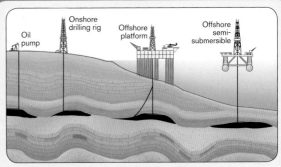

This illustration shows some of the different kinds of onshore and offshore drilling equipment. The type of drilling equipment depends on whether the oil or natural gas is in the ground or under the ocean.

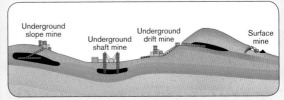

The mining of coal made the industrial revolution possible, and coal still provides a major energy source. Work that people once did using picks and shovels is now done with mechanized equipment. This diagram shows some kinds of coal mines currently in use.

LIGHTS OUT

In 2012, India experienced one of its worst blackouts ever, leaving some 600 million people in the dark. The blackout, which lasted a few hours, was caused by strain on an aging power grid. To avoid future blackouts, power needs to be delivered more efficiently. One possible solution? Focusing on alternative energy sources, like solar power and wind farms.

A train disabled by a massive power outage in India, July 2012

Alternative Power

WIND

Strong winds blowing through California's (U.S.A.) mountains spin windmill blades on an energy farm, powering giant turbines that generate electricity for the state.

HYDROELECTRIC

Hydroelectric plants, such as this one at Santiago del Estero in Argentina, use dams to harness running water to generate clean, renewable energy.

GEOTHERMAL

Geothermal power, from groundwater heated by molten rock, provides energy for this power plant in Iceland. Swimmers enjoy the warm waters of a lake created by the power plant.

SOLAR

Solar panels on Samso Island in Denmark capture and store energy from the sun, an environmentally friendly alternative to fossil fuels.

BIODIESEL

This Aero L-29 Delfin, nicknamed BioJet 1, was the first jet aircraft powered by 100 percent biodiesel fuel. Biodiesel—which can be made from vegetable oil, animal fats, or french-fry grease—is cleaner and emits fewer pollutants than fossil fuels do into the air.

Try This! Trash OR Treasure?

Give your junk a makeover! Celebrate Earth Day with your family on April 22 by creating these cool decorations from recycled materials.

1 Beanbag Chair

WHAT TO DO

1. Fill the sack with packing peanuts until it's completely stuffed.
2. Tie the drawstring tightly. Now *sack out* on your new beanbag chair.

YOU WILL NEED

- LARGE DRAWSTRING LAUNDRY BAG OR SANTA SACK
- LOTS OF LEFTOVER PACKING PEANUTS

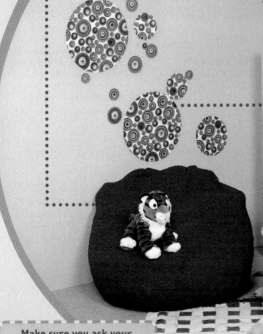

Make sure you ask your parents for permission before starting this project.

2 Disco Ball

WHAT TO DO

1. Straighten the paper clip and bend it into a U-shape. Dip both ends of the clip in glue, then stick them into the Styrofoam ball.
2. With a parent's help, use scissors to cut the CDs into irregular one-inch pieces. (Be very careful of sharp edges!)
3. Rest the ball on top of a bowl to keep it from rolling. Dab glue in the center of the less shiny side of a CD piece. Press onto the ball. Repeat until half of the ball is covered. Let dry.
4. Repeat on the other half of the ball. Tie the string around the paper clip loop, and hang near a window or light. Then start practicing your dance moves.

YOU WILL NEED

- LARGE PAPER CLIP
- TACKY GLUE
- 8-INCH (20-CM) STYRO-FOAM BALL
- 8 TO 10 OLD CDs (ASK FOR PERMISSION TO USE THEM)
- STRING

3 Magazine Pockets

WHAT TO DO

1. With a box standing upright, make a pencil mark on the edge of the box, five inches (13 cm) from the bottom. Draw a diagonal line to the opposite top corner of the box. Draw a matching line on the opposite side of the box.
2. Cut along the lines and remove the box top.
3. Wrap the box in wrapping paper or comics. Glue or tape in place. Your *National Geographic Kids* magazines finally have a home.

YOU WILL NEED

- EMPTY CEREAL BOXES
- OLD NEWSPAPERS OR LEFTOVER WRAPPING PAPER
- GLUE OR CLEAR TAPE

4 Wall Decals

WHAT TO DO

1. Ask your parents for permission to stick things on the wall. Cut different shapes out of the wrapping paper.
2. Peel the backing off the contact paper, then stick the design side of the wrapping paper to the sticky side of the contact paper. Restick the backing onto the contact paper.
3. Cut out each decal, leaving a quarter-inch (6-mm) border of contact paper around it. Stick the decals to the wall. Then stand back and admire your new look.

YOU WILL NEED

- LEFTOVER WRAPPING PAPER
- CLEAR, REPOSITIONABLE CONTACT PAPER

5 WAYS YOU CAN GO GREEN!

Do your part to save energy and protect the planet!

1 **Lower the thermostat** by two degrees in colder weather (or raise it two degrees in hotter weather). This could keep one ton of carbon dioxide out of the environment each year.

2 **Go green at lunch** by using Earth-friendly items such as reusable sandwich bags and cloth napkins.

3 **Unplug appliances you're not using.** Even if they're turned off, some appliances can still drain energy.

4 **Helping out with the laundry?** Hang your clean, wet clothes on a drying rack or clothesline to save energy typically spent in the dryer.

5 **Wipe down surfaces with cloth—** not paper towels. Even better? Repurpose old towels and t-shirts into dust rags.

5 WAYS YOU CAN GO BLUE!

Don't let the water entering our homes go thoughtlessly down the drain. Do your part to save water and protect the planet!

1 **Turn off the tap while you brush your teeth.** You'll save more than two gallons (7.5 L) a minute!

2 **Sip from a refillable water bottle** so you have fewer glasses to wash at the end of the day.

3 **Accidentally drop an ice cube?** Don't toss it. Place it in a house plant instead.

4 **Take shorter showers.** By cutting them down by two minutes, you can save up to 150 gallons (568 L) of water per month.

5 **Check around your house for leaks** in faucets, showerheads, pipes, and toilets. If you find one, talk to your parents about fixing them—fast.

STUMP YOUR PARENTS

GOING GREEN QUIZ

How eco-friendly are your parents? If they can't answer these questions, maybe *they* should take a lesson in going green. (Psst: Have them check out this chapter if they're stumped.) ANSWERS BELOW

1 Which animals are affected by habitat destruction?
a. sloth
b. toucan
c. polar bear
d. all of the above

2 Tropical rain forests cover about how much of Earth's land surface?
a. 2%
b. 5%
c. 7%
d. 12%

3 Where does geothermal power come from?
a. nuclear plants
b. groundwater heated by molten rock
c. the sun
d. long underwear

4 True or false? Earth is getting flatter.

5 Which is not a source of biodiesel fuel?
a. vegetable oil
b. animal fat
c. french-fry grease
d. chocolate syrup

6 Which activity will reduce your carbon footprint?
a. eating a cheeseburger
b. texting
c. riding a bike
d. wearing smaller shoes

ANSWERS:
1. d; 2. c; 3. b; 4. True. Earth is getting wider at the Equator and flatter at the Poles; 5. d; 6. c.

Write a Letter That Gets Results

Knowing how to write a good letter is a useful skill. It will come in handy anytime you want to persuade someone to understand your point of view. Whether you're emailing your congressperson, or writing a letter for a school project or to your grandma, a great letter will help you get your message across. Most important, a well-written letter leaves a good impression.

Check out the example below for the elements of a good letter.

Your address

Date

Salutation
Always use "Dear" followed by the person's name; use Mr., Mrs., Ms., or Dr. as appropriate.

Introductory paragraph
Give the reason you're writing the letter.

Body
The longest part of the letter, which provides evidence that supports your position. Be persuasive!

Closing paragraph
Sum up your argument.

Complimentary closing
Sign off with "Sincerely" or "Thank you."

Your signature

Christopher Jones
916 Green Street
Los Angeles, CA 90045

March 31, 2013

Dear Mr. School Superintendent,

I am writing to you about how much excess energy our school uses and to offer a solution.

Every day, we leave the computers on in the classroom, the TVs are plugged in all the time, and the lights are on all day. All of this adds up to a lot of wasted energy, which is not only harmful for the Earth as it increases the amount of harmful greenhouse gas emissions into the environment, but it's also costly to the school. In fact, I read that schools spend more on energy bills than on computers and textbooks combined!

I am suggesting that we start an Energy Patrol to monitor the use of lighting, air-conditioning, heating, and other energy systems within our school. My idea is to have a group of students dedicated to figuring out ways we can cut back our energy use in the school. We can do room checks, provide reminders to students and teachers to turn off lights and computers, replace old lightbulbs with energy-efficient products, and even reward the classrooms that do the most to save energy.

Above all, I think our school could help the environment tremendously by cutting back on how much energy we use. Let's see an Energy Patrol at our school soon. Thank you.

Sincerely,

Christopher Jones

Christopher Jones

COMPLIMENTARY CLOSINGS

Sincerely, Sincerely yours, Thank you, Regards, Best wishes, Respectfully,

Perched 7,710 feet (2,350 m) high in the Andes Mountains
in Peru, the ancient city Machu Picchu was built by the Inca
around 1450. It was rediscovered by Hiram Bingham in 1911.

History Happens

PACKING FOR THE AFTERLIFE

BOATS

Egyptians believed the sun god traveled to the afterlife each night by boat. Entombed model boats—and even full-size versions—helped the dead make that same voyage.

IMAGINE HOW YOU'D

FEEL IF YOU BOARDED A PLANE FOR A LONG TRIP

and realized you forgot to pack. To the ancient Egyptians, who viewed death as the start of a great journey, passing into the afterlife unprepared was equally unsettling. That's why family and friends filled the tombs of their dearly departed with everything they would need in the hereafter.

Graves of poor Egyptians were packed with just the essentials: food, cosmetics, and clothes. The ornate burial chambers of pharaohs overflowed with treasures and art. Browse these grave goodies recovered from ancient Egyptian tombs.

FOOD

Family members left food offerings outside a tomb to nourish their loved one's spirit. Paintings of feasts on tomb walls or sculptures of food trays were thought to provide magical bottomless buffets.

GAMES

Board games like Senet provided eternal entertainment.

CLOTHES

Most tombs were stocked with chests of clothes, fine linens, sandals, and other attire. It would be unseemly to spend eternity naked, after all.

COFFINS

Coffins were carved in the likeness of the deceased so that spirits could recognize their own bodies.

SERVANTS

Summoned to life by a spell, carved figures known as shabtis served as laborers in the afterlife. One pharaoh's tomb contained nearly a thousand of these ancient action figures.

JEWELRY

The adage "you can't take it with you" would have horrified wealthy Egyptians, who packed their tombs with their favorite jewelry.

227

THE LOST CITY OF POMPEII

When will the volcano that buried this ancient civilization blow again?

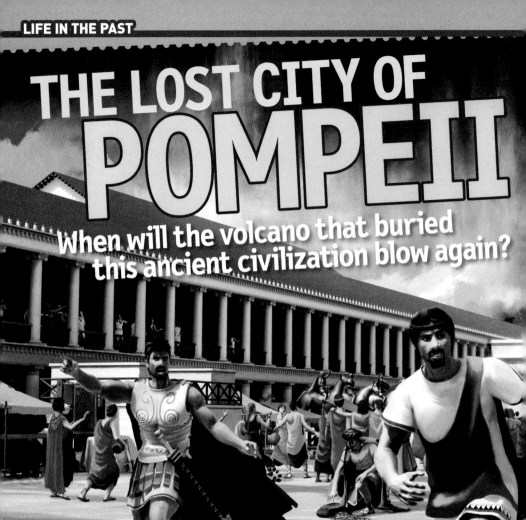

A deafening boom roars through Pompeii's crowded marketplace. The ground shakes violently, throwing the midday shoppers off balance and toppling stands of fish and meat. People start screaming and pointing toward Mount Vesuvius, a massive volcano that rises above the bustling city, located in what is now southern Italy.

Vesuvius has been silent for nearly 2,000 years, but it roars back to life, shooting ash and smoke into the air. Almost overnight, the city and most of its residents have vanished under a blanket of ash and lava.

Now, almost 2,000 years later, scientists agree that Vesuvius is overdue for another major eruption—but no one knows when it will happen. Three million people live in the volcano's shadow, in the modern-day city of Naples, Italy. Correctly predicting when the eruption will take place will mean the difference between life and death for many.

THE SKY IS FALLING

Thanks to excavations that started in 1748 and continue to this day, scientists have been able to re-create almost exactly what happened in Pompeii on that terrible day.

"The thick ash turned everything black," says Pompeii expert Andrew Wallace-Hadrill.

"People couldn't see the sun. All the landmarks disappeared. They didn't have the foggiest idea which way they were going."

Some people ran for their lives, clutching their valuable coins and jewelry. Other people took shelter in their homes. But the debris kept falling. Piles grew as deep as nine feet (2.7 m) in some places, blocking doorways and caving in roofs.

Around midnight, the first of four searing-hot clouds, or surges, of ash, pumice, rock, and toxic gas rushed down the mountainside. Traveling toward Pompeii at up to 180 miles an hour (290 kph), it scorched everything in its path. Around 7 a.m., 18 hours after the

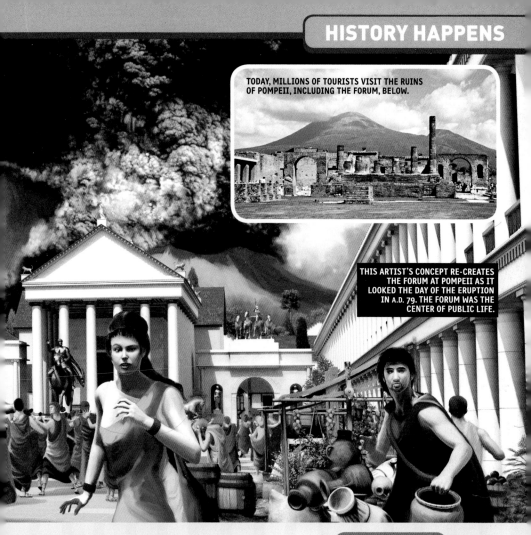

TODAY, MILLIONS OF TOURISTS VISIT THE RUINS OF POMPEII, INCLUDING THE FORUM, BELOW.

THIS ARTIST'S CONCEPT RE-CREATES THE FORUM AT POMPEII AS IT LOOKED THE DAY OF THE ERUPTION IN A.D. 79. THE FORUM WAS THE CENTER OF PUBLIC LIFE.

eruption, the last fiery surge buried the city.

LOST AND FOUND

Visiting the ruins of Pompeii today is like going back in time. The layers of ash actually helped preserve buildings, artwork, and even the forms of bodies. "It gives you the feeling you can reach out and touch the ancient world," Wallace-Hadrill says.

There are kitchens with pots on the stove and bakeries with loaves of bread—now turned to charcoal—still in the ovens. Narrow corridors lead to magnificent mansions with elaborate gardens and fountains. Mosaics, or designs made out of tiles, decorate the walls and floors.

WARNING SIGNS

Pompeii's destruction may be ancient history, but there's little doubt that disaster will strike again. Luckily, people living near Vesuvius today will likely receive evacuation warnings before the volcano blows.

Scientists are closely monitoring Vesuvius for shifts in the ground, earthquakes, and rising levels of certain gases, which could be signs of an upcoming eruption. The Italian government is also working on a plan to help people flee the area in the event of a natural disaster.

CREEPY CASTS

Volcanic ash settled around many of the victims at the moment of death. When the bodies decayed, holes remained inside the solid ash. Scientists poured plaster into the holes to preserve the shapes of the victims.

229

Ancient World ADVENTURE

ANGKOR WAT

WHERE: Cambodia
BUILT: A.D. 1113 to A.D.1150

COOL FACT: Created to honor the Hindu god Vishnu, Angkor Wat remains the largest religious complex in the world. It's still protected by a 4-mile (6.4-km) moat!

BOROBUDUR

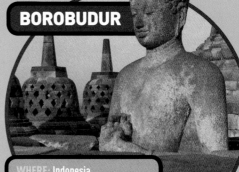

WHERE: Indonesia
BUILT: About A.D. 778 to A.D. 850

COOL FACT: The world's largest Buddhist monument, this temple is made from two million rocks and took about 75 years to build.

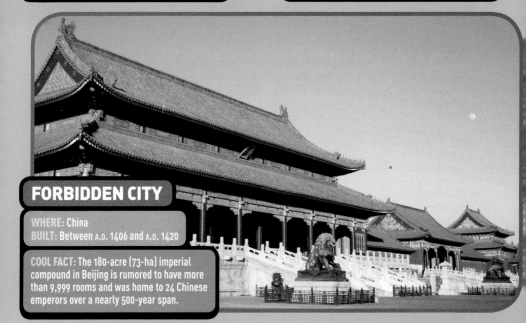

FORBIDDEN CITY

WHERE: China
BUILT: Between A.D. 1406 and A.D. 1420

COOL FACT: The 180-acre (73-ha) imperial compound in Beijing is rumored to have more than 9,999 rooms and was home to 24 Chinese emperors over a nearly 500-year span.

*E*ver wonder what it was like on Earth thousands of years ago? Check out these amazing ancient sites. Visiting them is like taking a time machine into the past!

PYRAMIDS AT GIZA

WHERE: Egypt
BUILT: About 2500 B.C.

COOL FACT: These massive pyramids—built as tombs for Egypt's pharaohs—are part of a complex that included a palace, temples, and boat pits. The largest pyramid is 481 feet (147 m) tall and is made from 2.3 million stone blocks.

PALENQUE

WHERE: Mexico
BUILT: About A.D. 500

COOL FACT: This ancient Maya city-state's buildings, including temples and tombs, were built without the use of metal tools, pack animals, or even the wheel.

TIMBUKTU

WHERE: Mali
BUILT: About A.D. 1100

COOL FACT: Once known as the fabled "City of Gold," Africa's Timbuktu was a center of learning and culture in the 15th and 16th centuries and is home to a still-standing university.

Bet you didn't know

(7) cool facts about castles

1 Disneyland's **Sleeping Beauty Castle** was **inspired** by Neuschwanstein Castle in Germany.

2 The **first castles** were built about **1,000** years ago.

3 The castle **barber** was also the **dentist.**

4 England's **Windsor Castle** is about **200 times larger** than a typical **U.S. house.**

5 The number of people who lived in some castles could have **filled** a **small village.**

6 Ireland's **Blarney Castle** has a **stone** that visitors **kiss** for **luck.**

7 Supplies were often **smuggled** into castles through **secret tunnels.**

232

COOL THINGS ABOUT
5 ANCIENT GREECE

ALTHOUGH THEY LIVED MORE THAN 2,000 YEARS AGO, the ancient Greeks were clearly ahead of their time. From science to sports, many Greek traditions are alive and well today. Here are some things that make this civilization stand out.

1 START-UP SCHOOL

In 387 B.C., the Greek philosopher Plato founded the Academy in Athens, which was the earliest example of a modern university. Students (including some women, against the traditions of the time) studied astronomy, biology, math, law, politics, and philosophy. Plato's hope was that the Academy would provide a place for all scholars to work toward better government in the Grecian cities. The Academy would become a center of learning for nearly 1,000 years.

2 OUTDOOR STAGE

The Greeks were among the first to perform plays. These performances sprung from festivals honoring their gods in which men would dress up, act out stories, and sing songs. They built large, outdoor theaters in most of their cities—some big enough to hold 15,000 people! The audience was so far away from the stage that the actors would wear elaborate costumes and sad- or happy-face masks so that people could see each character's expressions no matter where they were sitting.

3 CITY-STATES

Experts believe that ancient Greek civilization was likely begun nearly 4,000 years ago by the Mycenaeans of Crete, a Greek island. The ancient Greek Empire spread from Greece through Europe, and in 800 B.C. the Greeks began splitting their land into hundreds of city-states. Although most Greeks shared the same language and religion, each city-state maintained its own laws, customs, and rulers.

4 SUPERSTITIONS

The ancient Greeks were superstitious people. For instance, they originated the idea that breaking a mirror was bad luck. Believing mirrors showed the will of the gods, they thought a broken mirror meant the gods did not want you to see something unpleasant in your future. They also had unique ideas about food—some ancient Greeks would not eat beans because they believed they contained the souls of the dead.

5 ORIGINAL OLYMPICS

The ancient Greeks held many festivals in honor of their gods, including some serious sports competitions. The most famous took place in Olympia, Greece, starting in 776 B.C. Honoring the god Zeus, this two-day event—which inspired the modern-day Olympic Games—held contests in wrestling, boxing, long jump, javelin, discus, and chariot racing. Winners were given a wreath of leaves, free meals, and the best seats in the theater as prizes.

233

MYSTERY of the BURIED TREASURE

TRUE STORY

AN ANCIENT STASH OF GOLD AND SILVER WORTH MILLIONS OF DOLLARS IS UNCOVERED IN A FARMER'S FIELD.

Beep! The man stops suddenly as his metal detector sounds off. Something is buried under the English field he's been exploring. Is it a worthless piece of junk—or something far more valuable?

The man's discovery turns out to be more than 3,500 pieces of gold and silver treasure buried by ancient warriors at least 1,300 years ago. Archaeologists uncovered sword handles, helmet pieces, and shield decorations. Some were studded with jewels or engraved with animals.

The treasure is worth about $5.5 million. But archaeologists are more excited about what it could tell us about these ancient warriors.

MYSTERIOUS PEOPLE

The treasure was buried by people called the Anglo-Saxons, who settled in England after arriving from Germany starting around A.D. 410. Archaeologists think it may have belonged to the Anglo-Saxon ruler, King Penda of Mercia.

The Anglo-Saxons lived in the Dark Ages, once believed to be a time when little was happening in art or culture. But the treasure helps confirm that the Anglo-Saxon period was a time of great change and amazing artistry.

SECRETS OF THE TREASURE

Anglo-Saxons were considered fierce warriors, and they cared about their weapons. But the quality of the metalwork shows they were also artists. Craftsmen created tiny, detailed engravings without magnifying lenses.

The treasure may also shed new light on where Anglo-Saxons lived. Because it was found in western England, rather than in the south or east, where archaeologists believed early Anglo-Saxons settled, this may mean the people had traveled farther than once thought.

Still, archaeologists may have more questions than answers. Why weren't there any items belonging to women? Was the treasure buried for safekeeping, or to mark a victory?

The answers to these mysteries may come with further study, but more than anything, this discovery has brought the people of the Anglo-Saxon era to life.

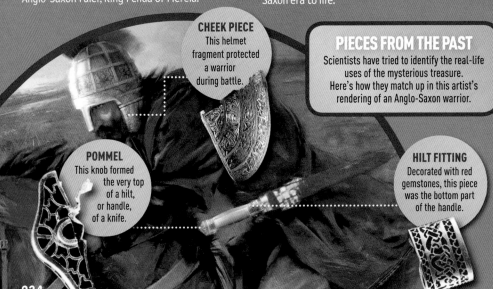

CHEEK PIECE
This helmet fragment protected a warrior during battle.

PIECES FROM THE PAST
Scientists have tried to identify the real-life uses of the mysterious treasure. Here's how they match up in this artist's rendering of an Anglo-Saxon warrior.

POMMEL
This knob formed the very top of a hilt, or handle, of a knife.

HILT FITTING
Decorated with red gemstones, this piece was the bottom part of the handle.

CURSE OF THE HOPE DIAMOND

Is the Hope Diamond, one of the world's most valuable jewels, the bearer of bad luck? Legend has it that the stone was stolen from the eye of a sacred statue in India, and Hindu gods cursed the stone to punish the thieves. You decide if the curse is rock solid or just a gem of a tale!

LOSING THEIR HEADS
The French royal family once owned the diamond, but not for too long. After King Louis XVI and his wife, Marie Antoinette, were imprisoned and beheaded during the French Revolution, the government confiscated the stone, which thieves later stole before it was bought by the wealthy Hope family.

LOST HOPE
Lord Francis Hope eventually inherited the diamond, and then his wife left him and he had to sell the pricey stone to help pay off his huge debts. But the gem still bears the Hope family name.

TEMPTING FATE
Millionaire Evalyn McLean bought the diamond in 1911. But luck was not on McLean's side, either. During her lifetime, two of her children died, her husband became mentally ill, and she fell into serious debt.

DOOMED DELIVERY
In 1958 a mailman named James Todd delivered the diamond to its present home—the Smithsonian Institution in Washington, D.C., U.S.A. Within a year Todd's wife died and his house burned down. Was it the curse?

REAL OR FAKE?
"The curse isn't true," says Richard Kurin, author of the book *Hope Diamond: The Legendary History of a Cursed Gem.* It may all just be an eerie coincidence, but one thing's for sure, "The Hope diamond is so valuable because it is a unique stone and because of its famous story," says Kurin.

WHERE DO DIAMONDS COME FROM?

Natural diamonds form about a hundred miles (160 km) underground and are the hardest known natural substance. Under extreme heat and pressure, carbon atoms are squeezed together into the hard, clear crystals. Volcanic eruptions carry the diamonds toward the Earth's surface, where they are mined for use in industrial tools and sparkly jewelry.

235

Secrets of the

SCIENTISTS USE CUTTING-EDGE TECHNOLOGY TO UNCOVER NEW EVIDENCE ABOUT HOW THE SHIP SANK.

Sunday, April 14, 1912: The R.M.S. *Titanic* steams across the North Atlantic Ocean. The 882-foot (269-m)-long passenger ship carries 2,208 people on its maiden voyage from Southampton, England, to New York City, in the United States of America.

Suddenly, a dark shape appears. An iceberg scrapes the ship, and within three hours, the *Titanic* sinks. Almost 1,500 people lose their lives.

Scientists have closely studied the *Titanic*'s wreck on the ocean floor since it was discovered in 1985. Recently, National Geographic Explorer-in-Residence James Cameron—the director of the movie *Titanic*—assembled a team of experts to examine the shipwreck anew. Using 3-D modeling and state-of-the-art technology, the experts reveal new clues about how the *Titanic* sank.

FLOODING

It might have been possible for the ship to sink more slowly, allowing more people to survive. Many of the ship's portholes were found open—most likely because passengers were airing out their rooms and never closed them. This caused the ship to take on water faster.

Something similar also may have happened in one of the grand lobbies, where a large door was found open. "The size of the door is twice the size of the original iceberg damage," Cameron says. "This would have sped up the sinking of the ship."

BREAKING

As the *Titanic* took on water, the front of the ship, called the bow, sank below the surface, causing the back, or stern, to lift into the air. The great stress broke the ship in half. "When the *Titanic* broke in half and the bow pulled away, the

EXPLORER JAMES CAMERON PILOTS AN UNDERWATER VEHICLE CALLED A SUBMERSIBLE.

bottom likely remained attached to the back of the ship until it, too, was pulled apart," Cameron says.

SINKING

In its final resting place, the bow looks remarkably intact. But the stern looks like a bomb destroyed it. Why? The bow was filled with water when it sank, so the pressure was the same on the inside as the outside. The stern, however, sank with lots of air inside and imploded from the pressure.

FINAL IMPACT

The sinking ship created a massive trail of water that followed it downward at 20 to 25 miles an hour (32 to 40 kph). Experts think that this water trail pummeled the *Titanic* after it hit bottom. "Millions of gallons of water came pushing down on it," Cameron says.

With all this new information, is our understanding of the *Titanic* tragedy complete? "I think we have a very good picture of what happened," Cameron says. "But there will always be mysteries."

Titanic

TITANIC · 19 · · 12 · LONDON

SUPERSIZE SHIP
The *Titanic* was almost as long as three football fields. With its smoke-stacks, the ship was as tall as a 17-story building.

TITANIC

WHAT IF...

Scientists know a lot about how the *Titanic* sank, but other factors contributed as well.

SAILING SCHEDULE
The *Titanic* set sail more than three weeks behind schedule. If the ship had left on time, an iceberg probably wouldn't have been in its path.

FROM CALM TO CHAOS
The sea was unusually calm on April 14, 1912. Waves would have made the iceberg easier to spot.

MISSED MESSAGES
Two messages were telegraphed from other ships to warn the *Titanic* of icebergs, but they never reached the captain.

We asked oceanographer and National Geographic Explorer-in-Residence Robert Ballard, who led the team that discovered the *Titanic* in 1985, what it felt like to make the discovery of the century.

"My first reaction was one of excitement and celebration. But we were at the **very spot** on the **cold North Atlantic Ocean** where it all happened. So then we had **a quiet moment of remembrance."**

WAR!

Since the beginning of time, different countries, territories, and cultures have feuded with each other over land, power, and politics. Major military conflicts include the following wars:

1095–1291 THE CRUSADES
Starting late in the 11th century, these wars over religion were fought in the Middle East for nearly 200 years.

1337–1453 HUNDRED YEARS' WAR
France and England battled over rights to land for more than a century before the French eventually drove the English out in 1453.

1754–1763 FRENCH AND INDIAN WAR (part of Europe's Seven Years' War)
A nine-year war between the British and French for control of North America.

1775–1783 AMERICAN REVOLUTION
Thirteen British colonies in America united to reject the rule of the British government and to form the United States of America.

1861–1865 AMERICAN CIVIL WAR
Occurred when the northern states (the Union) went to war with the southern states, which had seceded, or withdrew, to form the Confederate States of America. Slavery was one of the key issues in the Civil War.

1910–1920 MEXICAN REVOLUTION
The people of Mexico revolted against the rule of dictator President Porfirio Díaz, leading to his eventual defeat and to a democratic government.

1914–1918 WORLD WAR I
The assassination of Austria's Archduke Ferdinand by a Serbian nationalist sparked this wide-spreading war. The U.S. entered after Germany sunk the British ship *Lusitania*, killing more than 120 Americans.

1918–1920 RUSSIAN CIVIL WAR
A conflict pitting the Communist Red Army against the foreign-backed White Army. The Red Army won after four hostile years, leading to the establishment of the Union of Soviet Socialist Republics (U.S.S.R.) in 1922.

1936–1939 SPANISH CIVIL WAR
Aid from Italy and Germany helped the Nationalists gain victory over the Communist-supported Republicans. The war resulted in the loss of more than 300,000 lives and increased tension in Europe leading up to World War II.

1939–1945 WORLD WAR II
This massive conflict in Europe, Asia, and North Africa involved many countries that aligned with the two sides: the Allies and the Axis. After the bombing of Pearl Harbor in Hawaii in 1941, the U.S. entered the war on the side of the Allies. More than 50 million people died during the war.

1946–1949 CHINESE CIVIL WAR
Also known as the "War of Liberation," this pitted the Communist and Nationalist parties in China against each other. The Communists won.

1950–1953 KOREAN WAR
Kicked off when the Communist forces of North Korea, with backing from the Soviet Union, invaded their democratic neighbor to the south. A coalition of 16 countries from the United Nations stepped in to support South Korea.

WORLD WAR I
100th Anniversary

1950s–1975 VIETNAM WAR
Fought between the Communist North, supported by its allies including China, and the government of South Vietnam, supported by the United States and other anticommunist nations.

1967 SIX-DAY WAR
A battle for land between Israel and the states of Egypt, Jordan, and Syria. The outcome resulted in Israel's gaining control of coveted territory, including the Gaza Strip and the West Bank.

1990–1991 PERSIAN GULF WAR
When Iraq invaded the country of Kuwait over oil conflicts, a coalition of 32 nations stepped in to destroy Iraq's forces.

1991–PRESENT SOMALI CIVIL WAR
Began when Somalia's last president, a dictator named Mohamed Siad Barre, was overthrown. The war has led to years of fighting and anarchy.

2001–PRESENT WAR IN AFGHANISTAN
After attacks in the United States by the terrorist group al Qaeda, a coalition of more than 40 countries invaded Afghanistan to find Osama bin Laden and other al Qaeda members. Bin Laden was killed in a U.S. covert operation in 2011.

2003–2011 WAR IN IRAQ
A coalition led by the U.S., and including Britain, Australia, and Spain, invaded Iraq over suspicions that Iraq had weapons of mass destruction.

It started with two shots.
The shots that rang out on June 28, 1914, sparked one of the bloodiest conflicts in history, World War I. Exactly one month after a Serbian nationalist shot and killed Archduke Franz Ferdinand of Austria and his wife, Austria-Hungary declared war on Serbia. The result was a four-year war that pitted the Central Powers (Germany, Austria-Hungary, and the Ottoman Empire) against the Allied Powers (Great Britain, France, Russia, Italy, Japan, and eventually the United States). All told, the war involved 70 million military troops from countries around the world and marked the introduction of modern warfare, like chemical weapons, machine guns, and tanks. By the time the war ended with the defeat of the Central Powers in November 1918, an estimated 8.5 million troops had been killed with another 21 million wounded.

Now, 100 years later, the anniversary of the start of World War I will be commemorated with special services, dedications, and memorials to remember this epic event and honor those who fought and died in the world's first truly global conflict.

The Constitution & the Bill of Rights

The United States Constitution was written in 1787 by a group of political leaders from the 13 states that made up the U.S. at the time. Thirty-nine men, including Benjamin Franklin and James Madison, signed the document to create a national government. While some feared the creation of a strong federal government, all 13 states eventually ratified, or approved, the Constitution, making it the law of the land. The Constitution has three major parts: the preamble, the articles, and the amendments.

THE PREAMBLE outlines the basic purposes of the government: *We the People of the United States, in order to form a more perfect Union, establish justice, insure domestic tranquility, provide for the common defense, promote the general welfare, and secure the blessings of liberty to ourselves and our posterity, do ordain and establish this Constitution for the United States of America.*

SEVEN ARTICLES outline the powers of Congress, the President, and the court system:

Article I outlines the legislative branch—the Senate and the House of Representatives—and its powers and responsibilities.
Article II outlines the executive branch—the Presidency—and its powers and responsibilities.
Article III outlines the judicial branch—the court system—and its powers and responsibilities.

Article IV describes the individual states' rights and powers.
Article V outlines the amendment process.
Article VI establishes the Constitution as the law of the land.
Article VII gives the requirements for the Constitution to be approved.

THE AMENDMENTS, or additions to the Constitution, were put in later as needed. In 1791, the first ten amendments, known as the Bill of Rights, were added. Since then another 17 amendments have been added. This is the Bill of Rights:

1st Amendment: guarantees freedom of religion, speech, and the press, and the right to assemble and petition
2nd Amendment: discusses the militia and the right of people to bear arms
3rd Amendment: prohibits the military or troops from using private homes without consent
4th Amendment: protects people and their homes from search, arrest, or seizure without probable cause or a warrant
5th Amendment: grants people the right to have a trial and prevents punishment before prosecution;

protects private property from being taken without compensation
6th Amendment: guarantees the right to a speedy and public trial
7th Amendment: guarantees a trial by jury in certain cases
8th Amendment: forbids "cruel and unusual punishments"
9th Amendment: states that the Constitution is not all-encompassing and does not deny people other, unspecified rights
10th Amendment: grants the powers not covered by the Constitution to the states and the people

Bet you didn't know

WHEN THE **Constitution** was signed, the **population** of the **U.S.** was **4 MILLION. It is now more than 311 MILLION.**

The **U.S. Constitution** HAS BEEN AMENDED **17 TIMES** since 1791.

GEORGE
WASHINGTON'S
REAL LOOK

WITH HELP FROM SCIENCE, THESE WAX FIGURES SOLVE THE MYSTERY OF WHAT THE FIRST U.S. PRESIDENT LOOKED LIKE.

Did George Washington really look like the portrait on the dollar bill, which appears above? Without photos, no one knew for sure. So officials at Mount Vernon, Washington's Virginia estate, called the experts. Using scientific methods, they accurately re-created Washington at the ages of 19, 45 (big picture), and 57. Here's how they gave Washington a makeover.

FACE In 1785, artist Jean Antoine Houdon created a mask of Washington after laying plaster-soaked gauze over his face. The mask was a near-perfect match of Washington's face, so scientists scanned it into a computer to create a 3-D image (right) that accurately showed Washington's facial features.

HAIR Because Washington often powdered his hair, not many people knew what his real hair color was. That's why experts examined Washington's hair samples (left, in center) and written descriptions by people who knew him. That confirmed once and for all that the President had reddish brown hair.

JAW Washington started losing his teeth around age 24, which meant that his jaw changed shape over time. To determine what Washington's jawline would have looked like at 19, anthropologist Jeffrey Schwartz examined two sets of Washington's false teeth, which were scanned into a computer.

The result? Turns out the real George Washington was thinner than many artists portrayed him. And his face was actually broader and longer than how it looks on the dollar bill. "Basically," Schwartz says, "no one portrait represents him faithfully from head to toe."

Washington, age 19

Washington, age 57

Branches of Government

The **UNITED STATES GOVERNMENT** is divided into three branches: **executive, legislative,** and **judicial.** The system of checks and balances is a way to control power and to make sure one branch can't take the reins of government. For example, most of the President's actions require the approval of Congress. Likewise, the laws passed in Congress must be signed by the President before they can take effect.

White House

Executive Branch

The Constitution lists the central powers of the President: to serve as Commander in Chief of the armed forces; make treaties with other nations; grant pardons; inform Congress on the state of the union; and appoint ambassadors, officials, and judges. The executive branch includes the President and the governmental departments. Originally there were three departments—State, War, and Treasury. Today there are 15 departments (see chart below).

Theodore Roosevelt had the West Wing built onto the White House in 1902 so he could have a quiet place to work. It now houses the official offices of the President and senior members of the Executive Office staff.

Government of the United States

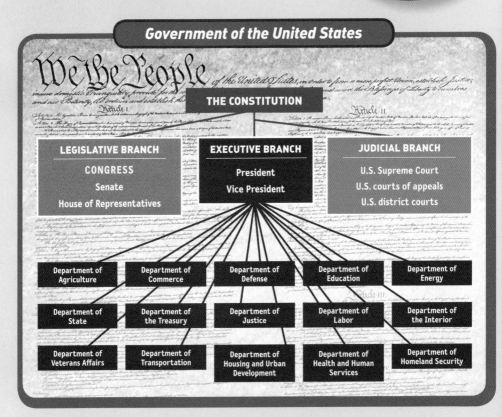

THE CONSTITUTION

LEGISLATIVE BRANCH	EXECUTIVE BRANCH	JUDICIAL BRANCH
CONGRESS	President	U.S. Supreme Court
Senate	Vice President	U.S. courts of appeals
House of Representatives		U.S. district courts

Department of Agriculture
Department of Commerce
Department of Defense
Department of Education
Department of Energy

Department of State
Department of the Treasury
Department of Justice
Department of Labor
Department of the Interior

Department of Veterans Affairs
Department of Transportation
Department of Housing and Urban Development
Department of Health and Human Services
Department of Homeland Security

Legislative Branch

This branch is made up of Congress—the Senate and the House of Representatives. The Constitution grants Congress the power to make laws. Congress is made up of elected representatives from each state. Each state has two representatives in the Senate, while the number of representatives in the House is determined by the size of the state's population. Washington, D.C., and the territories elect nonvoting representatives to the House of Representatives. The Founding Fathers set up this system as a compromise between big states—which wanted representation based on population—and small states—which wanted all states to have equal representation rights.

The U.S. Capitol in Washington, D.C.

Judicial Branch

The judicial branch is composed of the federal court system—the U.S. Supreme Court, the courts of appeals, and the district courts. The Supreme Court is the most powerful court. Its motto is "Equal Justice Under Law." This influential court is responsible for interpreting the Constitution and applying it to the cases that it hears. The decisions of the Supreme Court are absolute—they are the final word on any legal question.

There are nine justices on the Supreme Court. They are appointed by the President of the United States and confirmed by the Senate.

The U.S. Supreme Court Building in Washington, D.C.

Bet you didn't know

PRESIDENTIAL ELECTIONS

Grover Cleveland was elected President in 1884 and again in 1892, becoming the only U.S. President to serve two nonconsecutive terms.

There are some 50 recognized political parties in the United States.

Psephophobia is the fear of voting.

The 1960 U.S. presidential election was the first to include all 50 states.

In 1984, Ronald Reagan defeated Walter Mondale in one of the biggest landslides in U.S history.

More Americans voted in 2008 than in any other presidential election.

The President of the United States

is the chief of the executive branch, the Commander in Chief of the U.S. armed forces, and head of the federal government. Elected every four years, the President is the highest policy-maker in the nation. The 22nd Amendment (1951) says that no person may be elected to the office of President more than twice. There have been 44 Presidencies and 43 Presidents.

JAMES MONROE
5th President of the United States ★ *1817–1825*

BORN April 28, 1758, in Westmoreland County, VA
POLITICAL PARTY Democratic-Republican
NO. OF TERMS two
VICE PRESIDENT Daniel D. Tompkins
DIED July 4, 1831, in New York, NY

GEORGE WASHINGTON
1st President of the United States ★ *1789–1797*

BORN Feb. 22, 1732, in Pope's Creek, Westmoreland County, VA
POLITICAL PARTY Federalist
NO. OF TERMS two
VICE PRESIDENT John Adams
DIED Dec. 14, 1799, at Mount Vernon, VA

JOHN QUINCY ADAMS
6th President of the United States ★ *1825–1829*

BORN July 11, 1767, in Braintree (now Quincy), MA
POLITICAL PARTY Democratic-Republican
NO. OF TERMS one
VICE PRESIDENT John Caldwell Calhoun
DIED Feb. 23, 1848, at the U.S. Capitol, Washington, DC

JOHN ADAMS
2nd President of the United States ★ *1797–1801*

BORN Oct. 30, 1735, in Braintree (now Quincy), MA
POLITICAL PARTY Federalist
NO. OF TERMS one
VICE PRESIDENT Thomas Jefferson
DIED July 4, 1826, in Quincy, MA

ANDREW JACKSON
7th President of the United States ★ *1829–1837*

BORN March 15, 1767, in the Waxhaw region, NC and SC
POLITICAL PARTY Democrat
NO. OF TERMS two
VICE PRESIDENTS 1st term: John Caldwell Calhoun
2nd term: Martin Van Buren
DIED June 8, 1845, in Nashville, TN

THOMAS JEFFERSON
3rd President of the United States ★ *1801–1809*

BORN April 13, 1743, at Shadwell, Goochland (now Albemarle) County, VA
POLITICAL PARTY Democratic-Republican
NO. OF TERMS two
VICE PRESIDENTS 1st term: Aaron Burr
2nd term: George Clinton
DIED July 4, 1826, at Monticello, Charlottesville, VA

MARTIN VAN BUREN
8th President of the United States ★ *1837–1841*

BORN Dec. 5, 1782, in Kinderhook, NY
POLITICAL PARTY Democrat
NO. OF TERMS one
VICE PRESIDENT Richard M. Johnson
DIED July 24, 1862, in Kinderhook, NY

JAMES MADISON
4th President of the United States ★ *1809–1817*

BORN March 16, 1751, at Belle Grove, Port Conway, VA
POLITICAL PARTY Democratic-Republican
NO. OF TERMS two
VICE PRESIDENTS 1st term: George Clinton
2nd term: Elbridge Gerry
DIED June 28, 1836, at Montpelier, Orange County, VA

WILLIAM HENRY HARRISON
9th President of the United States ★ *1841*

BORN Feb. 9, 1773, in Charles City County, VA
POLITICAL PARTY Whig
NO. OF TERMS one (cut short by death)
VICE PRESIDENT John Tyler
DIED April 4, 1841, in the White House, Washington, DC

JOHN TYLER
10th President of the United States ★ 1841–1845
BORN March 29, 1790, in Charles City County, VA
POLITICAL PARTY Whig
NO. OF TERMS one (partial)
VICE PRESIDENT none
DIED Jan. 18, 1862, in Richmond, VA

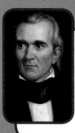

JAMES K. POLK
11th President of the United States ★ 1845–1849
BORN Nov. 2, 1795, near Pineville, Mecklenburg County, NC
POLITICAL PARTY Democrat
NO. OF TERMS one
VICE PRESIDENT George Mifflin Dallas
DIED June 15, 1849, in Nashville, TN

ZACHARY TAYLOR
12th President of the United States ★ 1849–1850
BORN Nov. 24, 1784, in Orange County, VA
POLITICAL PARTY Whig
NO. OF TERMS one (cut short by death)
VICE PRESIDENT Millard Fillmore
DIED July 9, 1850, in the White House, Washington, DC

MILLARD FILLMORE
13th President of the United States ★ 1850–1853
BORN Jan. 7, 1800, in Cayuga County, NY
POLITICAL PARTY Whig
NO. OF TERMS one (partial)
VICE PRESIDENT none
DIED March 8, 1874, in Buffalo, NY

FRANKLIN PIERCE
14th President of the United States ★ 1853–1857
BORN Nov. 23, 1804, in Hillsborough (now Hillsboro), NH
POLITICAL PARTY Democrat
NO. OF TERMS one
VICE PRESIDENT William Rufus De Vane King
DIED Oct. 8, 1869, in Concord, NH

JAMES BUCHANAN
15th President of the United States ★ 1857–1861
BORN April 23, 1791, in Cove Gap, PA
POLITICAL PARTY Democrat
NO. OF TERMS one
VICE PRESIDENT John Cabell Breckinridge
DIED June 1, 1868, in Lancaster, PA

ABRAHAM LINCOLN
16th President of the United States ★ 1861–1865
BORN Feb. 12, 1809, near Hodgenville, KY
POLITICAL PARTY Republican (formerly Whig)
NO. OF TERMS two (assassinated)
VICE PRESIDENTS 1st term: Hannibal Hamlin
2nd term: Andrew Johnson
DIED April 15, 1865, in Washington, DC

ANDREW JOHNSON
17th President of the United States ★ 1865–1869
BORN Dec. 29, 1808, in Raleigh, NC
POLITICAL PARTY Democrat
NO. OF TERMS one (partial)
VICE PRESIDENT none
DIED July 31, 1875, in Carter's Station, TN

PRESIDENTS BY THE NUMBERS

9 Presidents didn't attend college.

18 Presidents never served in the U.S. Congress.

43 was the age of the youngest elected President, John F. Kennedy.

69 was the age of the oldest elected President, Ronald Reagan.

$20 was the price of a speeding ticket given to Ulysses S. Grant for riding his horse too fast.

$25,000 was George Washington's salary in 1789—equal to about $615,000 today.

$400,000 was Barack Obama's salary in 2012.

ULYSSES S. GRANT

18th President of the United States ★ *1869–1877*

BORN April 27, 1822,
in Point Pleasant, OH

POLITICAL PARTY Republican

NO. OF TERMS two

VICE PRESIDENTS 1st term: Schuyler Colfax
2nd term: Henry Wilson

DIED July 23, 1885, in Mount McGregor, NY

RUTHERFORD B. HAYES

19th President of the United States ★ *1877–1881*

BORN Oct. 4, 1822,
in Delaware, OH

POLITICAL PARTY Republican

NO. OF TERMS one

VICE PRESIDENT William Almon Wheeler

DIED Jan. 17, 1893, in Fremont, OH

JAMES A. GARFIELD

20th President of the United States ★ *1881*

BORN Nov. 19, 1831, near Orange, OH

POLITICAL PARTY Republican

NO. OF TERMS one (assassinated)

VICE PRESIDENT Chester A. Arthur

DIED Sept. 19, 1881, in Elberon, NJ

CHESTER A. ARTHUR

21st President of the United States ★ *1881–1885*

BORN Oct. 5, 1829, in Fairfield, VT

POLITICAL PARTY Republican

NO. OF TERMS one (partial)

VICE PRESIDENT none

DIED Nov. 18, 1886, in New York, NY

GROVER CLEVELAND

22nd and 24th President of the United States
1885–1889 ★ *1893–1897*

BORN March 18, 1837, in Caldwell, NJ

POLITICAL PARTY Democrat

NO. OF TERMS two (nonconsecutive)

VICE PRESIDENTS 1st administration:
Thomas Andrews Hendricks
2nd administration:
Adlai Ewing Stevenson

DIED June 24, 1908, in Princeton, NJ

BENJAMIN HARRISON

23rd President of the United States ★ *1889–1893*

BORN Aug. 20, 1833,
in North Bend, OH

POLITICAL PARTY Republican

NO. OF TERMS one

VICE PRESIDENT Levi Parsons Morton

DIED March 13, 1901, in Indianapolis, IN

WILLIAM MCKINLEY

25th President of the United States ★ *1897–1901*

BORN Jan. 29, 1843, in Niles, OH

POLITICAL PARTY Republican

NO. OF TERMS two (assassinated)

VICE PRESIDENTS 1st term:
Garret Augustus Hobart
2nd term:
Theodore Roosevelt

DIED Sept. 14, 1901, in Buffalo, NY

THEODORE ROOSEVELT

26th President of the United States ★ *1901–1909*

BORN Oct. 27, 1858, in New York, NY

POLITICAL PARTY Republican

NO. OF TERMS one, plus balance of
McKinley's term

VICE PRESIDENTS 1st term: none
2nd term: Charles
Warren Fairbanks

DIED Jan. 6, 1919, in Oyster Bay, NY

WILLIAM HOWARD TAFT

27th President of the United States ★ *1909–1913*

BORN Sept. 15, 1857, in Cincinnati, OH

POLITICAL PARTY Republican

NO. OF TERMS one

VICE PRESIDENT James Schoolcraft
Sherman

DIED March 8, 1930, in Washington, DC

WOODROW WILSON

28th President of the United States ★ *1913–1921*

BORN Dec. 29, 1856,
in Staunton, VA

POLITICAL PARTY Democrat

NO. OF TERMS two

VICE PRESIDENT Thomas Riley Marshall

DIED Feb. 3, 1924, in Washington, DC

WARREN G. HARDING

29th President of the United States ★ *1921–1923*

BORN Nov. 2, 1865, in Caledonia (now Blooming Grove), OH

POLITICAL PARTY Republican

NO. OF TERMS one (died while in office)

VICE PRESIDENT Calvin Coolidge

DIED Aug. 2, 1923, in San Francisco, CA

HARRY S. TRUMAN

33rd President of the United States ★ *1945–1953*

BORN May 8, 1884, in Lamar, MO

POLITICAL PARTY Democrat

NO. OF TERMS one, plus balance of Franklin D. Roosevelt's term

VICE PRESIDENTS 1st term: none
2nd term: Alben William Barkley

DIED Dec. 26, 1972, in Independence, MO

CALVIN COOLIDGE

30th President of the United States ★ *1923–1929*

BORN July 4, 1872, in Plymouth, VT

POLITICAL PARTY Republican

NO. OF TERMS one, plus balance of Harding's term

VICE PRESIDENTS 1st term: none
2nd term: Charles Gates Dawes

DIED Jan. 5, 1933, in Northampton, MA

DWIGHT D. EISENHOWER

34th President of the United States ★ *1953–1961*

BORN Oct. 14, 1890, in Denison, TX

POLITICAL PARTY Republican

NO. OF TERMS two

VICE PRESIDENT Richard M. Nixon

DIED March 28, 1969, in Washington, DC

HERBERT HOOVER

31st President of the United States ★ *1929–1933*

BORN Aug. 10, 1874, in West Branch, IA

POLITICAL PARTY Republican

NO. OF TERMS one

VICE PRESIDENT Charles Curtis

DIED Oct. 20, 1964, in New York, NY

JOHN F. KENNEDY

35th President of the United States ★ *1961–1963*

BORN May 29, 1917, in Brookline, MA

POLITICAL PARTY Democrat

NO. OF TERMS one (assassinated)

VICE PRESIDENT Lyndon B. Johnson

DIED Nov. 22, 1963, in Dallas, TX

FRANKLIN D. ROOSEVELT

32nd President of the United States ★ *1933–1945*

BORN Jan. 30, 1882, in Hyde Park, NY

POLITICAL PARTY Democrat

NO. OF TERMS four (died while in office)

VICE PRESIDENTS 1st & 2nd terms: John Nance Garner; 3rd term: Henry Agard Wallace; 4th term: Harry S. Truman

DIED April 12, 1945, in Warm Springs, GA

LYNDON B. JOHNSON

36th President of the United States ★ *1963–1969*

BORN Aug. 27, 1908, near Stonewall, TX

POLITICAL PARTY Democrat

NO. OF TERMS one, plus balance of Kennedy's term

VICE PRESIDENTS 1st term: none
2nd term: Hubert Horatio Humphrey

DIED Jan. 22, 1973, near San Antonio, TX

COMMUNICATOR IN CHIEF

FIRST PRESIDENT **to receive a telegraph:** Martin Van Buren, in 1838.

FIRST PRESIDENT **heard on the radio:** Warren Harding, in 1922.

FIRST PRESIDENT **to appear on television:** Franklin D. Roosevelt, in 1939.

FIRST PRESIDENT **to send an email from the White House:** Bill Clinton, in 1993.

FIRST PRESIDENT **to Tweet:** Barack Obama, in 2011.

RICHARD NIXON
37th President of the United States ★ *1969–1974*
BORN Jan. 9, 1913, in Yorba Linda, CA
POLITICAL PARTY Republican
NO. OF TERMS two (resigned)
VICE PRESIDENTS 1st term & 2nd term (partial): Spiro Theodore Agnew; 2nd term (balance): Gerald R. Ford
DIED April 22, 1994, in New York, NY

GERALD R. FORD
38th President of the United States ★ *1974–1977*
BORN July 14, 1913, in Omaha, NE
POLITICAL PARTY Republican
NO. OF TERMS one (partial)
VICE PRESIDENT Nelson Aldrich Rockefeller
DIED Dec. 26, 2006, in Rancho Mirage, CA

JIMMY CARTER
39th President of the United States ★ *1977–1981*
BORN Oct. 1, 1924, in Plains, GA
POLITICAL PARTY Democrat
NO. OF TERMS one
VICE PRESIDENT Walter Frederick (Fritz) Mondale

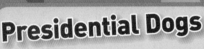

Presidential Dogs

When it comes to pets, which kind of pooches have the Presidents picked?

Airedale terrier: **Warren G. Harding**
Beagle: **Lyndon B. Johnson**
Collie: **Calvin Coolidge**
French poodle: **Richard Nixon**
German shepherd: **Herbert Hoover**
Golden retriever: **Gerald R. Ford**
King Charles spaniel: **Ronald Reagan**
Portuguese water dog: **Barack Obama**
Scottish terrier: **George W. Bush**
Weimaraner: **Dwight D. Eisenhower**

RONALD REAGAN
40th President of the United States ★ *1981–1989*
BORN Feb. 6, 1911, in Tampico, IL
POLITICAL PARTY Republican
NO. OF TERMS two
VICE PRESIDENT George H. W. Bush
DIED June 5, 2004, in Los Angeles, CA

GEORGE H. W. BUSH
41st President of the United States ★ *1989–1993*
BORN June 12, 1924, in Milton, MA
POLITICAL PARTY Republican
NO. OF TERMS one
VICE PRESIDENT James Danforth (Dan) Quayle III

WILLIAM J. CLINTON
42nd President of the United States ★ *1993–2001*
BORN Aug. 19, 1946, in Hope, AR
POLITICAL PARTY Democrat
NO. OF TERMS two
VICE PRESIDENT Albert Gore, Jr.

GEORGE W. BUSH
43rd President of the United States ★ *2001–2009*
BORN July 6, 1946, in New Haven, CT
POLITICAL PARTY Republican
NO. OF TERMS two
VICE PRESIDENT Richard Bruce Cheney

BARACK OBAMA
44th President of the United States ★ *2009–present*
BORN Aug. 4, 1961, in Honolulu, HI
POLITICAL PARTY Democrat
NO. OF TERMS two
VICE PRESIDENT Joseph Biden

FAST FACT
Maurice Sendak's *Where the Wild Things Are* is one of Barack Obama's favorite children's books.

The Indian Experience

A Navajo man in traditional costume, Monument Valley, Arizona/Utah, U.S.A.

American Indians are indigenous to North and South America—they are the people who were here before Columbus and other European explorers came to these lands. They lived in nations, tribes, and bands across both continents. For decades following the arrival of Europeans in 1492, American Indians clashed with the newcomers who had ruptured the Indians' way of living.

Tribal Land

During the 19th century, both United States legislation and military action restricted the movement of American Indians, forcing them to live on reservations and attempting to dismantle tribal structures. For centuries Indians were often displaced or killed, or became assimilated into the general U.S. population. In 1924 the Indian Citizenship Act granted citizenship to all American Indians. Unfortunately, this was not enough to end the social discrimination and mistreatment that many Indians have faced. Today, American Indians living in the U.S. still face many challenges.

Healing the Past

Many members of the 560-plus recognized tribes in the United States live primarily on reservations. Some tribes have more than one reservation, while others have none. Together these reservations make up less than 3 percent of the nation's land area. The tribal governments on reservations have the right to form their own governments and enforce laws, similar to individual states. Many feel that this sovereignty is still not enough to right the wrongs of the past: They hope for a change in the U.S. government's relationship with American Indians.

American Indians invented kayaks, snowshoes, and lacrosse.

Navajo "code talkers" communicated secret information for the U.S. Army and Marines during World War II.

249

CIVIL RIGHTS

Although the Constitution protects the civil rights of American citizens, it has not always been able to protect all Americans from persecution or discrimination. During the first half of the 20th century, many Americans, particularly African Americans, were subjected to widespread discrimination and racism. By the mid-1950s, many people were eager to end the bonds of racism and bring freedom to all men and women.

The civil rights movement of the 1950s and 1960s sought to end the racial discrimination against African Americans, especially in the southern states. The movement wanted to restore the fundamentals of economic and social equality to those who had been oppressed.

The Little Rock Nine

The Little Rock Nine study during the weeks when they were blocked from school.

September 4, 1957, marked the first day of school at Little Rock Central High in Little Rock, Arkansas. But this was no ordinary back-to-school scene: Armed soldiers surrounded the entrance, awaiting the arrival of Central's first-ever African-American students. The welcome was not warm, however, as the students—now known as the Little Rock Nine—were refused entry into the school by the soldiers and a group of protesters, angry about the potential integration. This did not deter the students, and they gained the support of President Dwight D. Eisenhower to eventually earn their right to go to an integrated school. Today, the Little Rock Nine are still considered civil rights icons for challenging a racist system—and winning!

Key Events in the Civil Rights Movement

1954	The Supreme Court case *Brown* v. *Board of Education* declares school segregation illegal.
1955	Rosa Parks refuses to give up her bus seat to a white passenger and spurs a bus boycott.
1957	The Little Rock Nine help to integrate schools.
1960	Four black college students begin sit-ins at a restaurant in Greensboro, North Carolina.
1961	Freedom Rides to southern states begin as a way to protest segregation in transportation.
1963	Martin Luther King, Jr., leads the famous March on Washington.
1964	The Civil Rights Act, signed by President Lyndon B. Johnson, prohibits discrimination based on race, color, religion, sex, and national origin.
1967	Thurgood Marshall becomes the first African American to be named to the Supreme Court.
1968	President Lyndon B. Johnson signs the Civil Rights Act of 1968, which prohibits discrimination in the sale, rental, and financing of housing.

Champions of Civil Rights:
Prominent figures who emerged from the civil rights movement included Rosa Parks, John F. Kennedy, Malcolm X, and Martin Luther King, Jr. Here's more about these powerful leaders.

ROSA PARKS 1913 (Alabama, U.S.A.) – 2005 (Michigan, U.S.A.)

After refusing to give up her bus seat to a white passenger, activist Parks sparked a 381-day boycott of the city bus line in Montgomery, Alabama. This eventually led to the 1956 Supreme Court ruling declaring segregation illegal on public buses, giving Parks the unofficial title of "The Mother of the Modern-Day Civil Rights Movement."

Did you know? At the time of her arrest, Parks was 42 and on her way home from work as a seamstress. Aside from being arrested, she was fined $14 for refusing to give up her seat.

JOHN F. KENNEDY 1917 (Massachusetts, U.S.A.) – 1963 (Texas, U.S.A.)

As President, Kennedy used executive orders and pleas to the public to show his support of civil rights. This included sending 400 U.S. Marshals to Alabama in 1961 to protect the "Freedom Riders," a group of men and women who boarded buses, trains, and planes to the Deep South to test the 1960 U.S. Supreme Court ruling outlawing racial segregation. Kennedy was assassinated during a presidential motorcade in Dallas, Texas, on November 22, 1963.

Did you know? Kennedy was the first U.S. President born in the 20th century.

MALCOLM X 1925 (Nebraska, U.S.A.) – 1965 (New York, U.S.A.)

A preacher and talented public speaker, Malcolm X believed that people would be set free of racism by working together, and encouraged his African-American followers to be proud of their race. He also advocated peace and unity among all people, regardless of the color of their skin. While giving a speech in Harlem, New York, Malcolm X was shot and killed by three members of the Nation of Islam, the religious organization he once belonged to.

Did you know? Malcolm X was born with the last name "Little," but changed it to "X" once he joined the Nation of Islam.

MARTIN LUTHER KING, JR. 1929 (Georgia, U.S.A.) – 1968 (Tennessee, U.S.A.)

Civil rights leader Dr. Martin Luther King, Jr., born in Atlanta, Georgia, in 1929, never backed down in his stand against racism. He dedicated his life to achieving equality and justice for Americans of all colors. From a family of preachers, King experienced racial prejudice early in life. As an adult fighting for civil rights, his speeches, marches, and mere presence motivated people to fight for justice for all. His March on Washington in 1963 was one of the largest activist gatherings in our nation's history. King was assassinated by James Earl Ray on April 4, 1968.

Did you know? King began attending Morehouse College in Atlanta, Georgia, when he was 15 years old.

WOMEN
Fighting for Equality

EQUALITY OF RIGHTS UNDER THE LAW SHALL NOT BE DENIED OR ABRIDG
BY THE UNITED STATES OR BY ANY STATE ON ACCOUNT OF SE

Women march for equality
in Washington, D.C.

Today, women make up about half of the country's workforce. But a little over a century ago, less than 20 percent worked outside the home. In fact, they didn't even have the right to vote!

That began to change in the mid-1800s when women, led by pioneers like Elizabeth Cady Stanton and Susan B. Anthony, started speaking up about inequality. They organized public demonstrations, gave speeches, published documents, and wrote newspaper articles to express their ideas. In 1848, about 300 people attended the Seneca Falls Convention in New York to address the need for equal rights. By the late 1800s, the National American Woman Suffrage Association had made great strides toward giving women the freedom to vote. One by one, states began allowing women to vote. By 1920, the U.S. Constitution was amended, giving women across the country the ability to cast a vote during any election.

But the fight for equality did not end there. In the 1960s and 1970s, the women's rights movement experienced a rebirth, as feminists protested against injustices in areas such as the workplace and in education.

While these efforts enabled women to make great strides in our society, the efforts to even the playing field among men and women continue today.

In 2012, Saudi Arabia sent female athletes to the Olympic Games for the first time.

Black South African women gained the right to vote in 1996.

252

Girls at a suffrage meeting, ca 1920

Key Events in Women's History

1848: **Elizabeth Cady Stanton** and **Lucretia Mott** organize the Seneca Falls Convention in New York. Attendees rally for equitable laws, equal educational and job opportunities, and the right to vote.

1920: **The 19th Amendment**, guaranteeing women the right to vote, is ratified.

1964: **Title VII of the Civil Rights Act of 1964,** which prohibits employment discrimination on the basis of sex, is successfully amended.

1966: **The National Organization for Women** (NOW), the largest feminist organization in the United States, is founded by women, including writer Betty Friedan; Rev. Pauli Murray, the first African-American female Episcopal priest; and Shirley Chisholm, the first African-American woman to run for president of the United States.

1971: **Gloria Steinem** heads up the National Women's Political Caucus, which encourages women to be active in government. She also launches *Ms.*, a magazine about women's issues.

1972: Congress approves **the Equal Rights Amendment** (ERA), proposing that women and men have equal rights under the law. It is ratified by 35 of the necessary 38 states, and is still not part of the U.S. Constitution.

1981: President Ronald Reagan appoints **Sandra Day O'Connor** as the first female Supreme Court justice.

1984: Democrat **Geraldine Ferraro** is nominated as a major party's first female vice presidential candidate.

1996: **Madeleine Albright** is appointed the first female Secretary of State.

2005: **Condoleezza Rice** becomes the first African-American woman to be appointed Secretary of State.

Amelia Bloomer Changes Style

While women were fighting for equal rights in the 19th century, they were doing so wearing confining corsets and layers of heavy petticoats underneath their dresses. But thanks to women's rights activist Amelia Bloomer, women's clothing eventually became a lot more comfortable. Bloomer, who tackled pressing women's issues in her newspaper *The Lily*, suggested a new style of looser tops and skirts that stopped at the knee with a pair of pants underneath. The style stuck—and short pants worn under a skirt or dress are still known as "bloomers" to this day.

Woman in bloomers

Madame President

Though no woman has ever been elected President of the United States, dozens have thrown their hats in the ring. Victoria Woodhull was the first in 1872. And in recent years, some women have nearly reached the coveted position. For example, in Hillary Rodham Clinton's 2008 run for the Democratic nomination for U.S. President, she came closer to winning the nomination of a major political party in the United States than any other woman had. That same year, Sarah Palin—the governor of Alaska—ran for Vice President on the Republican ticket alongside presidential contender John McCain. And in the 2012 presidential election, Minnesota Congresswoman Michele Bachmann was an early frontrunner for the Republican nomination, but later dropped out of the race. So when will a woman become the first female President of the United States? Only time will tell!

Hillary Rodham Clinton

STUMP YOUR PARENTS

HISTORY HAPPENS QUIZ

Is world history a mystery to your folks? Quiz them on this chapter's info to see if they're caught up on the past.

ANSWERS BELOW

1 Which royal couple once owned the Hope Diamond?
a. Queen Victoria and Prince Albert
b. King Louis XVI and Marie Antoinette
c. Queen Isabella and King Ferdinand II
d. Prince William and Kate Middleton

2 **True or false?** A castle barber was also the doctor.

3 When did excavations begin at Pompeii?
a. 1653
b. 1748
c. 1923
d. before the dawn of time

4 Which movie director assembled a team of experts to examine the *Titanic* shipwreck?
a. Steven Spielberg　c. Martin Scorsese
b. Danny Boyle　　　d. James Cameron

5 A Greek amphitheater could hold how many people?
a. 500
b. 5,000
c. 15,000
d. 150,000

6 Built around A.D. 1000, Timbuktu was once known as the "City of Gold." Where is it located?
a. Mali
b. Tanzania
c. Indonesia
d. at the end of the rainbow

ANSWERS:
1. b; 2. False. The barber was also the dentist; 3. b; 4. d; 5. c; 6. a

Brilliant Biographies

A biography is the story of a person's life. It can be a brief summary or a long book. Biographers—those who write biographies—use many different sources to learn about their subjects. You can write your own biography of a famous person whom you find inspiring.

How to Get Started

Choose a subject you find interesting. If you think Cleopatra is cool, you have a good chance of getting your reader interested, too. If you're bored by ancient Egypt, your reader will be snoring after your first paragraph.

Your subject can be almost anyone: an author, an inventor, a celebrity, a politician, or a member of your family. To find someone to write about, ask yourself these simple questions:

1. Whom do I want to know more about?
2. What did this person do that was special?
3. How did this person change the world?

Do Your Research

- Find out as much about your subject as possible. Read books, news articles, and encyclopedia entries. Watch video clips and movies, and search the Internet. Conduct interviews, if possible.
- Take notes, writing down important facts and interesting stories about your subject.

Write the Biography

- Come up with a title. Include the person's name.
- Write an introduction. Consider asking a probing question about your subject.
- Include information about the person's childhood. When was this person born? Where did he or she grow up? Whom did he or she admire?
- Highlight the person's talents, accomplishments, and personal attributes.
- Describe the specific events that helped to shape this person's life. Did this person ever have a problem and overcome it?
- Write a conclusion. Include your thoughts about why it is important to learn about this person.
- Once you have finished your first draft, revise and then proofread your work.

Author J. K. Rowling

Here's a SAMPLE BIOGRAPHY of J. K. Rowling, author of the *Harry Potter* series. Of course, there is so much more for you to discover, and write about on your own!

J. K. Rowling—Author

Joanne "Jo" Rowling was born on July 31, 1965, in Gloucestershire, England, the oldest of two children to her mother, Anne, and father, Peter James.

Joanne grew up writing fantasy stories and reading them to her younger sister, Dianne. But she did not set out to be a writer. She studied French at the University of Exeter and worked as both a researcher for Amnesty International, a nonprofit organization, and as a teacher. It wasn't until she was stuck on a delayed train between Manchester and London that the idea for *Harry Potter* popped into her head. She began writing as soon as she returned to her home in London, but it took six years before the book was completed and eventually published.

Rowling lives in Scotland with her husband, Neil, daughters Jessica and Mackenzie, and son, David. She finished the final novel in the *Harry Potter* series in 2007, but she continues to write and remains one of the world's most well-known—and wealthiest—authors.

Hot air balloons soar above "fairy chimneys" formed from ancient volcanic rock in Göreme, Cappadocia, Turkey.

Geography
Rocks

KINDS OF MAPS

Maps are special tools that geographers use to tell a story about Earth. Maps can be used to show just about anything related to places. Some maps show physical features, such as mountains or vegetation. Maps can also show climates or natural hazards and other things we cannot easily see. Other maps illustrate different features on Earth—political boundaries, urban centers, and economic systems.

AN IMPERFECT TOOL

Maps are not perfect. A globe is a scale model of Earth with accurate relative sizes and locations. Because maps are flat, they involve distortions of size, shape, and direction. Also, cartographers—people who create maps—make choices about what information to include. Because of this, it is important to study many different types of maps to learn the complete story of Earth. Three commonly found kinds of maps are shown on this page.

PHYSICAL MAPS. Earth's natural features—landforms, water bodies, and vegetation—are shown on physical maps. The map above uses color and shading to illustrate mountains, lakes, rivers, and deserts of western Africa. Country names and borders are added for reference, but they are not natural features.

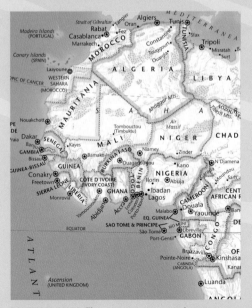

POLITICAL MAPS. These maps represent characteristics of the landscape created by humans, such as boundaries, cities, and place-names. Natural features are added only for reference. On the map above, capital cities are represented with a star inside a circle, while other cities are shown with black dots.

THEMATIC MAPS. Patterns related to a particular topic or theme, such as population distribution, appear on these maps. The map above displays the region's climate zones, which range from tropical wet (bright green) to tropical wet and dry (light green) to semiarid (dark yellow) to arid or desert (light yellow).

258

GEOGRAPHIC FEATURES

From roaring rivers to parched deserts, from underwater canyons to jagged mountains, Earth is covered with beautiful and diverse environments. Here are examples of the most common types of geographic features found around the world.

DESERT

Deserts are land features created by climate, specifically by a lack of water. Here, a camel caravan crosses the Sahara in North Africa.

VALLEY

Valleys, cut by running water or moving ice, may be broad and flat or narrow and steep, such as the Indus River Valley in Ladakh, India (above).

RIVER

As a river moves through flatlands, it twists and turns. Above, the Rio Los Amigos winds through a rain forest in Peru.

MOUNTAIN

Mountains are Earth's tallest landforms, and Mount Everest (above) rises highest of all, at 29,035 feet (8,850 m) above sea level.

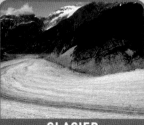

GLACIER

Glaciers—"rivers" of ice—such as Alaska's Hubbard Glacier (above) move slowly from mountains to the sea. Global warming is shrinking them.

CANYON

Steep-sided valleys called canyons are created mainly by running water. Buckskin Gulch in Utah (above) is the deepest slot canyon in the American Southwest.

WATERFALL

Waterfalls form when a river reaches an abrupt change in elevation. Above, Kaieteur Falls, in Guyana, has a sheer drop of 741 feet (226 m).

THE POLITICAL WORLD

Earth's land area is made up of seven continents, but people have divided much of the land into smaller political units called countries. Australia is a continent made up of a single country, and Antarctica is set aside for scientific research. But the other five continents include almost 200 independent countries. The political map shown here depicts boundaries—imaginary lines created by treaties—that separate countries. Some boundaries, such as the one between the United States and Canada, are very stable and have been recognized for many years.

ARC

Queen Elizabeth Is.

Chukchi Sea

Beaufort Sea

Baffin Bay

Greenland (Denmark)

RUSSIA

Alaska (U.S.)

Great Bear Lake

Great Slave Lake

ARCTIC

ICELAN

60°

Bering Sea

Gulf of Alaska

C A N A D A

Hudson Bay

Labrador Sea

UN KING

Lake Winnipeg

IRELA

Great Salt Lake

FR

UNITED STATES

See Europe map for more detail.

PORT.

MOR

30°

TROPIC OF CANCER

Gulf of Mexico

BAHAMAS

DOMINCAN REP.

Western Sahara (Morocco)

Hawai'i (U.S.)

MEXICO

CUBA

HAITI

Puerto Rico (U.S.)

ST. KITTS & NEVIS
ANTIGUA & BARBUDA
Guadeloupe (France)
DOMINICA
Martinique (France)
BARBADOS
ST. VINCENT & THE GRENADINES
TRINIDAD AND TOBAGO

MAURITANIA

CAPE VERDE

SENEGAL

JAMAICA

HONDURAS

Caribbean Sea

ST. LUCIA

GUATEMALA
EL SALVADOR

NICARAGUA

GRENADA

GAMBIA

GUINEA-BISSAU

COSTA RICA

PANAMA

VENEZUELA

GUYANA

GUINEA

COLOMBIA

French Guiana (France)

SIERRA LEONE

PACIFIC

SURINAME

LIBERIA

0°

EQUATOR

150°

120°

90°

Galápagos Islands (Ecuador)

ECUADOR

CÔTE D'IVOIRE (IVORY COAST)

KIRIBATI

OCEAN

EQ. GUIN

Marquesas Islands (France)

PERU

B R A Z I L

SAO

PRI

SAMOA

American Samoa (U.S.)

French Polynesia (France)

BOLIVIA

ATLANTIC

TONGA

PARAGUAY

OCEAN

TROPIC OF CAPRICORN

URUGUAY

30°

CHILE

ARGENTINA

0 miles 2000
0 kilometers 3000
Winkel Tripel Projection

Chatham Is. (N.Z.)

Falkland Islands (U.K.)

Tierra del Fuego

Strait of Magellan

Drake Passage

AN

60°

Weddell Sea

Ross Sea

A N

Other boundaries, such as the one between Ethiopia and Eritrea in northeast Africa, are relatively new and still disputed. Countries come in all shapes and sizes. Russia and Canada are giants; others, such as Luxembourg, are small. Some countries are long and skinny—look at Chile in South America! Still other countries—such as Indonesia and Japan in Asia—are made up of groups of islands. The political map is a clue to the diversity that makes Earth so fascinating.

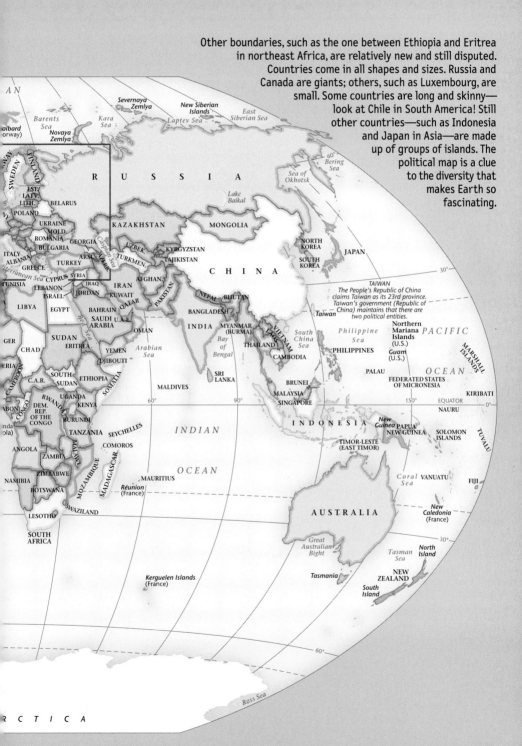

TAIWAN
The People's Republic of China claims Taiwan as its 23rd province. Taiwan's government (Republic of China) maintains that there are two political entities.

THE PHYSICAL WORLD

Earth is dominated by large landmasses called continents—seven in all—and by an interconnected global ocean that is divided into four parts by the continents. More than 70 percent of Earth's surface is covered by oceans, and the remaining 30 percent is made up of land areas.

Different landforms give variety to the surface of the continents. The Rockies and the Andes mark the western edge of the Americas, and the Himalaya tower above southern Asia. The Plateau of Tibet forms the rugged core of Asia, while

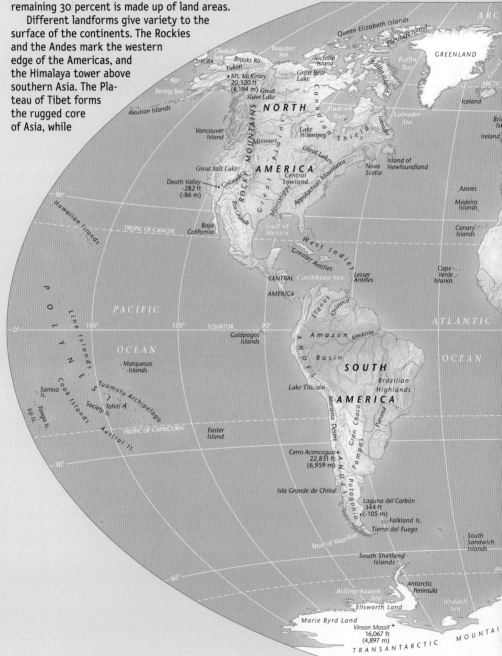

the Northern European Plain extends from the North Sea to the Ural Mountains. Much of Africa is a plateau, and dry plains cover large areas of Australia. Mountains rise more than 16,000 feet (4,877 m) above Antarctica's massive ice sheets. Mountains and trenches make the ocean floors as varied as any continent. A mountain chain called the Mid-Atlantic Ridge runs the length of the Atlantic Ocean. In the western Pacific, trenches drop deep into the ocean floor.

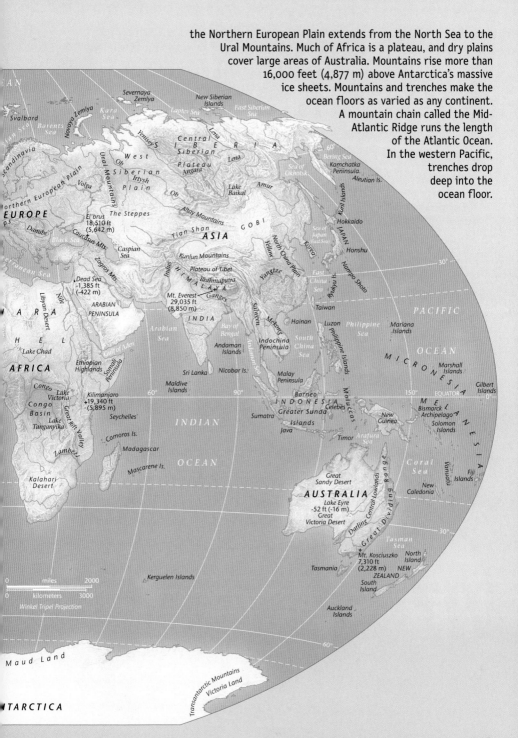

Wacky World →

Check out these **bizarre roadside attractions** from around the globe.

Eiffel Tower? Great Pyramid? Puh-lease! These unusual landmarks definitely would be something to write home about on your next international vacation. Take a look at some postcard-worthy attractions.

Headington Shark
Where: Headington, England
Why it's wacky: Just when you thought it was safe to go into the attic . . . a shark plunges through the roof! Two cranes lifted this fake shark over a house and lowered it into a hole that fits the creature's body perfectly.

Porcelain Dragon
Where: Yangzou, China
Why it's wacky: This dragon— a symbol of good luck in Chinese culture—is made of more than 2,800 plates, bowls, spoons, and cups attached to a metal frame about as long as a blue whale.

PLATES, SPOONS, BOWLS!

Check out this hilarious but real road sign near the Dead Sea, one of the saltiest bodies of water on Earth, in Jordan.

WARNING

EXTREMELY SALTY WATER

Hand of the Desert

Where: Atacama Desert, Chile
Why it's wacky: This three-story giant hand—built to draw visitors to the nearby city of Antofagasta—is strong enough to withstand both the blistering desert heat and freezing nighttime temperatures.

Larry the Lobster

Where: Kingston, South East, Australia
Why it's wacky: Visitors to the Big Lobster restaurant are welcomed by this 56-foot (17-m)-tall crustacean, towering over the building. Larry is one of Australia's "Big Things"— a series of giant tourist attractions along the country's roads.

ZANY HOTELS

These three weird-but-cool places are so wacky they'll make a huge splash on anyone's vacation. Hold your breath and dive in!

CHECK OUT THESE FUN WATER-THEMED PLACES TO STAY ON VACATION.

② MAGIC MOUNTAIN LODGE

WHERE: Puerto Fuy, Chile

WHY IT'S COOL: This 66-foot (20-m)-tall hotel looks like a volcano. But instead of lava, a waterfall erupts from the top and continuously cascades down the sides. Inspired by nearby Mocho Choshuenco volcano and Huilo-Huilo Falls, the lodge draws its waterfall from a local river.

① BURJ AL ARAB

WHERE: Dubai, United Arab Emirates

WHY IT'S COOL: No beach? No problem! The builders of the Burj Al Arab made their own island so that this sail-shaped hotel appears to be cruising 919 feet (280 m) into the Arabian Gulf. A simulated submarine ride takes you to a seafood restaurant with a giant aquarium.

INSIDE

③ CAPSULE HOTEL

WHERE: The Hague, Netherlands

WHY IT'S COOL: You *could* call these orange saucers UFOs—Unusual Floating Objects! These floating hotel rooms were once rescue capsules for workers on offshore oil rigs. Docked in a canal, the basic capsule comes with a seat, a toilet, and a hammock made from old fishing nets. A "superdeluxe" version livens things up with a DVD player, disco ball, and karaoke machine!

The coolest vacations on the planet

TRIPS AROUND THE WORLD

SOUTH AFRICA

WHAT YOU'LL DO Go on safari to see zebras, lions, and elephants; get face-to-face with a great white shark. (Don't worry—you'll be in a cage.)

ACT LIKE A LOCAL Cheer on a local soccer team—just make sure to call it football, not soccer.

SAY HELLO (in Zulu) *sawubona* (sow-BOH-nah)

ITALY

WHAT YOU'LL DO Float down Venice's canals in a gondola; pretend you're watching ancient gladiators battle at the Colosseum in Rome.

ACT LIKE A LOCAL Grab some gelato—like ice cream only creamier—while taking a late-afternoon stroll.

SAY HELLO (in Italian) *ciao* (CHOW)

HAWAII

WHAT YOU'LL DO Snorkel with sea turtles and tropical fish; hike on an active volcano at Hawaii Volcanoes National Park.

ACT LIKE A LOCAL Catch some waves on a surfboard, just as Hawaiians have done for hundreds of years.

SAY HELLO (in Hawaiian) *aloha* (ah-LOH-hah)

Is it REAL or is it LEGOLAND?

I magine a world built entirely out of LEGOS. At LEGOLAND parks in places like Malaysia, Germany, and Denmark, you can check out some of the most recognizable spots on the planet, made from ... you guessed it ... LEGOS! In honor of the newest LEGOLAND in Orlando, Florida, U.S.A., check out these three fun LEGO landmarks—and how they stack up to their real-life counterparts.

GOLDEN GATE BRIDGE
Named after the Golden Gate strait, the waterway linking the San Francisco Bay to the Pacific Ocean, this bridge opened in 1937 to give people an easier way to cross the bay.

BUILDING BLOCKS
LEGO VERSION: 400,023 bricks
THE REAL DEAL: 83,000 tons (75,000 t) of steel, 389,000 cubic yards (297,000 m³) of concrete

HOW LONG IT TOOK
LEGO VERSION: About 280 hours
THE REAL DEAL: Just over four years

HOW BIG IS IT?
LEGO VERSION: 21 feet (6.4 m) long, 9.6 feet (2.9 m) tall
THE REAL DEAL: 1.7 miles (2.7 km) long, 746 feet (227 m) tall

The LEGOLAND bridge features recordings of sea lions that sound just like the pinnipeds that gather not far from the real Golden Gate Bridge year-round.

THE WHITE HOUSE

Built between 1792 and 1800, the White House has been home to almost every U.S. President, even after it was set on fire during the War of 1812. Over time, it also has undergone lots of construction and renovation— such as adding an indoor pool!

The builders of this white house model stashed LEGO figures of themselves inside the columns that hold up the roof.

BUILDING BLOCKS
LEGO VERSION: 201,346 bricks
THE REAL DEAL: 600,000 bricks

HOW LONG IT TOOK
LEGO VERSION: 290 hours
THE REAL DEAL: 8 to 9 years

HOW BIG IS IT?
LEGO VERSION: 5.5 feet (1.7 m) long, 2 feet (0.6 m) tall
THE REAL DEAL: 168 feet (51 m) long, 70 feet (21 m) tall on its highest side

THE ENTIRE LEGOLAND TIMES SQUARE IS MADE OF 283,146 BRICKS.

At LEGOLAND's Time Square, you can see a billboard for the "musical" The Sound of Plastic.

ONE TIMES SQUARE

ONE TIMES SQUARE

One Times Square is one of the most recognizable buildings in New York City, thanks to the billboards that cover it. Some 80 percent of all Big Apple visitors come to Times Square, even though it only covers about 0.1 percent of the city.

BUILDING BLOCKS
LEGO VERSION: 63,500 bricks
THE REAL DEAL: 9,715 tons (8,813 t) of bricks, 41,462 tons (37, 613 t) of total material

HOW LONG IT TOOK
LEGO VERSION: 225 hours
THE REAL DEAL: About a year

HOW BIG IS IT?
LEGO VERSION: 4.5 feet (1.4 m) high
THE REAL DEAL: 250 feet (76 m) high

SPOTLIGHT ON
AFRICA

Researchers have discovered two-million-year-old human remains in Africa.

Gorillas burp when they're happy.

Mountain gorilla

The massive continent of Africa, where humankind began millions of years ago, is second to only Asia in size. Stretching nearly as far from west to east as it does from north to south, Africa is home to both the longest river in the world (the Nile) and the largest hot desert on Earth (Sahara).

Zulu woman in native costume

Home of the Bling

More diamonds are found in Africa than anywhere else in the world. Miners in South Africa recently unearthed a 500-carat diamond the size of a chicken egg!

Lots of Languages

Some 2,000 languages are spoken in Africa—more than any other continent. South Africa alone has 11 official languages. More than 130 languages and dialects are spoken in Chad.

Extreme Heat

Dallol, Ethiopia, is considered one of the hottest places in the world. The high temperature in that city typically tops 100°F (37.8°C) daily.

Unique Animals

Ninety percent of the animals found on the island of Madagascar evolved there and nowhere else. Many are endangered, including some of the numerous species of lemurs.

Top 5 Largest Animals

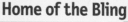

1. African elephant
   up to 14,000 pounds (6,350 kg)

2. Hippopotamus
   up to 8,000 pounds (3,630 kg)

3. White rhinoceros
   up to 7,920 pounds (3,600 kg)

4. Black rhinoceros
   up to 3,080 pounds (1,400 kg)

5. Giraffe
   up to 2,800 pounds (1,270 kg)

Downtown Johannesburg in South Africa

AFRICA

PHYSICAL

LAND AREA
11,608,000 sq mi
(30,065,000 sq km)

HIGHEST POINT
Kilimanjaro, Tanzania
19,340 ft (5,895 m)

LOWEST POINT
Lake Assal, Djibouti
-512 ft (-156 m)

LONGEST RIVER
Nile
4,241 mi (6,825 km)

LARGEST LAKE
Victoria
26,800 sq mi
(69,500 sq km)

POLITICAL

POPULATION
1,072,254,000

LARGEST COUNTRY
Algeria
919,595 sq mi
(2,381,741 sq km)

LARGEST METROPOLITAN AREA
Lagos, Nigeria
Pop. 11,223,000

MOST DENSELY POPULATED COUNTRY
Mauritius 1,639 people
per sq mi (633 per sq km)

ASIA

EUROPE

Atlantic Ocean

Azores
(Portugal)

Madeira Islands
(Portugal)

Canary Islands
(Spain)

Strait of Gibraltar

Rabat ⊛
Casablanca ⊛
•Fez
MOROCCO
•Marrakech

Western
Sahara
(Morocco)

MAURITANIA
⊛Nouakchott

CAPE
VERDE

Oran •
Constantine •
Algiers
⊛

ALGERIA

MALI
•Tombouctou
(Timbuktu)

Tunis
⊛
TUNISIA

Tripoli
⊛

Benghazi •

LIBYA

Mediterranean Sea

NIGER

CHAD

Alexandria •
Cairo
⊛
Port
Said •
Nile
River

EGYPT

Red Sea

Africa–Asia
boundary

SUDAN
Omdurman

ERITREA

TROPIC OF CANCER

SOMALIA

Mogadishu
(historic capital;
no central
government
since 1991)

Victoria

SEYCHELLES

MAURITIUS
Port Louis
Réunion
(France)

Addis
Ababa

ETHIOPIA

COMOROS
Moroni

Antananarivo

MADAGASCAR

Indian
Ocean

Juba

SOUTH
SUDAN

UGANDA

Kampala

KENYA

Nairobi

Kilimanjaro
19,340 ft
(5,895 m)

Mombasa

Dar es Salaam

Mozambique Channel

Lake
Victoria

Kigali

RWANDA

BURUNDI
Bujumbura

Dodoma

TANZANIA

MALAWI
Lilongwe

CENTRAL
AFRICAN REPUBLIC

Bangui

Kisangani

DEMOCRATIC
REPUBLIC
OF THE CONGO

Lubumbashi

Kananga

Mbuji-Mayi

Kolwezi

Kitwe

ZAMBIA

Lusaka

Harare

ZIMBABWE

MOZAMBIQUE

Maputo

SWAZILAND

Lobamba

Mbabane

Maseru

LESOTHO

Durban

CAMEROON

Yaoundé

Douala

Libreville

GABON

Brazzaville

CONGO

Kinshasa

Pointe-Noire

Cabinda
(Angola)

Luanda

ANGOLA

NAMIBIA

Windhoek

BOTSWANA

Gaborone

Pretoria
(Tshwane)

Johannesburg

Bloemfontein

SOUTH
AFRICA

Port
Elizabeth

Cape Town

NIGERIA

Abuja

Ogbomosho

Lagos

Porto-
Novo

BENIN

TOGO

GHANA

Accra

Lomé

Cotonou

Malabo

EQUATORIAL GUINEA

SÃO TOMÉ & PRÍNCIPE

São Tomé

SIERRA
LEONE

Freetown

Conakry

LIBERIA

Monrovia

CÔTE D'IVOIRE
(IVORY COAST)

Yamoussoukro

Abidjan

Atlantic
Ocean

St. Helena
(U.K.)

Ascension
(U.K.)

EQUATOR

TROPIC OF CAPRICORN

Azimuthal Equal-Area Projection

Map Key

- ⊛ National capital
- • Other city
- ▲ Highest point
- ▼ Lowest point

800 Miles

800 Kilometers

SPOTLIGHT ON
ANTARCTICA

Chinstrap
penguin

Antarctica experiences icequakes, which are like earthquakes that occur within an ice sheet.

Chinstrap penguins are named for the narrow black band under their heads.

This frozen continent may be a cool place to visit, but unless you're a penguin, you probably wouldn't want to hang out in Antarctica for long. The fact that it's the coldest, windiest, and driest continent helps explain why humans never colonized this ice-covered land surrounding the South Pole.

Once an Argentine scientific research station, Almirante Brown is now a popular stop for tourists.

Lava Bombs

Mount Erebus is Earth's southernmost volcano. This 12,448-feet (3,794-m)-tall peak constantly sputters heat and gas and sometimes spews 6.5-foot (2-m)-wide lava bombs!

Under the Ice

Hidden underneath Antarctica's icy surface are some 70 lakes as well as a recently discovered rift that's 60 miles (100 km) long, 6 miles (10 km) across, and up to a mile (1.6 km) deep.

Extreme Weather

Parts of Antarctica are covered in ice up to 2.5 miles (4 km) deep, and wind gusts here can reach up to 200 miles per hour (322 kph)!

Penguin Population

There are nearly 600,000 Emperor penguins living on Antarctica. These 4-foot (1.2 m)-tall flightless birds are the only warm-blooded animals to stay on the continent during the bitter winter.

Extreme Antarctica

Highest recorded temperature
59°F (15°C), 1974

Lowest recorded temperature
-129°F (-89.2°C), 1983

Leopard seal

275

PHYSICAL

LAND AREA
5,100,000 sq mi
(13,209,000 sq km)

HIGHEST POINT
Vinson Massif
16,067 ft (4,897 m)

LOWEST POINT
Bentley Subglacial
Trench
-8,383 ft (-2,555 m)

COLDEST PLACE
Ridge A, annual
average temperature
-94°F (-70°C)

**AVERAGE
PRECIPITATION ON
THE POLAR PLATEAU**
Less than 2 in (5 cm)
per year

POLITICAL

POPULATION
There are no indig-
enous inhabitants,
but there are both
permanent and
summer-only staffed
research stations.

**NUMBER OF
INDEPENDENT
COUNTRIES** 0

**NUMBER OF
COUNTRIES
CLAIMING LAND** 7

**NUMBER OF
COUNTRIES
OPERATING YEAR-
ROUND RESEARCH
STATIONS** 20

**NUMBER OF YEAR-
ROUND RESEARCH
STATIONS** 39

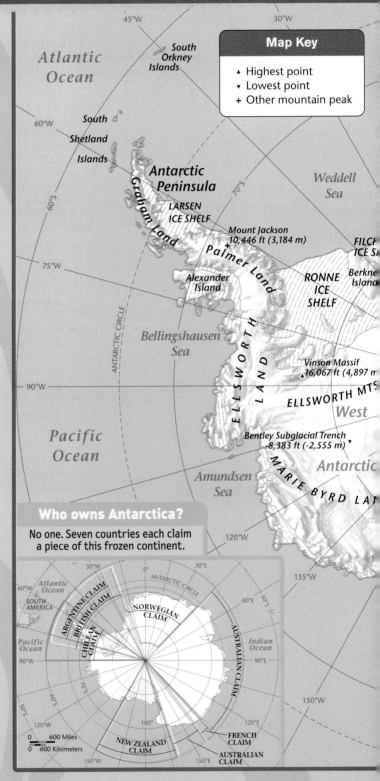

Map Key

▲ Highest point
▼ Lowest point
+ Other mountain peak

Atlantic Ocean

South Orkney Islands

South Shetland Islands

60°W

45°W

30°W

Antarctic Peninsula

Graham Land

LARSEN ICE SHELF

70°S

Weddell Sea

Mount Jackson
10,446 ft (3,184 m)

Palmer Land

FILCH
ICE S

75°W

Alexander Island

RONNE ICE SHELF

Berkne
Island

ANTARCTIC CIRCLE

60°S

Bellingshausen Sea

ELLSWORTH LAND

Vinson Massif
▲16,067 ft (4,897 m

90°W

ELLSWORTH MTS
West

Pacific Ocean

Bentley Subglacial Trench
-8,383 ft (-2,555 m) ▼

MARIE BYRD LAN

Antarctic

Amundsen Sea

120°W

135°W

Who owns Antarctica?

No one. Seven countries each claim
a piece of this frozen continent.

30°W   0°   30°E
ANTARCTIC CIRCLE

60°W
Atlantic Ocean

SOUTH AMERICA

ARGENTINE CLAIM

BRITISH CLAIM

CHILEAN CLAIM

NORWEGIAN CLAIM

60°E

Indian Ocean

AUSTRALIAN CLAIM

90°E

Pacific Ocean

90°W

120°W

180°

120°E

NEW ZEALAND CLAIM

150°W

FRENCH CLAIM

AUSTRALIAN CLAIM

150°E

0   600 Miles
0   600 Kilometers

ANTARCTICA

FIMBUL
ICE SHELF

RIISER-LARSEN
ICE SHELF

QUEEN MAUD LAND

ENDERBY
LAND

15°E

0°

30°E

45°E

60°E

*Indian
Ocean*

Valkyrie
Dome

Lambert
Glacier

MacKenzie Bay

AMERY ICE SHELF

75°E

AMERICAN

HIGHLAND

Ridge A +

POLAR PLATEAU

East

WEST
ICE SHELF

90°E

South Pole

Antarctica

SHACKLETON
ICE SHELF

T R A N S A N T A R C T I C   M O U N T A I N S

80°S

ROSS
ICE
SHELF

Roosevelt
Island

Taylor
Glacier

Ross Island

Mount Erebus
12,448 ft
(3,794 m)

*Ross
Sea*

VICTORIA LAND

Talos
Dome

W I L K E S   L A N D

70°S

105°E

120°E

60°S

*Indian
Ocean*

180°

• South
Magnetic
Pole (2013)

135°E

150°E

600 Miles

600 Kilometers

Azimuthal Equidistant Projection

SPOTLIGHT ON
ASIA

Downtown Shanghai
in eastern China

Shanghai
means
"above the sea"
in Chinese.

In Malaysia,
bats outnumber
any other mammal,
including
humans.

Made up of 46 countries, Asia is the world's largest continent. And just how big is it? From western Turkey to the eastern tip of Russia, Asia spans nearly half the globe! Home to four billion citizens—that's three out of five people on the planet—Asia's population is bigger than all the other continents combined.

Clouded leopard

On the Border

Asia is the only continent that shares borders with two other continents: Africa and Europe. Here a marker identifies the border between Europe and Asia in western Russia.

Culture Club

The first-ever civilization started in Sumer (right), in what is now Iraq. Today, Asia's peoples practice a huge variety of religions. Plus, hundreds of languages—from Arabic to Xiang—are spoken here.

Go Bananas

Bananas have grown in Southeast Asia for over 7,000 years. Today, the Philippines is one of the world's largest exporters of the fruit.

Pandas in Peril

Wild pandas are only found in Asia, but their numbers are dwindling. Because of poaching and deforestation, fewer than 2,000 giant pandas live in the mountain forests of China.

Asia's Tallest Buildings

Burj Khalifa	Makkah Clock Royal Tower	Taipei 101	Shanghai World Financial Center	International Commerce Centre
Dubai, U.A.E. 2,717 feet (828 m)	Mecca, Saudi Arabia 1,972 feet (601 m)	Taiwan 1,667 feet (508 m)	Shanghai, China 1,614 feet (492 m)	Hong Kong, China 1,588 feet (484 m)

Mongolian horse rider

PHYSICAL

LAND AREA
17,208,000 sq mi
(44,570,000 sq km)

HIGHEST POINT
Mount Everest,
China–Nepal
29,035 ft (8,850 m)

LOWEST POINT
Dead Sea,
Israel–Jordan
-1,385 ft (-422 m)

LONGEST RIVER
Yangtze, China
3,880 mi (6,244 km)

**LARGEST LAKE
ENTIRELY IN ASIA**
Lake Baikal, Russia
12,200 sq mi
(31,500 sq km)

POLITICAL

POPULATION
4,260,894,000

**LARGEST
METROPOLITAN AREA**
Tokyo, Japan
Pop. 37,217,000

**LARGEST COUNTRY
ENTIRELY IN ASIA**
China
3,705,405 sq mi
(9,596,960 sq km)

**MOST DENSELY
POPULATED COUNTRY**
Singapore
20,761 people
per sq mi
(8,021 per sq km)

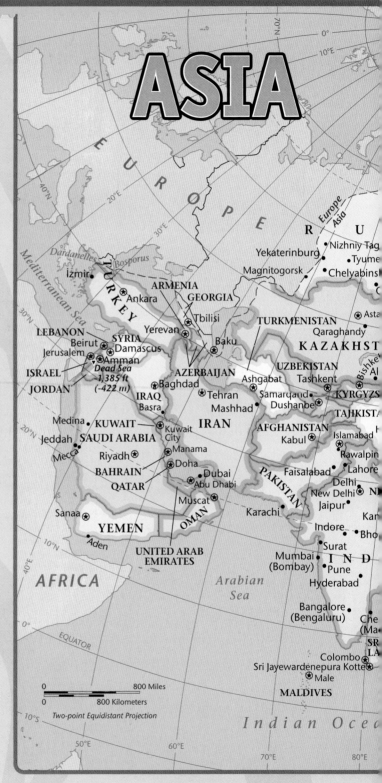

ASIA

EUROPE

EUROPE
Asia

Yekaterinburg • Nizhniy Tag
Magnitogorsk • Tyume
• Chelyabins

Dardanelles
Mediterranean Sea
İzmir
TURKEY
Ankara
ARMENIA
GEORGIA
Tbilisi
Yerevan
Baku
TURKMENISTAN
Qaraghandy
KAZAKHST
• Asta

LEBANON
Beirut
Jerusalem
Damascus
Amman
Dead Sea
-1,385 ft
(-422 m)
SYRIA
AZERBAIJAN
Baghdad
IRAQ
Basra
• Tehran
Mashhad
IRAN
UZBEKISTAN
Ashgabat
Tashkent
Samarqand
Dushanbe
KYRGYZS
Bishke
TAJIKISTA
AFGHANISTAN
Kabul
Islamabad
Rawalpin

ISRAEL
JORDAN

Medina
KUWAIT
Jeddah
SAUDI ARABIA
Mecca
Riyadh
BAHRAIN
QATAR
Kuwait
City
Manama
Doha
Dubai
Abu Dhabi
Muscat
PAKISTAN
Faisalabad
Karachi
Lahore
Delhi
New Delhi
Jaipur
Kar

Sanaa
YEMEN
Aden
OMAN
UNITED ARAB
EMIRATES
Indore
Surat
Mumbai
(Bombay)
Pune
Hyderabad
Bho
IND

AFRICA
Arabian
Sea
Bangalore
(Bengaluru)
Che
(Ma
SR
LA

EQUATOR
Colombo
Sri Jayewardenepura Kotte
Male
MALDIVES

0   800 Miles
0   800 Kilometers
Two-point Equidistant Projection

Indian Oce

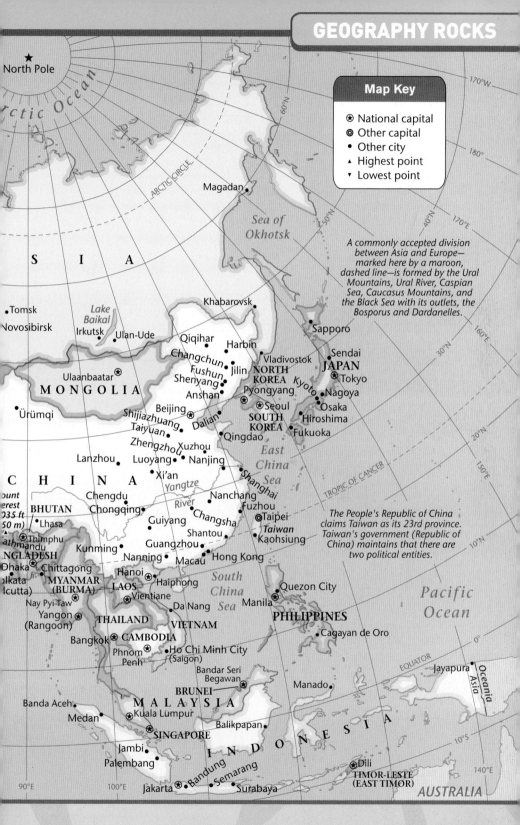

★ North Pole

Arctic Ocean

Map Key

⊛ National capital
◎ Other capital
• Other city
▲ Highest point
▼ Lowest point

A S I A

Magadan

Sea of Okhotsk

A commonly accepted division between Asia and Europe—marked here by a maroon, dashed line—is formed by the Ural Mountains, Ural River, Caspian Sea, Caucasus Mountains, and the Black Sea with its outlets, the Bosporus and Dardanelles.

•Tomsk
•Novosibirsk

Lake Baikal

Irkutsk Ulan-Ude

Khabarovsk

Sapporo

Qiqihar Harbin

Changchun Jilin

Vladivostok

Sendai

JAPAN

⊛Tokyo

Fushun

NORTH KOREA

Ulaanbaatar ⊛

M O N G O L I A

Shenyang Anshan

Pyongyang

Kyoto

Nagoya

•Ürümqi

Beijing ⊛

Shijiazhuang

Dalian

⊛Seoul

SOUTH KOREA

Osaka

Hiroshima

Taiyuan

Qingdao

Fukuoka

Zhengzhou Xuzhou

East China Sea

Lanzhou Luoyang •Nanjing

C H I N A

Xi'an

Yangtze

Shanghai

ount erest 235 ft 50 m)

Chengdu

Chongqing

River

Nanchang

Fuzhou

BHUTAN

•Lhasa

Guiyang

Changsha

◎Taipei

athmandu

•Thimphu

Taiwan

NGLADESH

Kunming

Shantou

Kaohsiung

Dhaka ⊛

Chittagong

Nanning

Guangzhou

Macau Hong Kong

lkata lcutta)

MYANMAR (BURMA)

Hanoi ⊛

LAOS

Haiphong

South China Sea

Nay Pyi Taw

Vientiane ◎

Quezon City

Yangon (Rangoon)

THAILAND

Da Nang

Manila ⊛

VIETNAM

PHILIPPINES

Pacific Ocean

Bangkok ⊛

CAMBODIA

•Cagayan de Oro

Phnom Penh

⊛ •Ho Chi Minh City (Saigon)

Bandar Seri Begawan

Manado•

Jayapura•

Oceania Asia

Banda Aceh•

BRUNEI

M A L A Y S I A

EQUATOR

0°

Medan•

Kuala Lumpur ⊛

Balikpapan

SINGAPORE ⊛

I N D O N E S I A

Jambi•

Palembang•

Bandung

Semarang

Dili ◎

TIMOR-LESTE (EAST TIMOR)

Jakarta ⊛

Surabaya

AUSTRALIA

The People's Republic of China claims Taiwan as its 23rd province. Taiwan's government (Republic of China) maintains that there are two political entities.

TROPIC OF CANCER

ARCTIC CIRCLE

SPOTLIGHT ON
AUSTRALIA,
NEW ZEALAND, AND OCEANIA

In some remote areas of Australia, airplanes double as ambulances.

The Lord of the Rings trilogy and *The Hobbit* were filmed in New Zealand (below).

Bay of Many Islands, Queen Charlotte Sound, Marlborough Sounds, South Island, New Zealand

G'day, mate! This vast region, covering almost 3.3 million square miles (8.5 million sq km), includes Australia—the world's smallest and flattest continent—and New Zealand, as well as a fleet of mostly tiny islands scattered across the Pacific Ocean. Also known as "Down Under," all of the countries in this region are in the Southern Hemisphere, and below the Equator.

Aborigine children in ceremonial dress

Animal Kingdom

In Australia, there are 10,000 species of spiders and more than 60 species of kangaroos and their close relatives. More sheep live in New Zealand and Australia than people.

Rock Stars

Most of Australia is a rural desert, also known as the outback. Here you can also find a giant rock formation called Uluru, or Ayers Rock, which appears to change color during the day.

Aborigine Astronomers

Australia's Aborigines—the oldest continuous culture in the world—are also some of the world's first astronomers. They mapped the constellations thousands of years ago.

Giant Reef

The Great Barrier Reef, found off the east coast of Australia, is big enough to be seen from space. It's home to tons of sea life, like whales, dolphins, sea turtles, snakes, coral, and fish.

Most Coral Reefs by Country

1. **Indonesia**
   51,020 square miles
   (132,132 sq km)

2. **Australia**
   48,960 square miles
   (126,797 sq km)

3. **Philippines**
   25,060 square miles
   (64,900 sq km)

4. **France***
   14,280 square miles
   (36,982 sq km)

5. **Papua New Guinea**
   13,840 square miles
   (35,843 sq km)

*Most of France's coral reefs are in its overseas territories in the Pacific Ocean.

Koalas

PHYSICAL

LAND AREA
3,278,000 sq mi
(8,490,000 sq km)

HIGHEST POINT
Mount Wilhelm,
Papua New Guinea
14,793 ft (4,509 m)

LOWEST POINT
Lake Eyre, Australia
-52 ft (-16 m)

LONGEST RIVER
Murray-Darling,
Australia 2,310 mi
(3,718 km)

LARGEST LAKE
Lake Eyre, Australia
3,741 sq mi
(9,690 sq km)

POLITICAL

POPULATION
36,620,000

**LARGEST
METROPOLITAN AREA**
Sydney, Australia
Pop. 4,543,000

LARGEST COUNTRY
Australia
2,969,906 sq mi
(7,692,024 sq km)

**MOST DENSELY
POPULATED COUNTRY**
Nauru
1,256 people per sq
mi (485 per sq km)

Map Key
- ⊛ National capital
- • Other city
- ▲ Highest point
- ▼ Lowest point

A S I A

Northern Mariana
Islands (U.S.)
• Capital Hill

Guam (U.S.)

M i c r o n e s i a

PALAU
Melekeok

Yap
Islands

Truk Islands

C a r o l i n e   I s l a n d

FEDERATED STATES
OF MICRONESIA

M e l

Oceania–Asia
boundary

PAPUA NEW GUINEA
▲ Mount Wilhelm
14,793 ft
(4,509 m)

Honia

Solomon Island

Port Moresby ⊛

Coral Sea
Islands
Territory
(Australia)

C o r a l   S e a

A U S T R A L I A

Brisbane

-52 ft
(-16 m)
▼ Lake
Eyre

Perth •

Darling River

Lord Howe
Island
(Australia)

Sydney

Adelaide •
Murray River

Canberra ⊛

Tasn
Se

Melbourne •

Indian
Ocean

Tasmania

Hobart •

0   800 Miles
0   800 Kilometers

Mercator Projection

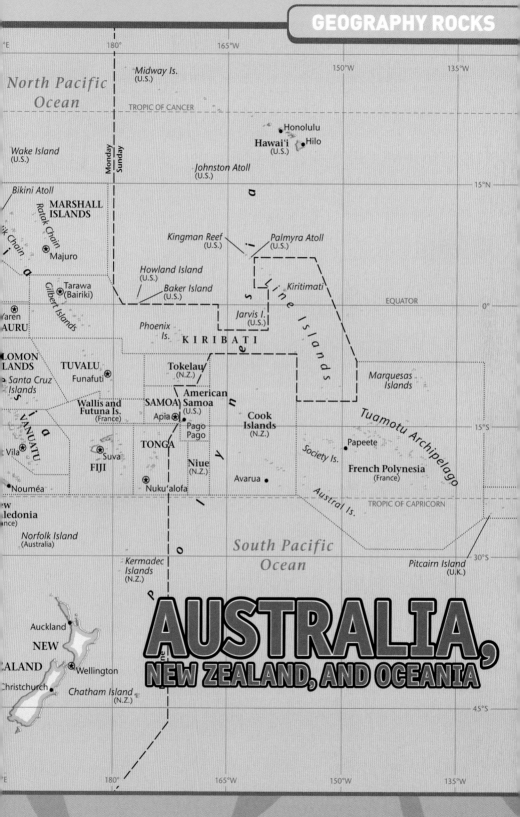

North Pacific
Ocean

Midway Is.
(U.S.)

TROPIC OF CANCER

Honolulu
Hawai'i
Hilo
(U.S.)

Wake Island
(U.S.)

Monday Sunday

Johnston Atoll
(U.S.)

15°N

Bikini Atoll

MARSHALL
ISLANDS

Ratak Chain

Kingman Reef
(U.S.)

Palmyra Atoll
(U.S.)

Chain

Majuro

Howland Island
(U.S.)

Kiritimati

Line Islands

Tarawa
(Bairiki)

Baker Island
(U.S.)

Gilbert Islands

EQUATOR
0°

Varen
AURU

Jarvis I.
(U.S.)

Phoenix
Is.

KIRIBATI

LOMON
LANDS

TUVALU

Tokelau
(N.Z.)

Marquesas
Islands

Santa Cruz
Islands

Funafuti

American
Samoa
(U.S.)

VANUATU

Wallis and
Futuna Is.
(France)

SAMOA

Apia

Pago
Pago

Cook
Islands
(N.Z.)

Tuamotu Archipelago

15°S

Vila

Suva

TONGA

Society Is.

Papeete

FIJI

Niue
(N.Z.)

Avarua

French Polynesia
(France)

Nouméa

Nuku'alofa

Austral Is.

TROPIC OF CAPRICORN

w
ledonia
nce)

Norfolk Island
(Australia)

South Pacific
Ocean

30°S

Kermadec
Islands
(N.Z.)

Pitcairn Island
(U.K.)

Auckland

NEW

AUSTRALIA,
NEW ZEALAND, AND OCEANIA

ALAND

Wellington

Christchurch

Chatham Island
(N.Z.)

45°S

180°

165°W

150°W

135°W

SPOTLIGHT ON
EUROPE

The floor of the Colosseum's arena featured several trapdoors.

It takes 65 tons (59 t) of paint to cover Paris's Eiffel Tower.

The Colosseum in Rome, Italy, is an amphitheater opened by Emperor Titus in A.D. 80.

A cluster of islands and peninsulas jutting west from Asia, Europe is bordered by the Atlantic and Arctic Oceans and more than a dozen seas. Here, you'll find a variety of scenery, from mountains to countryside to coastlines. Aside from unique landscapes, Europe is also known for its rich culture and fascinating history that make it one of the most-visited continents on the planet.

Ukrainian girl in traditional dress

Cool Castles

Europe's landscape is dotted with fortresses. Many are still in use, like the 900-year-old Windsor Castle— home to the Queen of England—Europe's longest-occupied palace.

Spot On

Dalmatians get their name from Dalmatia, a region of Croatia along the Adriatic Sea. The spotted canines have served as border guard dogs during conflicts in the region.

Tiny Territory

Occupying only 0.2 sq mi (0.4 sq km) Vatican City, in Rome, is the world's smallest country. It also has the smallest population of any country on the planet, with some 800 people living there.

Great Big Sea

About the same size as Japan, the Caspian Sea is the world's biggest body of water surrounded by land. It's home to sturgeon, endangered fish whose eggs (roe) are used to make caviar.

Europe's 6 Most-Visited Cities*

1. London, England
   16.9 million visitors

2. Paris, France
   16 million visitors

3. Istanbul, Turkey
   11.6 million visitors

4. Madrid, Spain
   9.7 million visitors

5. Frankfurt, Germany
   8.1 million visitors

6. Rome, Italy
   7.8 million visitors

*2012

Alpine ibex

PHYSICAL

LAND AREA
3,841,000 sq mi
(9,947,000 sq km)

HIGHEST POINT
El'brus, Russia
18,510 ft (5,642 m)

LOWEST POINT
Caspian Sea
-92 ft (-28 m)

LONGEST RIVER
Volga, Russia
2,290 mi
(3,685 km)

**LARGEST LAKE
ENTIRELY IN
EUROPE**
Ladoga, Russia
6,900 sq mi
(17,872 sq km)

POLITICAL

POPULATION
740,110,000

**LARGEST
METROPOLITAN AREA**
Moscow, Russia
Pop. 11,621,000

**LARGEST COUNTRY
ENTIRELY IN
EUROPE**
Ukraine
233,090 sq mi
(603,700 sq km)

**MOST DENSELY
POPULATED COUNTRY**
Monaco
45,000 people per sq
mi (18,000 per sq km)

Map Key

⊗ National capital
• Other city
▫ Small country
▲ Highest point
▼ Lowest point

Reykjavík
ICELAND

Norwegian Sea

Faroe Islands (Denmark)

Shetland Islands

Orkney Islands

SCOTLAND
Glasgow
Edinburgh

N. IRELAND
Belfast

North Sea

IRELAND
Dublin ⊗

UNITED KINGDOM

Liverpool • Manchester
WALES Birmingham
Cardiff • ENGLAND
London ⊗

The Hague
Amsterdam
NETH.
Hamb...

DENM...
Kiel

Brussels ⊗
BELGIUM
GERMA...
Frank...
LUX.

⊗ Paris

• Nantes

FRANCE

Atlantic Ocean

Bay of Biscay

Zürich
Bern ⊗
SWITZ.
Muni...
LIECH.

• Bordeaux
Lyon •

Milan
• Turin   Veni...
• Genoa
SAN
MARINO
ITA...

Oporto
PORTUGAL
Bilbao •
• Valladolid
ANDORRA
• Zaragoza

• Toulouse
MONACO ▫
Marseille
Nice

Lisbon ⊗
Madrid ⊗
SPAIN

Barcelona

Corsica (France)
VATICAN
CITY
Rome

Valencia •

Seville •
Murcia •
Málaga •
Balearic Is. (Spain)

Sardinia (Italy)

Mediterran...
Paler...

Gibraltar (U.K.)

0 ___ 400 Miles
0 ___ 400 Kilometers
Azimuthal Equidistant Projection

AFRICA

Val...
M...

EUROPE

A commonly accepted division between Asia and Europe—marked here by a maroon, dashed line—is formed by the Ural Mountains, Ural River, Caspian Sea, Caucasus Mountains, and the Black Sea with its outlets, the Bosporus and Dardanelles.

Barents Sea
Murmansk
Arkhangel'sk
RUSSIA
ASIA
Asia
Europe

FINLAND
SWEDEN
Lake Ladoga
Helsinki
St. Petersburg
Tallinn
ESTONIA
Stockholm
borg
Baltic Sea
enhagen
Rīga
LATVIA
LITHUANIA
Kaliningrad
(Russia)
Kaunas
Vilnius
Minsk
Gdańsk
in
POLAND
Warsaw
BELARUS
Homyel'
Bydgoszcz
Łódź
Wrocław
Kraków
rague
Kiev
CH REP.
ECHIA)
L'viv
UKRAINE
SLOVAKIA
a
Bratislava
RIA
Budapest
HUNGARY
bliana
Zagreb
ROATIA
ROMANIA
OSNIA &
GOVINA
Sarajevo
SERBIA
Belgrade
Bucharest
MONTENEGRO
Podgorica
KOSOVO
Prishtina
BULGARIA
Varna
Tirana
Skopje
Sofia
es
ALBANIA
MACED.
Thessaloníki
Dardanelles
GREECE
essina
ania
Athens
a
Crete
Nicosia
CYPRUS

Tver'
Yaroslavl'
Volga River
Kazan'
Ufa
Moscow
Nizhniy Novgorod
Ryazan'
Penza
Samara
Orenburg
Vitsyebsk
Smolensk
Bryansk
Saratov
KAZAKHSTAN
Kursk
Poltava
Kharkiv
Volgograd
Vinnytsya
Donets'k
Astrakhan'
Dnipropetrovs'k
Rostov
MOLDOVA
Chişinău
-92 ft
(-28 m)
Caspian Sea
Odesa
El'brus
Groznyy
Simferopol'
(5,642 m) 18,510 ft
Sevastopol'
Sochi
GEORGIA
Baku
Black Sea
AZERBAIJAN
Bosporus
T U R K E Y
Istanbul

20°E
30°E
40°E
50°E
60°E
70°E
60°N
50°N
40°N

SPOTLIGHT ON
NORTH AMERICA

Canada produced enough maple syrup in one year to fill more than 15 Olympic-size pools.

More than 1.9 billion cars have crossed the Golden Gate Bridge since it opened in 1937.

Golden Gate Bridge, San Francisco, California, U.S.A.

From the Great Plains of the United States and Canada to the rain forests of Panama, North America stretches 5,500 miles (8,850 km) from north to south. The third largest continent, North America can be divided into five regions: the mountainous west (including parts of Mexico and Central America's western coast), the Great Plains, the Canadian Shield, the varied eastern region (including Central America's lowlands and coastal plains), and the Caribbean.

Mexican children perform mariachi music.

Hole-y Moly

At 6,000 feet (1,800 m) deep, 18 miles (29 km) wide, and 277 miles (446 km) long, the Grand Canyon in Arizona, U.S.A., is one of the largest canyons of its kind.

Cool Cats

Jaguars, the Western Hemisphere's largest and most powerful cats, are native to North America. The threatened animals have been recently spotted in Mexico and in Arizona, U.S.A.

Twister Target

The United States experiences and records more tornadoes than any other nation. More than 1,000 twisters touch down in the U.S. each year.

Salty Lake

A popular tourist destination, Little Manitou Lake in Saskatchewan, Canada, is so salty that you can't sink in it. The lake's salt content is five times more concentrated than the ocean's.

Fun in the Sun

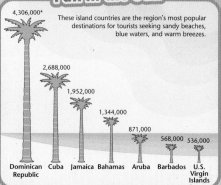

These island countries are the region's most popular destinations for tourists seeking sandy beaches, blue waters, and warm breezes.

Country	International tourist arrivals, 2011
Dominican Republic	4,306,000*
Cuba	2,688,000
Jamaica	1,952,000
Bahamas	1,344,000
Aruba	871,000
Barbados	568,000
U.S. Virgin Islands	536,000

*International tourist arrivals, 2011

Monarch butterfly

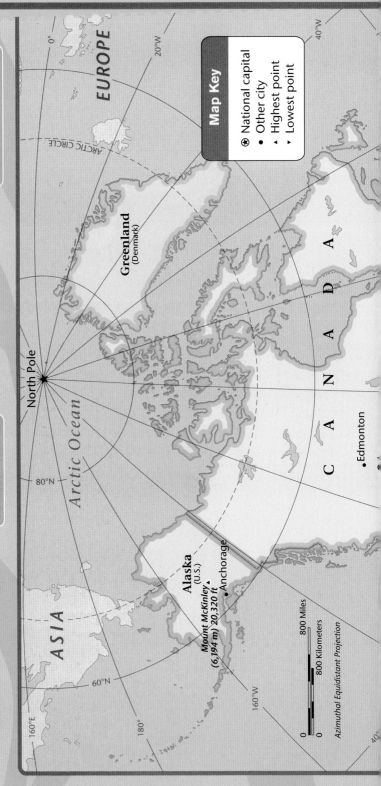

PHYSICAL

LAND AREA
9,449,000 sq mi
(24,474,000 sq km)

HIGHEST POINT
Mount McKinley, Alaska
20,320 ft (6,194 m)

LOWEST POINT
Death Valley, California
-282 ft (-86 m)

LONGEST RIVER
Mississippi–Missouri,
United States
3,710 mi (5,970 km)

LARGEST LAKE
Lake Superior,
U.S.–Canada
31,700 sq mi
(82,100 sq km)

POLITICAL

POPULATION
551,014,000

LARGEST COUNTRY
Canada
3,855,103 sq mi
(9,984,670 sq km)

LARGEST METROPOLITAN AREA
Mexico City, Mexico
Pop. 20,446,000

**MOST DENSELY POPULATED
COUNTRY**
Barbados/1,668 people
per sq mi (644 per sq km)

Map Key

⊛ National capital
• Other city
▲ Highest point
▼ Lowest point

EUROPE

ASIA

CANADA

Greenland
(Denmark)

North Pole

Arctic Ocean

ARCTIC CIRCLE

80°N

60°N

Alaska
(U.S.)

Mount McKinley
(6,194 m) 20,320 ft
• Anchorage

• Edmonton

0°

20°W

40°W

160°E

180°

160°W

800 Miles
800 Kilometers

Azimuthal Equidistant Projection

292

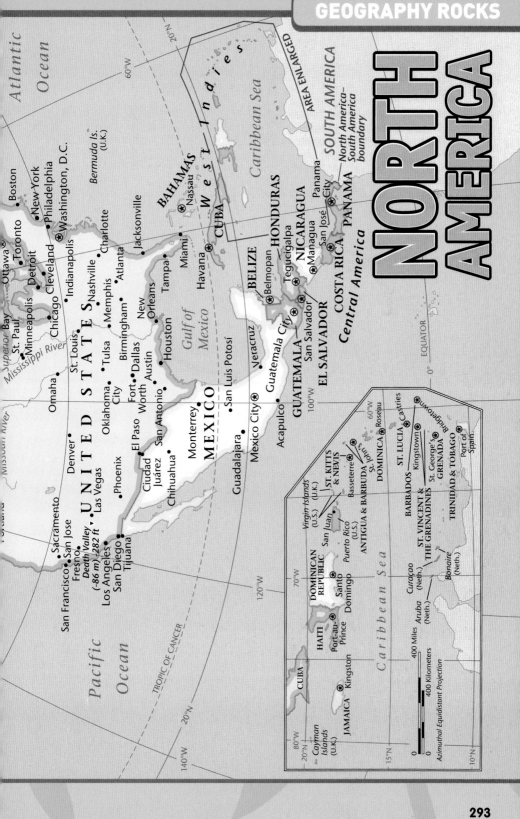

NORTH AMERICA

Atlantic Ocean

Pacific Ocean

SOUTH AMERICA

AREA ENLARGED

North America–
South America
boundary

West Indies

Caribbean Sea

Central America

*Bermuda Is.
(U.K.)*

BAHAMAS
Nassau ⊕

CUBA
Havana ⊕

BELIZE
Belmopan ⊕

HONDURAS
Tegucigalpa ⊕

GUATEMALA
Guatemala City ⊕

EL SALVADOR
San Salvador ⊕

NICARAGUA
Managua ⊕

COSTA RICA
San José ⊕

PANAMA
Panama City ⊕

UNITED STATES

Boston
New York
Philadelphia
Washington, D.C. ⊛
Baltimore
Charlotte
Jacksonville
Indianapolis
Atlanta
Nashville
Cleveland
Detroit
Ottawa
Toronto
Superior Bay
St. Paul
Minneapolis
Chicago
Memphis
Birmingham
Tampa
Miami
St. Louis
Omaha
Oklahoma City
Tulsa
Dallas
Fort Worth
Austin
San Antonio
New Orleans
Houston
Denver
Las Vegas
Death Valley
(−86 m) −282 ft ▼
Phoenix
El Paso
Sacramento
San Jose
Fresno
San Francisco
Los Angeles
San Diego
Tijuana

Mississippi River
Missouri River

Gulf of Mexico

MEXICO
Mexico City ⊛
Monterrey
Guadalajara
Acapulco
Veracruz
San Luis Potosí
Ciudad Juárez
Chihuahua

EQUATOR
0°

TROPIC OF CANCER

20°N

20°N

0°W

20°W

40°W

60°W

80°W

100°W

120°W

140°W

N

Inset — West Indies

CUBA
JAMAICA
Kingston

Cayman Islands
(U.K.)

HAITI
Port-au-Prince

DOMINICAN REPUBLIC
Santo Domingo

Puerto Rico
(U.S.)
San Juan

Virgin Islands
(U.S.) (U.K.)

ST. KITTS & NEVIS
Basseterre

ANTIGUA & BARBUDA
St. John's ⊕

DOMINICA
Roseau ⊕

ST. LUCIA
Castries ⊕

BARBADOS
Bridgetown ⊕

ST. VINCENT & THE GRENADINES
Kingstown ⊕

GRENADA
St. George's ⊕

TRINIDAD & TOBAGO
Port of Spain ⊕

Aruba
(Neth.)

Curaçao
(Neth.)

Bonaire
(Neth.)

Caribbean Sea

400 Miles
400 Kilometers
0
0
Azimuthal Equidistant Projection

80°W

70°W

60°W

20°N

15°N

10°N

293

SPOTLIGHT ON
SOUTH AMERICA

It takes several months for a baby toucan's large beak to reach full size.

Turtles the size of compact cars once roamed South America.

Toucans are found throughout South America's tropical forests.

South America is bordered by three major bodies of water—the Caribbean Sea, Atlantic Ocean, and Pacific Ocean. The world's fourth-largest continent extends over a range of climates from tropical in the north to subarctic in the south. South America produces a rich diversity of natural resources, like nuts, fruits, sugar, grains, coffee, and chocolate.

Peruvian girl in festival costume

Sky-High Cities

At 16,732 feet (5,100 m) above sea level, La Rinconada, Peru (right), is considered the world's highest town. At about 12,000 feet (3,657 m), La Paz, Bolivia, is the planet's highest capital.

Amazing Amazon

More water is carried by the Amazon than by the world's next ten biggest rivers combined. It's surrounded by Earth's largest rain forest, home to diverse species like this brown spider monkey.

Game On

In 2016, Rio de Janeiro, Brazil, will become the first South American city to host the Summer Olympics. The capital city will also hold the 2014 FIFA World Cup.

No Bones About It

In Peru, scientists discovered the remains of a megalodon, a 60-foot (18-m)-long whale-eating prehistoric shark. Another team unearthed 41-million-year-old rodent fossils.

Brazil, Deforestation by Year

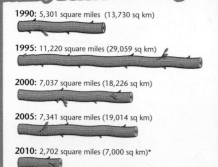

1990: 5,301 square miles (13,730 sq km)

1995: 11,220 square miles (29,059 sq km)

2000: 7,037 square miles (18,226 sq km)

2005: 7,341 square miles (19,014 sq km)

2010: 2,702 square miles (7,000 sq km)*

*Deforestation in Brazil's Amazon rain forest has been reduced significantly since 2005, when the Brazilian government started to adopt successful policies to help reduce it.

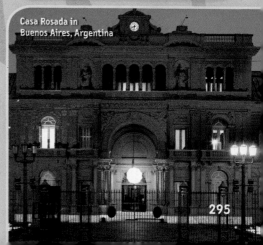

Casa Rosada in Buenos Aires, Argentina

PHYSICAL

LAND AREA
6,880,000 sq mi
(17,819,000 sq km)

HIGHEST POINT
Cerro Aconcagua,
Argentina
22,831 ft (6,959 m)

LOWEST POINT
Laguna del Carbón,
Argentina
-344 ft (-105 m)

LONGEST RIVER
Amazon
4,150 mi (6,679 km)

LARGEST LAKE
Lake Maracaibo,
Venezuela; 5,127 sq
mi (13,280 sq km)

POLITICAL

POPULATION
397,183,000

LARGEST COUNTRY
Brazil
3,287,612 sq mi
(8,514,877 sq km)

LARGEST METROPOLITAN AREA
São Paulo, Brazil
Pop. 19,924,000

**MOST DENSELY POPULATED
COUNTRY**
Ecuador / 135 people per
sq mi (52 per sq km)

Map Key

⊛ National capital
• Other city
▲ Highest point
▼ Lowest point

600 Miles
600 Kilometers
0
0

Azimuthal Equidistant Projection

Central
America

Caribbean
Sea

South America–
North America
boundary

EQUATOR

10°N

0°

10°S

50°W

60°W

70°W

80°W

Barranquilla
Maracaibo
Lake
Maracaibo

Caracas
Valencia
Barquisimeto

VENEZUELA

Medellín
• Bogotá
Cali

COLOMBIA

⊛ Quito
ECUADOR

Guayaquil

Trujillo

Lima ⊛

P E R U

Georgetown ⊛
GUYANA

Paramaribo ⊛
SURINAME

Cayenne
French Guiana
(France)

Manaus

Amazon River

B R A Z I L

Belém

Fortaleza

Natal

Recife

EQUATOR

SOUTH AMERICA

Atlantic
Ocean

TROPIC OF CAPRICORN

Belo
Horizonte

Rio de Janeiro
Nova Iguaçu
São Paulo
Santos

Curitiba

Porto Alegre

Montevideo

URUGUAY

Mar del Plata

PARAGUAY

Asunción

Santa
Fe

Rosario

Buenos Aires
La Plata

Santa Cruz

Sucre

San Miguel
de Tucumán

Córdoba

A
R
G
E
N
T
I
N
A

Cerro Aconcagua
▲ 22,831 ft
(6,959 m)

Valparaíso
Santiago

C
H
I
L
E

Laguna del Carbón
▼ 344 ft (-105 m)

Stanley

Falkland Islands
(U.K.)

South
Georgia
(U.K.)

Punta Arenas

Pacific
Ocean

20°S

30°S

40°S

50°S

20°W

30°W

40°W

50°W

60°W

70°W

80°W

90°W

100°W

297

COUNTRIES OF THE WORLD

The following pages present a general overview of all 195 independent countries recognized by the National Geographic Society, including the newest nation, South Sudan, which gained independence in 2011.

The flags of each independent country symbolize diverse cultures and histories. The statistical data cover highlights of geography and demography and provide a brief overview of each country. They present general characteristics and are not intended to be comprehensive. For example, not every language spoken in a specific country can be listed. Thus, languages shown are the most representative of that area. This is also true of the religions mentioned.

A country is defined as a political body with its own independent government, geographical space, and, in most cases, laws, military, and taxes.

Disputed areas such as Northern Cyprus and Taiwan, and dependencies of independent nations, such as Bermuda and Puerto Rico, are not included in this listing.

Note the color key at the bottom of the pages and the locator map below, which assign a color to each country based on the continent on which it is located. All information is accurate as of press time.

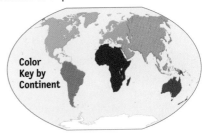

Color Key by Continent

Afghanistan

Area: 251,773 sq mi (652,090 sq km)
Population: 33,397,000
Capital: Kabul, pop. 3,097,000
Currency: afghani
Religions: Sunni Muslim, Shiite Muslim
Languages: Afghan Persian (Dari), Pashto, Turkic languages (primarily Uzbek and Turkmen), Baluchi, 30 minor languages (including Pashai)

Albania

Area: 11,100 sq mi (28,748 sq km)
Population: 2,832,000
Capital: Tirana, pop. 419,000
Currency: lek
Religions: Muslim, Albanian Orthodox, Roman Catholic
Languages: Albanian, Greek, Vlach, Romani, Slavic dialects

Algeria

Area: 919,595 sq mi (2,381,741 sq km)
Population: 37,402,000
Capital: Algiers, pop. 2,916,000
Currency: Algerian dinar
Religion: Sunni Muslim
Languages: Arabic, French, Berber dialects

Andorra

Area: 181 sq mi (469 sq km)
Population: 72,000
Capital: Andorra la Vella, pop. 23,000
Currency: euro
Religion: Roman Catholic
Languages: Catalan, French, Castilian, Portuguese

Angola

Area: 481,354 sq mi (1,246,700 sq km)
Population: 20,945,000
Capital: Luanda, pop. 5,068,000
Currency: kwanza
Religions: indigenous beliefs, Roman Catholic, Protestant
Languages: Portuguese, Bantu, and other African languages

Antigua and Barbuda

Area: 171 sq mi (442 sq km)
Population: 87,000
Capital: St. John's, pop. 27,000
Currency: East Caribbean dollar
Religions: Anglican, Seventh-day Adventist, Pentecostal, Moravian, Roman Catholic, Methodist, Baptist, Church of God, other Christian
Languages: English, local dialects

COLOR KEY Africa Australia, New Zealand, and Oceania

Argentina

Area: 1,073,518 sq mi
(2,780,400 sq km)
Population: 40,829,000
Capital: Buenos Aires,
pop. 13,528,000
Currency: Argentine peso
Religion: Roman Catholic
Languages: Spanish, English, Italian, German, French

Armenia

Area: 11,484 sq mi
(29,743 sq km)
Population: 3,282,000
Capital: Yerevan,
pop. 1,116,000
Currency: dram
Religions: Armenian Apostolic, other Christian
Language: Armenian

Australia

Area: 2,969,906 sq mi
(7,692,024 sq km)
Population: 22,035,000
Capital: Canberra,
pop. 399,000
Currency: Australian dollar
Religions: Roman Catholic, Anglican
Language: English

Austria

Area: 32,378 sq mi (83,858 sq km)
Population: 8,485,000
Capital: Vienna, pop. 1,720,000
Currency: euro
Religions: Roman Catholic, Protestant, Muslim
Language: German

Azerbaijan

Area: 33,436 sq mi
(86,600 sq km)
Population: 9,284,000
Capital: Baku, pop. 2,123,000
Currency: Azerbaijani manat
Religion: Muslim
Language: Azerbaijani (Azeri)

Bahamas

Area: 5,382 sq mi
(13,939 sq km)
Population: 362,000
Capital: Nassau, pop. 254,000
Currency: Bahamian dollar
Religions: Baptist, Anglican, Roman Catholic,
Pentecostal, Church of God
Languages: English, Creole

Bahrain

Area: 277 sq mi (717 sq km)
Population: 1,336,000
Capital: Manama, pop. 262,000
Currency: Bahraini dinar
Religions: Shiite Muslim, Sunni Muslim, Christian
Languages: Arabic, English, Farsi, Urdu

Bangladesh

Area: 55,598 sq mi
(143,998 sq km)
Population: 152,875,000
Capital: Dhaka, pop. 15,391,000
Currency: taka
Religions: Muslim, Hindu
Languages: Bangla (Bengali), English

Barbados

Area: 166 sq mi (430 sq km)
Population: 277,000
Capital: Bridgetown, pop. 122,000
Currency: Barbadian dollar
Religions: Anglican, Pentecostal, Methodist, other
Protestant, Roman Catholic
Language: English

Belarus

Area: 80,153 sq mi
(207,595 sq km)
Population: 9,457,000
Capital: Minsk, pop. 1,861,000
Currency: Belarusian ruble
Religions: Eastern Orthodox, other (includes Roman
Catholic, Protestant, Jewish, Muslim)
Languages: Belarusian, Russian

● Asia ● Europe ● North America ● South America

299

Belgium

Area: 11,787 sq mi (30,528 sq km)
Population: 11,120,000
Capital: Brussels, pop. 1,949,000
Currency: euro
Religions: Roman Catholic, other (includes Protestant)
Languages: Dutch, French

Belize

Area: 8,867 sq mi (22,965 sq km)
Population: 326,000
Capital: Belmopan, pop. 14,000
Currency: Belizean dollar
Religions: Roman Catholic, Protestant (includes Pentecostal, Seventh-day Adventist, Mennonite, Methodist)
Languages: Spanish, Creole, Mayan dialects, English, Garifuna (Carib), German

Benin

Area: 43,484 sq mi (112,622 sq km)
Population: 9,374,000
Capitals: Porto-Novo, pop. 314,000; Cotonou, pop. 924,000
Currency: Communauté Financière Africaine franc
Religions: Christian, Muslim, Vodoun
Languages: French, Fon, Yoruba, tribal languages

Bhutan

Area: 17,954 sq mi (46,500 sq km)
Population: 708,000
Capital: Thimphu, pop. 99,000
Currencies: ngultrum; Indian rupee
Religions: Lamaistic Buddhist, Indian- and Nepalese-influenced Hindu
Languages: Dzongkha, Tibetan dialects, Nepalese dialects

Bolivia

Area: 424,164 sq mi (1,098,581 sq km)
Population: 10,836,000
Capitals: La Paz, pop. 1,715,000; Sucre, pop. 307,000
Currency: boliviano
Religions: Roman Catholic, Protestant (includes Evangelical Methodist)
Languages: Spanish, Quechua, Aymara

Bosnia and Herzegovina

Area: 19,741 sq mi (51,129 sq km)
Population: 3,843,000
Capital: Sarajevo, pop. 389,000
Currency: konvertibilna marka (convertible mark)
Religions: Muslim, Orthodox, Roman Catholic
Languages: Bosnian, Croatian, Serbian

Botswana

Area: 224,607 sq mi (581,730 sq km)
Population: 1,850,000
Capital: Gaborone, pop. 202,000
Currency: pula
Religions: Christian, Badimo
Languages: Setswana, Kalanga

Brazil

Area: 3,287,612 sq mi (8,514,877 sq km)
Population: 194,334,000
Capital: Brasília, pop. 3,813,000
Currency: real
Religions: Roman Catholic, Protestant
Language: Portuguese

Brunei

Area: 2,226 sq mi (5,765 sq km)
Population: 413,000
Capital: Bandar Seri Begawan, pop. 16,000
Currency: Bruneian dollar
Religions: Muslim, Buddhist, Christian, other (includes indigenous beliefs)
Languages: Malay, English, Chinese

Bulgaria

Area: 42,855 sq mi (110,994 sq km)
Population: 7,240,000
Capital: Sofia, pop. 1,174,000
Currency: lev
Religions: Bulgarian Orthodox, Muslim
Languages: Bulgarian, Turkish, Roma

COLOR KEY ● Africa ● Australia, New Zealand, and Oceani

Burkina Faso

Area: 105,869 sq mi
(274,200 sq km)
Population: 17,482,000
Capital: Ouagadougou,
pop. 2,053,000
Currency: Communauté Financière Africaine franc
Religions: Muslim, indigenous beliefs, Christian
Languages: French, native African languages

Cambodia

Area: 69,898 sq mi (181,035 sq km)
Population: 14,953,000
Capital: Phnom Penh,
pop. 1,550,000
Currency: riel
Religion: Theravada Buddhist
Language: Khmer

Burundi

Area: 10,747 sq mi (27,834 sq km)
Population: 10,557,000
Capital: Bujumbura, pop. 605,000
Currency: Burundi franc
Religions: Roman Catholic, indigenous beliefs,
Muslim, Protestant
Languages: Kirundi, French, Swahili

Cameroon

Area: 183,569 sq mi
(475,442 sq km)
Population: 20,919,000
Capital: Yaoundé, pop. 2,432,000
Currency: Communauté Financière Africaine franc
Religions: indigenous beliefs, Christian, Muslim
Languages: 24 major African language groups,
English, French

You Are There!
Boromo, Burkina Faso

The beat of a tribal drum grows louder as you approach a clearing in a dusty field. There, you join a crowd of villagers surrounding a group of people wearing colorful costumes and giant wooden masks. The villagers whistle and clap while the masked people dance, jump, and tumble around to the rhythm of the drum.

This is *Fête des Masques*, or a mask festival celebrated by many tribes of Burkina Faso in western Africa during the dry season. In an ancient tradition, tribesmen ask their masks to protect their villages and to call for rain. Today's festivals—which can last for several days—feature elaborate dance-offs. It's considered a great honor to dance in the festival, but being able to watch it all unfold is just as cool.

Canada

Area: 3,855,101 sq mi
(9,984,670 sq km)
Population: 34,860,000
Capital: Ottawa, pop. 1,208,000
Currency: Canadian dollar
Religions: Roman Catholic, Protestant (includes United Church, Anglican), other Christian
Languages: English, French

Cape Verde

Area: 1,558 sq mi (4,036 sq km)
Population: 510,000
Capital: Praia, pop. 132,000
Currency: Cape Verdean escudo
Religions: Roman Catholic (infused with indigenous beliefs), Protestant (mostly Church of the Nazarene)
Languages: Portuguese, Crioulo

Central African Republic

Area: 240,535 sq mi
(622,984 sq km)
Population: 4,576,000
Capital: Bangui, pop. 740,000
Currency: Communauté Financière Africaine franc
Religions: indigenous beliefs, Protestant, Roman Catholic, Muslim
Languages: French, Sangho, tribal languages

Chad

Area: 495,755 sq mi
(1,284,000 sq km)
Population: 11,831,000
Capital: N'Djamena, pop. 1,079,000
Currency: Communauté Financière Africaine franc
Religions: Muslim, Catholic, Protestant, animist
Languages: French, Arabic, Sara, more than 120 languages and dialects

Chile

Area: 291,930 sq mi
(756,096 sq km)
Population: 17,403,000
Capital: Santiago, pop. 6,034,000
Currency: Chilean peso
Religions: Roman Catholic, Evangelical
Language: Spanish

China

Area: 3,705,405 sq mi
(9,596,960 sq km)
Population: 1,350,378,000
Capital: Beijing, pop. 15,594,000
Currency: renminbi (yuan)
Religions: Taoist, Buddhist, Christian
Languages: Standard Chinese or Mandarin, Yue, Wu, Minbei, Minnan, Xiang, Gan, Hakka dialects

5 cool things about CHINA

1. Twenty percent of the Earth's population lives in China.

2. Soup made from birds' nests is a Chinese delicacy.

3. After the Beijing Olympics in 2008, thousands of people in China named their babies after the Olympic mascots.

4. Seventy-five percent of the toys exported in the world are made in China.

5. China is the third country (after the United States and Russia) to launch a manned space flight.

Colombia

Area: 440,831 sq mi
(1,141,748 sq km)
Population: 47,415,000
Capital: Bogotá, pop. 8,743,000
Currency: Colombian peso
Religion: Roman Catholic
Language: Spanish

Comoros

Area: 863 sq mi (2,235 sq km)
Population: 773,000
Capital: Moroni, pop. 54,000
Currency: Comoran franc
Religion: Sunni Muslim
Languages: Arabic, French, Shikomoro

Congo

Area: 132,047 sq mi (342,000 sq km)
Population: 4,247,000
Capital: Brazzaville, pop. 1,611,000
Currency: Communauté Financière Africaine franc
Religions: Christian, animist
Languages: French, Lingala, Monokutuba, local languages

Costa Rica

Area: 19,730 sq mi (51,100 sq km)
Population: 4,481,000
Capital: San José, pop. 1,515,000
Currency: Costa Rican colón
Religions: Roman Catholic, Evangelical
Languages: Spanish, English

Côte d'Ivoire (Ivory Coast)

Area: 124,503 sq mi (322,462 sq km)
Population: 20,646,000
Capitals: Abidjan, pop. 4,288,000; Yamoussoukro, pop. 966,000
Currency: Communauté Financière Africaine franc
Religions: Muslim, indigenous beliefs, Christian
Languages: French, Dioula, other native dialects

Croatia

Area: 21,831 sq mi (56,542 sq km)
Population: 4,274,000
Capital: Zagreb, pop. 686,000
Currency: kuna
Religions: Roman Catholic, Orthodox
Language: Croatian

Cuba

Area: 42,803 sq mi (110,860 sq km)
Population: 11,219,000
Capital: Havana, pop. 2,116,000
Currency: Cuban peso
Religions: Roman Catholic, Protestant, Jehovah's Witnesses, Jewish, Santería
Language: Spanish

Cyprus

Area: 3,572 sq mi (9,251 sq km)
Population: 1,172,000
Capital: Nicosia, pop. 253,000
Currencies: euro; new Turkish lira in Northern Cyprus
Religions: Greek Orthodox, Muslim, Maronite, Armenian Apostolic
Languages: Greek, Turkish, English

CYPRUS is said to be the BIRTHPLACE of the mythical APHRODITE, the goddess of love.

Czech Republic (Czechia)

Area: 30,450 sq mi (78,866 sq km)
Population: 10,490,000
Capital: Prague, pop. 1,276,000
Currency: koruny
Religion: Roman Catholic
Language: Czech

Democratic Republic of the Congo

Area: 905,365 sq mi (2,344,885 sq km)
Population: 69,117,000
Capital: Kinshasa, pop. 8,798,000
Currency: Congolese franc
Religions: Roman Catholic, Protestant, Kimbanguist, Muslim, syncretic sects, indigenous beliefs
Languages: French, Lingala, Kingwana, Kikongo, Tshiluba

Denmark

Area: 16,640 sq mi (43,098 sq km)
Population: 5,590,000
Capital: Copenhagen, pop. 1,206,000
Currency: Danish krone
Religions: Evangelical Lutheran, other Protestant, Roman Catholic
Languages: Danish, Faroese, Greenlandic, German, English as second language

Djibouti

Area: 8,958 sq mi
(23,200 sq km)
Population: 923,000
Capital: Djibouti, pop. 496,000
Currency: Djiboutian franc
Religions: Muslim, Christian
Languages: French, Arabic, Somali, Afar

Dominican Republic

Area: 18,704 sq mi
(48,442 sq km)
Population: 10,135,000
Capital: Santo Domingo,
pop. 2,191,000
Currency: Dominican peso
Religion: Roman Catholic
Language: Spanish

Dominica

Area: 290 sq mi (751 sq km)
Population: 71,000
Capital: Roseau, pop. 14,000
Currency: East Caribbean
dollar
Religions: Roman Catholic, Seventh-day Adventist,
Pentecostal, Baptist, Methodist, other Christian
Languages: English, French patois

Ecuador

Area: 109,483 sq mi
(283,560 sq km)
Population: 14,865,000
Capital: Quito, pop. 1,622,000
Currency: U.S. dollar
Religion: Roman Catholic
Languages: Spanish, Quechua, other
Amerindian languages

You Are There!
The Galápagos Islands, Ecuador

Slip on a snorkel mask, fins, and a wet suit and dive under the waters surrounding the Galápagos Islands. Soon, you're face-to-face with a marine iguana, the only seagoing lizards on the planet. Watch as these scaly, spiky dark gray reptiles dive down to feast on algae and seaweed before hopping back on land to warm up on the rocks. You may even see them sneeze out a nose full of saltwater, which lands on their head. When the water dries, leaving the salt behind, these lizards get their trademark salty white "wigs."

But that's not all you see. The Galápagos Islands, located 600 miles (1,000 km) from mainland South America, are home to about 9,000 species of animals, including penguins, countless other birds, and the world's largest tortoise. So no matter where you roam, you're bound to spot something wild!

COLOR KEY ● Africa ● Australia, New Zealand, and Oceania

Egypt

Area: 386,874 sq mi
(1,002,000 sq km)
Population: 82,283,000
Capital: Cairo, pop. 11,169,000
Currency: Egyptian pound
Religions: Muslim (mostly Sunni), Coptic Christian
Languages: Arabic, English, French

El Salvador

Area: 8,124 sq mi
(21,041 sq km)
Population: 6,264,000
Capital: San Salvador,
pop. 1,605,000
Currency: U.S. dollar
Religions: Roman Catholic, Protestant
Languages: Spanish, Nahua

Equatorial Guinea

Area: 10,831 sq mi (28,051 sq km)
Population: 740,000
Capital: Malabo, pop. 137,000
Currency: Communauté
Financière Africaine franc
Religions: Christian (predominantly Roman Catholic),
pagan practices
Languages: Spanish, French, Fang, Bubi

Eritrea

Area: 45,406 sq mi
(117,600 sq km)
Population: 5,581,000
Capital: Asmara, pop. 712,000
Currency: nakfa
Religions: Muslim, Coptic Christian, Roman Catholic
Languages: Afar, Arabic, Tigre, Kunama, Tigrinya, other
Cushitic languages

Estonia

Area: 17,462 sq mi (45,227 sq km)
Population: 1,339,000
Capital: Tallinn, pop. 400,000
Currency: euro
Religions: Evangelical Lutheran, Orthodox
Languages: Estonian, Russian

Ethiopia

Area: 426,373 sq mi
(1,104,300 sq km)
Population: 86,960,000
Capital: Addis Ababa,
pop. 2,979,000
Currency: birr
Religions: Christian, Muslim, traditional
Languages: Amharic, Oromigna, Tigrinya, Guaragigna

Fiji

Area: 7,095 sq mi
(18,376 sq km)
Population: 844,000
Capital: Suva, pop. 177,000
Currency: Fijian dollar
Religions: Christian (Methodist, Roman Catholic,
Assembly of God), Hindu (Sanatan), Muslim (Sunni)
Languages: English, Fijian, Hindustani

Finland

Area: 130,558 sq mi
(338,145 sq km)
Population: 5,414,000
Capital: Helsinki, pop. 1,134,000
Currency: euro
Religion: Lutheran Church of Finland
Languages: Finnish, Swedish

France

Area: 210,026 sq mi
(543,965 sq km)
Population: 63,605,000
Capital: Paris, pop. 10,620,000
Currency: euro
Religions: Roman Catholic, Muslim
Language: French

Gabon

Area: 103,347 sq mi (267,667 sq km)
Population: 1,564,000
Capital: Libreville, pop. 686,000
Currency: Communauté Financière
Africaine franc
Religions: Christian, animist
Languages: French, Fang, Myene, Nzebi, Bapounou/
Eschira, Bandjabi

Gambia

Area: 4,361 sq mi (11,295 sq km)
Population: 1,825,000
Capital: Banjul, pop. 506,000
Currency: dalasi
Religions: Muslim, Christian
Languages: English, Mandinka, Wolof, Fula, other indigenous vernaculars

Grenada

Area: 133 sq mi (344 sq km)
Population: 115,000
Capital: St. George's, pop. 41,000
Currency: East Caribbean dollar
Religions: Roman Catholic, Anglican, other Protestant
Languages: English, French patois

Georgia

Area: 26,911 sq mi (69,700 sq km)
Population: 4,519,000
Capital: Tbilisi, pop. 1,121,000
Currency: lari
Religions: Orthodox Christian, Muslim, Armenian-Gregorian
Languages: Georgian, Russian, Armenian, Azeri, Abkhaz

There is an **UNDERWATER ART GALLERY** in Grenada's **MOLINIERE BAY.**

Germany

Area: 137,847 sq mi (357,022 sq km)
Population: 81,825,000
Capital: Berlin, pop. 3,462,000
Currency: euro
Religions: Protestant, Roman Catholic, Muslim
Language: German

Guatemala

Area: 42,042 sq mi (108,889 sq km)
Population: 15,044,000
Capital: Guatemala City, pop. 1,168,000
Currency: quetzal
Religions: Roman Catholic, Protestant, indigenous Maya beliefs
Languages: Spanish, 23 official Amerindian languages

Ghana

Area: 92,100 sq mi (238,537 sq km)
Population: 25,546,000
Capital: Accra, pop. 2,573,000
Currency: Ghana cedi
Religions: Christian (Pentecostal/Charismatic, Protestant, Roman Catholic, other), Muslim, traditional beliefs
Languages: Asante, Ewe, Fante, Boron (Brong), Dagomba, Dangme, Dagarte (Dagaba), Akyem, Ga, English

Guinea

Area: 94,926 sq mi (245,857 sq km)
Population: 11,498,000
Capital: Conakry, pop. 1,786,000
Currency: Guinean franc
Religions: Muslim, Christian, indigenous beliefs
Languages: French, ethnic languages

Greece

Area: 50,949 sq mi (131,957 sq km)
Population: 10,833,000
Capital: Athens, pop. 3,414,000
Currency: euro
Religion: Greek Orthodox
Languages: Greek, English, French

Guinea-Bissau

Area: 13,948 sq mi (36,125 sq km)
Population: 1,637,000
Capital: Bissau, pop. 423,000
Currency: Communauté Financière Africaine franc
Religions: indigenous beliefs, Muslim, Christian
Languages: Portuguese, Crioulo, African languages

COLOR KEY ● Africa ● Australia, New Zealand, and Oceania

Guyana

Area: 83,000 sq mi
(214,969 sq km)
Population: 796,000
Capital: Georgetown, pop. 127,000
Currency: Guyanese dollar
Religions: Christian, Hindu, Muslim
Languages: English, Amerindian dialects, Creole, Hindustani, Urdu

Honduras

Area: 43,433 sq mi
(112,492 sq km)
Population: 8,385,000
Capital: Tegucigalpa,
pop. 1,088,000
Currency: lempira
Religions: Roman Catholic, Protestant
Languages: Spanish, Amerindian dialects

Haiti

Area: 10,714 sq mi (27,750 sq km)
Population: 10,256,000
Capital: Port-au-Prince,
pop. 2,207,000
Currency: gourde
Religions: Roman Catholic, Protestant
(Baptist, Pentecostal, other)
Languages: French, Creole

Hungary

Area: 35,919 sq mi (93,030 sq km)
Population: 9,947,000
Capital: Budapest, pop. 1,737,000
Currency: forint
Religions: Roman Catholic, Calvinist, Lutheran
Language: Hungarian

You Are There!

The Parthenon, Athens, Greece

Want to know what life looked like more than 2,400 years ago? Then head to the Acropolis overlooking Athens, Greece, where ruins of buildings built in ancient times still stand. Here, you can walk around the grounds of the Parthenon, one of the world's most recognizable buildings. Originally constructed as a temple to the goddess Athena, the Parthenon (which has since served as a church, a fortress, and a place to store ammunition) has literally stood the test of time. The building has been shot at, blown up, set on fire, and rocked by earthquakes—and yet its columns still stand.

● Asia   ● Europe   ● North America   ● South America

Iceland

Area: 39,769 sq mi
(103,000 sq km)
Population: 320,000
Capital: Reykjavík, pop. 206,000
Currency: Icelandic krona
Religion: Lutheran Church of Iceland
Languages: Icelandic, English, Nordic
languages, German

Indonesia

Area: 742,308 sq mi
(1,922,570 sq km)
Population: 240,989,000
Capital: Jakarta, pop. 9,769,000
Currency: Indonesian rupiah
Religions: Muslim, Protestant, Roman Catholic
Languages: Bahasa Indonesia (modified form of Malay),
English, Dutch, Javanese, local dialects

India

Area: 1,269,221 sq mi (3,287,270 sq km)
Population: 1,259,721,000
Capital: New Delhi, pop. 22,654,000
(part of Delhi metropolitan area)
Currency: Indian rupee
Religions: Hindu, Muslim
Languages: Hindi, 21 other official languages,
Hindustani (popular Hindi/Urdu variant in the north)

Iran

Area: 636,296 sq mi
(1,648,000 sq km)
Population: 78,869,000
Capital: Tehran, pop. 7,304,000
Currency: Iranian rial
Religions: Shiite Muslim, Sunni Muslim
Languages: Persian, Turkic, Kurdish, Luri,
Baluchi, Arabic

You Are There!
Cliffs of Moher, Ireland

Rising 702 feet (214 m) from the churning Atlantic Ocean, the Cliffs of Moher offer some of the most magical views in all of Ireland. Follow the winding path along the top of the cliffs for a gentle hike to cool spots like O'Brien's Tower, one of the highest points around. Climb to the top of the tower to take in the stunning surroundings of Galway Bay and the rocky landscape of the nearby Aran Islands.

Another can't-miss destination? The Hag's Head rock formation, which is said to resemble an old woman staring out to sea.

COLOR KEY ● Africa ● Australia, New Zealand, and Ocean

Iraq

Area: 168,754 sq mi
(437,072 sq km)
Population: 33,703,000
Capital: Baghdad, pop. 6,036,000
Currency: Iraqi dinar
Religions: Shiite Muslim, Sunni Muslim
Languages: Arabic, Kurdish, Assyrian, Armenian

Japan

Area: 145,902 sq mi (377,887 sq km)
Population: 127,588,000
Capital: Tokyo, pop. 37,217,000
Currency: yen
Religions: Shinto, Buddhist
Language: Japanese

Ireland

Area: 27,133 sq mi
(70,273 sq km)
Population: 4,683,000
Capital: Dublin, pop. 1,121,000
Currency: euro
Religions: Roman Catholic, Church of Ireland
Languages: Irish (Gaelic), English

Jordan

Area: 34,495 sq mi
(89,342 sq km)
Population: 6,318,000
Capital: Amman, pop. 1,179,000
Currency: Jordanian dinar
Religions: Sunni Muslim, Christian
Languages: Arabic, English

Israel

Area: 8,550 sq mi (22,145 sq km)
Population: 7,906,000
Capital: Jerusalem, pop. 791,000
Currency: new Israeli sheqel
Religions: Jewish, Muslim
Languages: Hebrew, Arabic, English

Kazakhstan

Area: 1,049,155 sq mi
(2,717,300 sq km)
Population: 16,793,000
Capital: Astana, pop. 664,000
Currency: tenge
Religions: Muslim, Russian Orthodox
Languages: Kazakh (Qazaq), Russian

Italy

Area: 116,345 sq mi
(301,333 sq km)
Population: 60,950,000
Capital: Rome, pop. 3,298,000
Currency: euro
Religions: Roman Catholic, Protestant, Jewish, Muslim
Languages: Italian, German, French, Slovene

Kenya

Area: 224,081 sq mi (580,367 sq km)
Population: 43,013,000
Capital: Nairobi, pop. 3,363,000
Currency: Kenyan shilling
Religions: Protestant, Roman Catholic, Muslim,
indigenous beliefs
Languages: English, Kiswahili, many indigenous
languages

Jamaica

Area: 4,244 sq mi
(10,991 sq km)
Population: 2,716,000
Capital: Kingston, pop. 571,000
Currency: Jamaican dollar
Religions: Protestant (Church of God, Seventh-day
Adventist, Pentecostal, Baptist, Anglican, other)
Languages: English, English patois

Kiribati

Area: 313 sq mi (811 sq km)
Population: 105,000
Capital: Tarawa, pop. 44,000
Currency: Australian
dollar
Religions: Roman Catholic, Protestant
(Congregational)
Languages: I-Kiribati, English

Kosovo

Area: 4,203 sq mi (10,887 sq km)
Population: 2,290,000
Capital: Prishtina, pop. 600,000
Currency: euro
Religions: Muslim, Serbian Orthodox, Roman Catholic
Languages: Albanian, Serbian, Bosnian, Turkish, Roma

Kuwait

Area: 6,880 sq mi (17,818 sq km)
Population: 2,892,000
Capital: Kuwait City, pop. 2,406,000
Currency: Kuwaiti dinar
Religions: Sunni Muslim, Shiite Muslim
Languages: Arabic, English

> **MUTLA RIDGE, one of the tallest points in KUWAIT, is only 476 feet (145 m) high.**

Kyrgyzstan

Area: 77,182 sq mi (199,900 sq km)
Population: 5,668,000
Capital: Bishkek, pop. 839,000
Currency: som
Religions: Muslim, Russian Orthodox
Languages: Kyrgyz, Uzbek, Russian

Laos

Area: 91,429 sq mi (236,800 sq km)
Population: 6,521,000
Capital: Vientiane, pop. 810,000
Currency: kip
Religions: Buddhist, animist
Languages: Lao, French, English, various ethnic languages

Latvia

Area: 24,938 sq mi (64,589 sq km)
Population: 2,049,000
Capital: Riga, pop. 701,000
Currency: Latvian lat
Religions: Lutheran, Roman Catholic, Russian Orthodox
Languages: Latvian, Russian, Lithuanian

Lebanon

Area: 4,036 sq mi (10,452 sq km)
Population: 4,304,000
Capital: Beirut, pop. 2,022,000
Currency: Lebanese pound
Religions: Muslim, Christian
Languages: Arabic, French, English, Armenian

Lesotho

Area: 11,720 sq mi (30,355 sq km)
Population: 2,217,000
Capital: Maseru, pop. 239,000
Currencies: loti; South African rand
Religions: Christian, indigenous beliefs
Languages: Sesotho, English, Zulu, Xhosa

Liberia

Area: 43,000 sq mi (111,370 sq km)
Population: 4,245,000
Capital: Monrovia, pop. 750,000
Currency: Liberian dollar
Religions: Christian, indigenous beliefs, Muslim
Languages: English, some 20 ethnic languages

Libya

Area: 679,362 sq mi (1,759,540 sq km)
Population: 6,469,000
Capital: Tripoli, pop. 1,127,000
Currency: Libyan dinar
Religion: Sunni Muslim
Languages: Arabic, Italian, English

Liechtenstein

Area: 62 sq mi (160 sq km)
Population: 37,000
Capital: Vaduz, pop. 5,000
Currency: Swiss franc
Religions: Roman Catholic, Protestant
Languages: German, Alemannic dialect

Lithuania

Area: 25,212 sq mi
(65,300 sq km)
Population: 3,179,000
Capital: Vilnius, pop. 546,000
Currency: litas
Religions: Roman Catholic, Russian Orthodox
Languages: Lithuanian, Russian, Polish

Luxembourg

Area: 998 sq mi (2,586 sq km)
Population: 527,000
Capital: Luxembourg,
pop. 94,000
Currency: euro
Religions: Roman Catholic, Protestant,
Jewish, Muslim
Languages: Luxembourgish, German, French

5 cool things about LUXEMBOURG

1. At 998 square miles (2,586 sq km), Luxembourg is the second-smallest country in the European Union after Malta.

2. You could drive the length of Luxembourg in an hour and a half.

3. Luxembourg is the only country in the world ruled by a grand duke.

4. Luxembourg has three official languages: French, German, and Luxembourgish.

5. There are about 150 banks in Luxembourg, but only one university.

Macedonia

Area: 9,928 sq mi
(25,713 sq km)
Population: 2,064,000
Capital: Skopje, pop. 499,000
Currency: Macedonian denar
Religions: Macedonian Orthodox, Muslim
Languages: Macedonian, Albanian, Turkish

Madagascar

Area: 226,658 sq mi
(587,041 sq km)
Population: 21,929,000
Capital: Antananarivo,
pop. 1,987,000
Currency: Madagascar ariary
Religions: indigenous beliefs, Christian, Muslim
Languages: English, French, Malagasy

Malawi

Area: 45,747 sq mi
(118,484 sq km)
Population: 15,883,000
Capital: Lilongwe, pop. 772,000
Currency: Malawian kwacha
Religions: Christian, Muslim
Languages: Chichewa, Chinyanja, Chiyao, Chitumbuka

Malaysia

Area: 127,355 sq mi (329,847 sq km)
Population: 28,975,000
Capital: Kuala Lumpur,
pop. 1,556,000
Currency: ringgit
Religions: Muslim, Buddhist, Christian, Hindu
Languages: Bahasa Malaysia, English, Chinese, Tamil, Telugu, Malayalam, Panjabi, Thai, indigenous languages

Maldives

Area: 115 sq mi (298 sq km)
Population: 331,000
Capital: Male, pop. 132,000
Currency: rufiyaa
Religion: Sunni Muslim
Languages: Maldivian Dhivehi, English

Mali

Area: 478,841 sq mi (1,240,192 sq km)
Population: 16,014,000
Capital: Bamako, pop. 2,037,000
Currency: Communauté Financière Africaine franc
Religions: Muslim, indigenous beliefs
Languages: Bambara, French, numerous African languages

Marshall Islands

Area: 70 sq mi (181 sq km)
Population: 55,000
Capital: Majuro, pop. 31,000
Currency: U.S. dollar
Religions: Protestant, Assembly of God, Roman Catholic
Language: Marshallese

Malta

Area: 122 sq mi (316 sq km)
Population: 399,000
Capital: Valletta, pop. 198,000
Currency: euro
Religion: Roman Catholic
Languages: Maltese, English

Mauritania

Area: 397,955 sq mi (1,030,700 sq km)
Population: 3,623,000
Capital: Nouakchott, pop. 786,000
Currency: ouguiya
Religion: Muslim
Languages: Arabic, Pulaar, Soninke, French, Hassaniya, Wolof

You Are There!

Chichén Itzá, Mexico

Think pyramids are only found in Egypt? Think again! You can find another ancient pyramid in Mexico, the 1,100-year-old Temple Kukulcan. The standout symbol of the ancient Maya city of Chichén Itzá, this nine-level, 79-foot (24-m)-tall pyramid is also known as *El Castillo* (the castle). It's believed that the pyramid was built as a tribute to the sacred quetzal bird. In fact, if you stand in front of the pyramid and clap, the resulting echo sounds a lot like the call of the now-threatened bird.

COLOR KEY ● Africa ● Australia, New Zealand, and Oceania

Mauritius

Area: 788 sq mi (2,040 sq km)
Population: 1,291,000
Capital: Port Louis, pop. 151,000
Currency: Mauritian rupee
Religions: Hindu, Roman Catholic, Muslim, other Christian
Languages: Creole, Bhojpuri, French

Mexico

Area: 758,449 sq mi (1,964,375 sq km)
Population: 116,147,000
Capital: Mexico City, pop. 20,446,000
Currency: Mexican peso
Religions: Roman Catholic, Protestant
Languages: Spanish, Mayan, other indigenous languages

Micronesia

Area: 271 sq mi (702 sq km)
Population: 107,000
Capital: Palikir, pop. 7,000
Currency: U.S. dollar
Religions: Roman Catholic, Protestant
Languages: English, Trukese, Pohnpeian, Yapese, other indigenous languages

Moldova

Area: 13,050 sq mi (33,800 sq km)
Population: 4,114,000
Capital: Chisinau, pop. 677,000
Currency: Moldovan leu
Religion: Eastern Orthodox
Languages: Moldovan, Russian, Gagauz

Monaco

Area: 0.8 sq mi (2.0 sq km)
Population: 36,000
Capital: Monaco, pop. 35,000
Currency: euro
Religion: Roman Catholic
Languages: French, English, Italian, Monegasque

Mongolia

Area: 603,909 sq mi (1,564,116 sq km)
Population: 2,873,000
Capital: Ulaanbaatar, pop. 1,184,000
Currency: togrog/tugrik
Religions: Buddhist Lamaist, Shamanist, Christian
Languages: Khalkha Mongol, Turkic, Russian

Montenegro

Area: 5,333 sq mi (13,812 sq km)
Population: 622,000
Capital: Podgorica, pop. 156,000
Currency: euro
Religions: Orthodox, Muslim, Roman Catholic
Languages: Serbian (Ijekavian dialect), Bosnian, Albanian, Croatian

Morocco

Area: 172,414 sq mi (446,550 sq km)
Population: 32,597,000
Capital: Rabat, pop. 1,843,000
Currency: Moroccan dirham
Religion: Muslim
Languages: Arabic, Berber dialects, French

Mozambique

Area: 308,642 sq mi (799,380 sq km)
Population: 23,702,000
Capital: Maputo, pop. 1,150,000
Currency: metical
Religions: Roman Catholic, Muslim, Zionist Christian
Languages: Emakhuwa, Xichangana, Portuguese, Elomwe, Cisena, Echuwabo, other local languages

Myanmar (Burma)

Area: 261,218 sq mi (676,552 sq km)
Population: 54,585,000
Capitals: Nay Pyi Taw, pop. 1,060,000; Yangon (Rangoon), pop. 4,457,000
Currency: kyat
Religions: Buddhist, Christian, Muslim
Languages: Burmese, minority ethnic languages

Namibia

Area: 318,261 sq mi
(824,292 sq km)
Population: 2,364,000
Capital: Windhoek, pop. 380,000
Currencies: Namibian dollar;
South African rand
Religions: Lutheran, other Christian, indigenous beliefs
Languages: Afrikaans, German, English

> **NAMIBIA is the driest country in sub-Saharan AFRICA.**

Nauru

Area: 8 sq mi (21 sq km)
Population: 10,000
Capital: Yaren, pop. 10,000
Currency: Australian dollar
Religions: Protestant, Roman Catholic
Languages: Nauruan, English

Nepal

Area: 56,827 sq mi
(147,181 sq km)
Population: 30,918,000
Capital: Kathmandu, pop. 1,015,000
Currency: Nepalese rupee
Religions: Hindu, Buddhist, Muslim, Kirant
Languages: Nepali, Maithali, Bhojpuri, Tharu,
Tamang, Newar, Magar

Netherlands

Area: 16,034 sq mi
(41,528 sq km)
Population: 16,749,000
Capital: Amsterdam, pop. 1,056,000
Currency: euro
Religions: Roman Catholic, Dutch Reformed,
Calvinist, Muslim
Languages: Dutch, Frisian

New Zealand

Area: 104,454 sq mi
(270,534 sq km)
Population: 4,437,000
Capital: Wellington, pop. 410,000
Currency: New Zealand dollar
Religions: Anglican, Roman Catholic, Presbyterian,
other Christian
Languages: English, Maori

Nicaragua

Area: 50,193 sq mi
(130,000 sq km)
Population: 5,955,000
Capital: Managua, pop. 970,000
Currency: gold cordoba
Religions: Roman Catholic, Evangelical
Language: Spanish

Niger

Area: 489,191 sq mi (1,267,000 sq km)
Population: 16,276,000
Capital: Niamey, pop. 1,297,000
Currency: Communauté
Financière Africaine franc
Religions: Muslim, other (includes indigenous
beliefs and Christian)
Languages: French, Hausa, Djerma

Nigeria

Area: 356,669 sq mi
(923,768 sq km)
Population: 170,124,000
Capital: Abuja, pop. 2,153,000
Currency: naira
Religions: Muslim, Christian, indigenous beliefs
Languages: English, Hausa, Yoruba, Igbo (Ibo), Fulani

North Korea

Area: 46,540 sq mi
(120,538 sq km)
Population: 24,589,000
Capital: Pyongyang,
pop. 2,843,000
Currency: North Korean won
Religions: Buddhist, Confucianist, some Christian
and syncretic Chondogyo
Language: Korean

Norway

Area: 125,004 sq mi
(323,758 sq km)
Population: 5,019,000
Capital: Oslo, pop. 915,000
Currency: Norwegian krone
Religion: Church of Norway (Lutheran)
Languages: Bokmal Norwegian, Nynorsk
Norwegian, Sami

Pakistan

Area: 307,374 sq mi
(796,095 sq km)
Population: 180,428,000
Capital: Islamabad, pop. 919,000
Currency: Pakistani rupee
Religions: Sunni Muslim, Shiite Muslim
Languages: Punjabi, Sindhi, Siraiki, Pashto, Urdu,
Baluchi, Hindko, English

Oman

Area: 119,500 sq mi
(309,500 sq km)
Population: 3,090,000
Capital: Muscat, pop. 743,000
Currency: Omani rial
Religions: Ibadhi Muslim, Sunni Muslim,
Shiite Muslim, Hindu
Languages: Arabic, English, Baluchi, Urdu, Indian dialects

Palau

Area: 189 sq mi (489 sq km)
Population: 21,000
Capital: Melekeok, pop. 1,000
Currency: U.S. dollar
Religions: Roman Catholic, Protestant, Modekngei,
Seventh-day Adventist
Languages: Palauan, Filipino, English, Chinese

You Are There!

Franz Josef Glacier, New Zealand

As your helicopter lifts into the cloudless sky, the landscape below rapidly changes from a lush green to an icy blue. You are flying high above New Zealand's Westland Tai Poutini National Park, home to the Franz Josef Glacier. Ranging from a height of 8,858 feet (2,700 m) above sea level down to just 787 feet (240 m), Franz Josef is one of the world's steepest glaciers. But it's also one of the most accessible, welcoming up to 2,700 visitors a day.

The best way to take in all of the glacier's glory? The chopper, of course, which gives you a brilliant bird's-eye view before landing. Then hike past funky formations, curving tunnels, and towering peaks—all formed by the majestic blue glacial ice.

● Asia ● Europe ● North America ● South America

Panama

Area: 29,157 sq mi (75,517 sq km)
Population: 3,610,000
Capital: Panama City, pop. 1,426,000
Currencies: balboa; U.S. dollar
Religions: Roman Catholic, Protestant
Languages: Spanish, English

5 cool things about PANAMA

1. Panama is a land bridge separating North and South America.

2. The Panama Canal, completed in 1914, joins the Atlantic and Pacific Oceans.

3. Trees with square trunks grow in the mountains west of Panama City.

4. Panama is home to the golden frog, which is thought to bring people good luck.

5. Panama City is the only major Latin American city with a rain forest just minutes from its downtown area.

Papua New Guinea

Area: 178,703 sq mi (462,840 sq km)
Population: 7,034,000
Capital: Port Moresby, pop. 343,000
Currency: kina
Religions: indigenous beliefs, Roman Catholic, Lutheran, other Protestant
Languages: Melanesian Pidgin, 820 indigenous languages

Paraguay

Area: 157,048 sq mi (406,752 sq km)
Population: 6,683,000
Capital: Asunción, pop. 2,139,000
Currency: guarani
Religions: Roman Catholic, Protestant
Languages: Spanish, Guarani

Peru

Area: 496,224 sq mi (1,285,216 sq km)
Population: 30,136,000
Capital: Lima, pop. 9,130,000
Currency: nuevo sol
Religion: Roman Catholic
Languages: Spanish, Quechua, Aymara, minor Amazonian languages

Philippines

Area: 115,831 sq mi (300,000 sq km)
Population: 96,218,000
Capital: Manila, pop. 11,862,000
Currency: Philippine peso
Religions: Roman Catholic, Muslim, other Christian
Languages: Filipino (based on Tagalog), English

Poland

Area: 120,728 sq mi (312,685 sq km)
Population: 38,195,000
Capital: Warsaw, pop. 1,723,000
Currency: zloty
Religion: Roman Catholic
Language: Polish

Portugal

Area: 35,655 sq mi (92,345 sq km)
Population: 10,561,000
Capital: Lisbon, pop. 2,843,000
Currency: euro
Religion: Roman Catholic
Languages: Portuguese, Mirandese

Qatar

Area: 4,448 sq mi (11,521 sq km)
Population: 1,882,000
Capital: Doha, pop. 567,000
Currency: Qatari rial
Religions: Muslim, Christian
Languages: Arabic; English commonly a second language

COLOR KEY ● Africa ● Australia, New Zealand, and Oceani

Romania

Area: 92,043 sq mi
(238,391 sq km)
Population: 21,408,000
Capital: Bucharest, pop. 1,937,000
Currency: new leu
Religions: Eastern Orthodox, Protestant,
Roman Catholic
Languages: Romanian, Hungarian

Russia

Area: 6,592,850 sq mi
(17,075,400 sq km)
Population: 143,165,000
Capital: Moscow, pop. 11,621,000
Currency: ruble
Religions: Russian Orthodox, Muslim
Languages: Russian, many minority languages

Note: Russia is in both Europe and Asia, but its capital is in Europe, so it is classified here as a European country.

Rwanda

Area: 10,169 sq mi
(26,338 sq km)
Population: 10,815,000
Capital: Kigali, pop. 1,004,000
Currency: Rwandan franc
Religions: Roman Catholic, Protestant,
Adventist, Muslim
Languages: Kinyarwanda, French, English, Kiswahili

Samoa

Area: 1,093 sq mi (2,831 sq km)
Population: 187,000
Capital: Apia, pop. 37,000
Currency: tala
Religions: Congregationalist, Roman Catholic,
Methodist, Church of Jesus Christ of Latter-day
Saints, Assembly of God, Seventh-day Adventist
Languages: Samoan (Polynesian), English

San Marino

Area: 24 sq mi (61 sq km)
Population: 32,000
Capital: San Marino, pop. 4,000
Currency: euro
Religion: Roman Catholic
Language: Italian

São Tomé and Príncipe

Area: 386 sq mi (1,001 sq km)
Population: 183,000
Capital: São Tomé,
pop. 64,000
Currency: dobra
Religions: Roman Catholic, Evangelical
Language: Portuguese

Saudi Arabia

Area: 756,985 sq mi
(1,960,582 sq km)
Population: 28,705,000
Capital: Riyadh, pop. 5,451,000
Currency: Saudi riyal
Religion: Muslim
Language: Arabic

Senegal

Area: 75,955 sq mi
(196,722 sq km)
Population: 13,108,000
Capital: Dakar, pop. 3,035,000
Currency: Communauté
Financière Africaine franc
Religions: Muslim, Christian (mostly Roman Catholic)
Languages: French, Wolof, Pulaar, Jola, Mandinka

Serbia

Area: 29,913 sq mi (77,474 sq km)
Population: 7,102,000
Capital: Belgrade, pop. 1,135,000
Currency: Serbian dinar
Religions: Serbian Orthodox, Roman Catholic, Muslim
Languages: Serbian, Hungarian

Seychelles

Area: 176 sq mi (455 sq km)
Population: 93,000
Capital: Victoria, pop. 27,000
Currency: Seychelles rupee
Religions: Roman Catholic, Anglican, other Christian
Languages: Creole, English

Sierra Leone

Area: 27,699 sq mi (71,740 sq km)
Population: 6,126,000
Capital: Freetown, pop. 941,000
Currency: leone
Religions: Muslim, indigenous beliefs, Christian
Languages: English, Mende, Temne, Krio

Slovakia

Area: 18,932 sq mi (49,035 sq km)
Population: 5,394,000
Capital: Bratislava, pop. 434,000
Currency: euro
Religions: Roman Catholic, Protestant, Greek Catholic
Languages: Slovak, Hungarian

Singapore

Area: 255 sq mi (660 sq km)
Population: 5,294,000
Capital: Singapore, pop. 5,188,000
Currency: Singapore dollar
Religions: Buddhist, Muslim, Taoist, Roman Catholic, Hindu, other Christian
Languages: Mandarin, English, Malay, Hokkien, Cantonese, Teochew, Tamil

Slovenia

Area: 7,827 sq mi (20,273 sq km)
Population: 2,058,000
Capital: Ljubljana, pop. 273,000
Currency: euro
Religions: Roman Catholic, Muslim, Orthodox
Languages: Slovene, Croatian, Serbian

You Are There!
Cape Town, South Africa

Cape Town, South Africa, was the first place Dutch explorers colonized on Africa's southern tip. Now Cape Town is one of the top tourist destinations in Africa. What's the draw? Hop a cableway up Table Mountain or hit a world-class beach, try skydiving or grab a sea kayak. Simply name your adventure, and you're bound to be able to do it in Cape Town!

COLOR KEY ● Africa ● Australia, New Zealand, and Oceani

Solomon Islands

Area: 10,954 sq mi
(28,370 sq km)
Population: 552,000
Capital: Honiara, pop. 68,000
Currency: Solomon Islands dollar
Religions: Church of Melanesia, Roman Catholic, South Seas Evangelical, other Christian
Languages: Melanesian pidgin, 120 indigenous languages

Somalia

Area: 246,201 sq mi
(637,657 sq km)
Population: 10,086,000
Capital: Mogadishu, pop. 1,554,000
Currency: Somali shilling
Religion: Sunni Muslim
Languages: Somali, Arabic, Italian, English

South Africa

Area: 470,693 sq mi (1,219,090 sq km)
Population: 51,147,000
Capitals: Pretoria (Tshwane), pop. 1,501,000; Bloemfontein, pop. 468,000; Cape Town, pop. 3,562,000
Currency: rand
Religions: Zion Christian, Pentecostal, Catholic, Methodist, Dutch Reformed, Anglican, other Christian
Languages: IsiZulu, IsiXhosa, Afrikaans, Sepedi, English

South Korea

Area: 38,321 sq mi
(99,250 sq km)
Population: 48,906,000
Capital: Seoul, pop. 9,736,000
Currency: South Korean won
Religions: Christian, Buddhist
Languages: Korean, English

South Sudan

Area: 248,777 sq mi (644,329 sq km)
Population: 9,385,000
Capital: Juba, pop. 269,000
Currency: South Sudan pound
Religions: animist, Christian
Languages: English, Arabic, regional languages (Dinke, Nuer, Bari, Zande, Shilluk)

Spain

Area: 195,363 sq mi (505,988 sq km)
Population: 46,195,000
Capital: Madrid, pop. 6,574,000
Currency: euro
Religion: Roman Catholic
Languages: Castilian Spanish, Catalan, Galician, Basque

Sri Lanka

Area: 25,299 sq mi
(65,525 sq km)
Population: 21,166,000
Capitals: Colombo, pop. 693,000; Sri Jayewardenepura Kotte, pop. 126,000
Currency: Sri Lankan rupee
Religions: Buddhist, Muslim, Hindu, Christian
Languages: Sinhala, Tamil

St. Kitts and Nevis

Area: 104 sq mi (269 sq km)
Population: 54,000
Capital: Basseterre, pop. 12,000
Currency: East Caribbean dollar
Religions: Anglican, other Protestant, Roman Catholic
Language: English

St. Lucia

Area: 238 sq mi (616 sq km)
Population: 169,000
Capital: Castries, pop. 21,000
Currency: East Caribbean dollar
Religions: Roman Catholic, Seventh-day Adventist, Pentecostal
Languages: English, French patois

St. Vincent and the Grenadines

Area: 150 sq mi (389 sq km)
Population: 108,000
Capital: Kingstown, pop. 31,000
Currency: East Caribbean dollar
Religions: Anglican, Methodist, Roman Catholic
Languages: English, French patois

Sudan

Area: 718,722 sq mi
(1,861,484 sq km)
Population: 33,494,000
Capital: Khartoum, pop. 4,632,000
Currency: Sudanese pound
Religions: Sunni Muslim, indigenous beliefs, Christian
Languages: Arabic, Nubian, Ta Bedawie, many diverse dialects of Nilotic, Nilo-Hamitic, Sudanic languages

Suriname

Area: 63,037 sq mi (163,265 sq km)
Population: 542,000
Capital: Paramaribo, pop. 278,000
Currency: Suriname dollar
Religions: Hindu, Protestant (predominantly Moravian), Roman Catholic, Muslim, indigenous beliefs
Languages: Dutch, English, Sranang Tongo, Hindustani, Javanese

Swaziland

Area: 6,704 sq mi (17,363 sq km)
Population: 1,220,000
Capitals: Mbabane, pop. 66,000; Lobamba, pop. 4,557
Currency: lilangeni
Religions: Zionist, Roman Catholic, Muslim
Languages: English, siSwati

Sweden

Area: 173,732 sq mi
(449,964 sq km)
Population: 9,513,000
Capital: Stockholm, pop. 1,385,000
Currency: Swedish krona
Religion: Lutheran
Languages: Swedish, Sami, Finnish

Switzerland

Area: 15,940 sq mi
(41,284 sq km)
Population: 7,994,000
Capital: Bern, pop. 353,000
Currency: Swiss franc
Religions: Roman Catholic, Protestant, Muslim
Languages: German, French, Italian, Romansh

Syria

Area: 71,498 sq mi (185,180 sq km)
Population: 22,531,000
Capital: Damascus, pop. 2,650,000
Currency: Syrian pound
Religions: Sunni, other Muslim (includes Alawite, Druze), Christian
Languages: Arabic, Kurdish, Armenian, Aramaic, Circassian

Tajikistan

Area: 55,251 sq mi
(143,100 sq km)
Population: 7,079,000
Capital: Dushanbe, pop. 739,000
Currency: somoni
Religions: Sunni Muslim, Shiite Muslim
Languages: Tajik, Russian

Tanzania

Area: 364,900 sq mi (945,087 sq km)
Population: 47,656,000
Capitals: Dar es Salaam, pop. 2,930,000; Dodoma, pop. 226,000
Currency: Tanzanian shilling
Religions: Muslim, indigenous beliefs, Christian
Languages: Kiswahili, Kiunguja, English, Arabic, local languages

Thailand

Area: 198,115 sq mi
(513,115 sq km)
Population: 69,892,000
Capital: Bangkok, pop. 8,426,000
Currency: baht
Religions: Buddhist, Muslim
Languages: Thai, English, ethnic dialects

Timor-Leste (East Timor)

Area: 5,640 sq mi
(14,609 sq km)
Population: 1,126,000
Capital: Dili, pop. 180,000
Currency: U.S. dollar
Religion: Roman Catholic
Languages: Tetum, Portuguese, Indonesian, English, indigenous languages

COLOR KEY ● Africa ● Australia, New Zealand, and Oceani

Togo

Area: 21,925 sq mi (56,785 sq km)
Population: 6,011,000
Capital: Lomé, pop. 1,524,000
Currency: Communauté Financière Africaine franc
Religions: indigenous beliefs, Christian, Muslim
Languages: French, Ewe, Mina, Kabye, Dagomba

Trinidad and Tobago

Area: 1,980 sq mi (5,128 sq km)
Population: 1,315,000
Capital: Port of Spain, pop. 66,000
Currency: Trinidad and Tobago dollar
Religions: Roman Catholic, Hindu, Anglican, Baptist
Languages: English, Caribbean Hindustani, French, Spanish, Chinese

Tonga

Area: 289 sq mi (748 sq km)
Population: 103,000
Capital: Nuku'alofa, pop. 25,000
Currency: pa'anga
Religion: Christian
Languages: Tongan, English

Tunisia

Area: 63,170 sq mi (163,610 sq km)
Population: 10,800,000
Capital: Tunis, pop. 790,000
Currency: Tunisian dinar
Religion: Muslim
Languages: Arabic, French

 **You Are There!** **Phang Nga Bay, Thailand**

Welcome to Thailand's Phang Nga Bay! This shallow bay in the Andaman Sea surrounds 42 small islands, including the popular "James Bond Island"— once a setting featured in the famous spy film series. And it's no wonder this bay served as a movie backdrop: After one glimpse of its turquoise water and towering limestone cliffs, you'll likely agree that you're as close to paradise as you can get. In 2004, the nearby island of Phuket was hit hard by a tsunami that devastated most of southern Thailand. But today, the island is back up and running—and welcoming more than five million visitors a year. Many of those visitors flock to Phang Nga Bay to kayak, snorkel, and spot wildlife like spinner dolphins and the blue-ringed octopus.

Turkey

Area: 300,948 sq mi
(779,452 sq km)
Population: 74,885,000
Capital: Ankara, pop. 4,194,000
Currency: new Turkish lira
Religion: Muslim (mostly Sunni)
Languages: Turkish, Kurdish, Dimli (Zaza), Azeri, Kabardian, Gagauz

5 cool things about TURKEY

1. Turkey is home to one of the earliest settlements on Earth, built 8,800 years ago.

2. Tulips were first grown in Turkey.

3. Istanbul, the largest city in Turkey, is partly in Europe and partly in Asia.

4. Turkey is one of the most earthquake-prone areas on the planet.

5. Turkey is the world's largest exporter of hazelnuts.

Turkmenistan

Area: 188,456 sq mi
(488,100 sq km)
Population: 5,170,000
Capital: Ashgabat, pop. 683,000
Currency: Turkmen manat
Religions: Muslim, Eastern Orthodox
Languages: Turkmen, Russian, Uzbek

Tuvalu

Area: 10 sq mi (26 sq km)
Population: 11,000
Capital: Funafuti, pop. 5,000
Currencies: Australian dollar; Tuvaluan dollar
Religion: Church of Tuvalu (Congregationalist)
Languages: Tuvaluan, English, Samoan, Kiribati

Uganda

Area: 93,104 sq mi
(241,139 sq km)
Population: 35,621,000
Capital: Kampala, pop. 1,659,000
Currency: Ugandan shilling
Religions: Protestant, Roman Catholic, Muslim
Languages: English, Ganda, other local languages, Kiswahili, Arabic

Ukraine

Area: 233,090 sq mi
(603,700 sq km)
Population: 45,556,000
Capital: Kiev, pop. 2,829,000
Currency: hryvnia
Religions: Ukrainian Orthodox, Orthodox, Ukrainian Greek Catholic
Languages: Ukrainian, Russian

United Arab Emirates

Area: 30,000 sq mi
(77,700 sq km)
Population: 8,106,000
Capital: Abu Dhabi, pop. 942,000
Currency: Emirati dirham
Religion: Muslim
Languages: Arabic, Persian, English, Hindi, Urdu

United Kingdom

Area: 93,788 sq mi
(242,910 sq km)
Population: 63,213,000
Capital: London, pop. 9,005,000
Currency: British pound
Religions: Anglican, Roman Catholic, Presbyterian, Methodist
Languages: English, Welsh, Scottish form of Gaelic

United States

Area: 3,794,083 sq mi
(9,826,630 sq km)
Population: 311,695,000
Capital: Washington, D.C., pop. 617,996
Currency: U.S. dollar
Religions: Protestant, Roman Catholic
Languages: English, Spanish

COLOR KEY ● Africa ● Australia, New Zealand, and Oceani

Uruguay

Area: 68,037 sq mi
(176,215 sq km)
Population: 3,381,000
Capital: Montevideo, pop. 1,672,000
Currency: Uruguayan peso
Religion: Roman Catholic
Language: Spanish

Uzbekistan

Area: 172,742 sq mi
(447,400 sq km)
Population: 29,780,000
Capital: Tashkent,
pop. 2,227,000
Currency: Uzbekistani sum
Religions: Muslim (mostly Sunni), Eastern Orthodox
Languages: Uzbek, Russian, Tajik

Vanuatu

Area: 4,707 sq mi (12,190 sq km)
Population: 258,000
Capital: Port Vila, pop. 47,000
Currency: vatu
Religions: Presbyterian, Anglican, Roman Catholic, other Christian, indigenous beliefs
Languages: more than 100 local languages, pidgin (known as Bislama or Bichelama)

Vatican City

Area: 0.2 sq mi (0.4 sq km)
Population: 798
Capital: Vatican City, pop. 798
Currency: euro
Religion: Roman Catholic
Languages: Italian, Latin, French

Venezuela

Area: 352,144 sq mi
(912,050 sq km)
Population: 29,718,000
Capital: Caracas, pop. 3,242,000
Currency: bolivar
Religion: Roman Catholic
Languages: Spanish, numerous indigenous dialects

Vietnam

Area: 127,844 sq mi
(331,114 sq km)
Population: 88,984,000
Capital: Hanoi, pop. 2,955,000
Currency: dong
Religions: Buddhist, Roman Catholic
Languages: Vietnamese, English, French, Chinese, Khmer

Yemen

Area: 207,286 sq mi
(536,869 sq km)
Population: 25,569,000
Capital: Sanaa, pop. 2,419,000
Currency: Yemeni rial
Religions: Muslim, including Shaf'i (Sunni) and Zaydi (Shiite)
Language: Arabic

Zambia

Area: 290,586 sq mi
(752,614 sq km)
Population: 13,711,000
Capital: Lusaka, pop. 1,802,000
Currency: Zambian kwacha
Religions: Christian, Muslim, Hindu
Languages: English, Bemba, Kaonda, Lozi, Lunda, Luvale, Nyanja, Tonga, about 70 other indigenous languages

Zimbabwe

Area: 150,872 sq mi
(390,757 sq km)
Population: 12,620,000
Capital: Harare, pop. 1,542,000
Currency: Zimbabwean dollar
Religions: Syncretic (part Christian, part indigenous beliefs), Christian, indigenous beliefs
Languages: English, Shona, Sindebele, tribal dialects

VENEZUELA'S ANGEL FALLS—the highest waterfall in the world—is twice as tall as the EMPIRE STATE BUILDING.

THE POLITICAL UNITED STATES

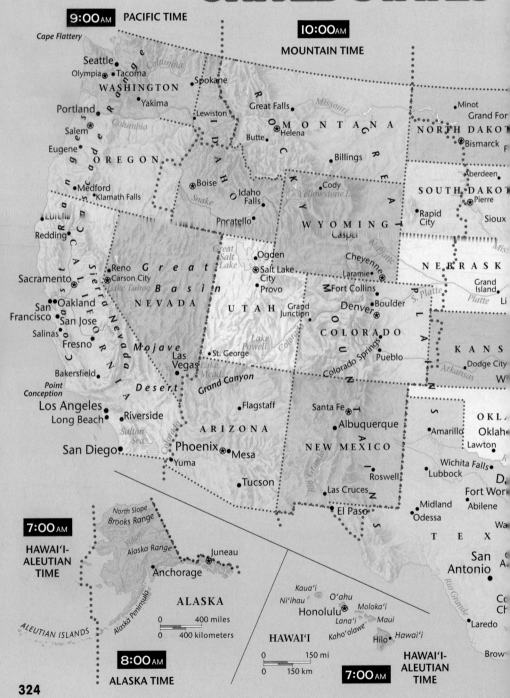

9:00 AM PACIFIC TIME

10:00 AM MOUNTAIN TIME

Cape Flattery

Seattle
Olympia • Tacoma
WASHINGTON
• Yakima
Portland
Salem
Eugene
OREGON
Medford
• Klamath Falls

Spokane
Lewiston
Great Falls •
MONTANA
Butte • Helena
• Billings

Minot
Grand For
NORTH DAKOT
• Bismarck

Boise
Idaho Falls
Pocatello
Snake
Cody
Yellowstone L.
WYOMING
Casper

Aberdeen
SOUTH DAKOT
• Pierre
Rapid City
Sioux

Redding
Reno
Carson City
Lake Tahoe
Great
Basin
NEVADA
Sacramento
San Francisco
Oakland
San Jose
Salinas
Fresno
Bakersfield
Point Conception
Los Angeles
Long Beach
Riverside
Salton Sea
San Diego

Great Salt Lake
Ogden
Salt Lake City
Provo
UTAH
Grand Junction
Lake Powell
Mojave
Las Vegas
Lake Mead
Desert
Grand Canyon
Flagstaff
ARIZONA
Phoenix • Mesa
Yuma
Tucson

Cheyenne
Laramie
Fort Collins
Denver • Boulder
COLORADO
Colorado Springs
Pueblo
S. Platte
N. Platte
Arkansas

NEBRASK
Grand Island
Platte
Li

KANS
Dodge City
W

Santa Fe
Albuquerque
NEW MEXICO
Las Cruces
El Paso
Roswell
Rio Grande

OKLA
Oklah
Lawton
Amarillo
Wichita Falls
Lubbock
Fort Wor
Midland Abilene
Odessa
Da
Wa
TEX
San Antonio
Co
Ch
Laredo
Brow

7:00 AM
HAWAI'I-ALEUTIAN TIME

North Slope
Brooks Range
Yukon
Alaska Range
Juneau
Anchorage
Alaska Peninsula
ALASKA
ALEUTIAN ISLANDS

0   400 miles
0   400 kilometers

Kaua'i
Ni'ihau O'ahu
Honolulu Moloka'i
Lana'i Maui
Kaho'olawe Hilo • Hawai'i
HAWAI'I

0   150 mi
0   150 km

HAWAI'I-ALEUTIAN TIME

8:00 AM ALASKA TIME

7:00 AM HAWAI'I-ALEUTIAN TIME

Like a giant quilt, the United States is made up of 50 states. Each is unique, but together they make a national fabric held together by a constitution and a federal government. State boundaries, outlined in dotted lines on the map, set apart internal political units within the country. The national capital—Washington, D.C.—is marked by a star in a double circle. The capital of each state is marked by a star in a single circle.

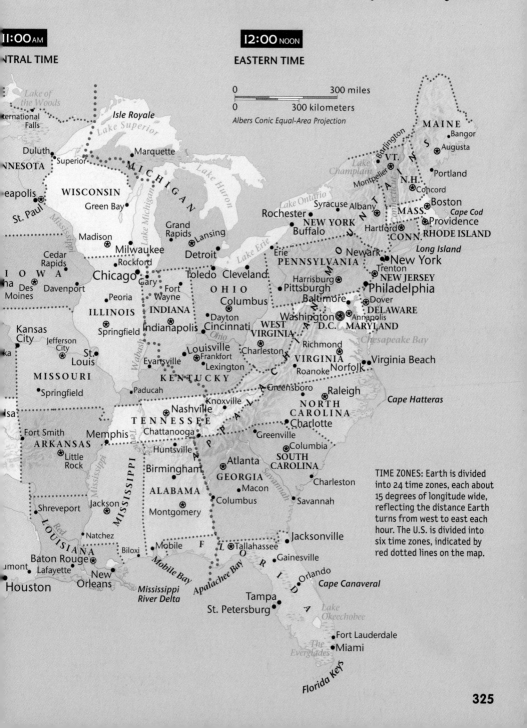

11:00 AM

NTRAL TIME

12:00 NOON

EASTERN TIME

0 — 300 miles
0 — 300 kilometers
Albers Conic Equal-Area Projection

Lake of the Woods · Isle Royale · MAINE · Bangor
ternational Falls · Lake Superior · Augusta
Duluth · Marquette · MICHIGAN · Lake Champlain · Burlington · VT. · Portland
NNESOTA · Superior · Montpelier · N.H. · Concord
eapolis · WISCONSIN · Green Bay · Lake Huron · Rochester · Syracuse · Albany · MASS. · Boston · Cape Cod
St. Paul · Madison · Grand Rapids · Lansing · NEW YORK · Buffalo · Hartford · Providence
Cedar Rapids · Milwaukee · Detroit · Lake Erie · Erie · PENNSYLVANIA · CONN. · RHODE ISLAND
I O W A · Rockford · Chicago · Toledo · Cleveland · Newark · Long Island
ha · Des Moines · Davenport · Peoria · Gary · Fort Wayne · O H I O · Harrisburg · Pittsburgh · Trenton · New York
Kansas City · ILLINOIS · INDIANA · Columbus · Dayton · Baltimore · NEW JERSEY · Philadelphia
ka · Jefferson City · Springfield · Indianapolis · Cincinnati · WEST · Washington · Dover · DELAWARE
St. Louis · Evansville · Louisville · Frankfort · VIRGINIA · D.C. · Annapolis · MARYLAND
MISSOURI · Lexington · Charleston · Richmond · Chesapeake Bay
Springfield · Paducah · KENTUCKY · VIRGINIA · Norfolk · Virginia Beach
sa · Knoxville · Roanoke · Greensboro · Raleigh · Cape Hatteras
Fort Smith · Nashville · NORTH CAROLINA · Charlotte
ARKANSAS · TENNESSEE · Chattanooga · Greenville
Little Rock · Huntsville · Columbia · SOUTH CAROLINA
Birmingham · Atlanta · Charleston
MISSISSIPPI · ALABAMA · GEORGIA · Macon · Savannah
Shreveport · Jackson · Columbus · Montgomery
Natchez · Mobile · Jacksonville
mont · LOUISIANA · Biloxi · Tallahassee · Gainesville
Baton Rouge · Mobile Bay · Apalachee Bay · Orlando · Cape Canaveral
Houston · New Orleans · Lafayette · Mississippi River Delta · Tampa · St. Petersburg · Lake Okeechobee
Fort Lauderdale · Miami · The Everglades · Florida Keys

TIME ZONES: Earth is divided into 24 time zones, each about 15 degrees of longitude wide, reflecting the distance Earth turns from west to east each hour. The U.S. is divided into six time zones, indicated by red dotted lines on the map.

THE PHYSICAL UNITED STATES

Mt. St. Helens +
8,366 ft
2,550 m

+ Mt. Rainier
14,411 ft
4,392 m

CASCADE RANGE

Snake

Columbia

Mt. Hood
11,239 ft
3,425 m

Great Sandy
Desert

Blue Mountains

Columbia Plateau

Flathead
Lake

Bitterroot Range

Salmon River
Mountains

Snake

Snake River Plain

Yellowstone
Lake

ROCKY

Milk

Fort Peck
Lake

Missouri

Yellowstone

Absaroka Range

Bighorn Mts.

Grand
Teton
13,770 ft
4,197 m

Geographical
Center of the 50
United States

Little Missouri

Missouri

Heart

White
Butte
3,506 ft
1,069 m

Lake
Sakakawea

Lake
Oahe

Missouri

Black
Hills

Harney
Peak
7,242 ft
2,207 m

White

Great Divide
Basin

Uinta Mts.

Great
Salt
Lake

Wasatch Range

Sacramento Valley

Sierra Nevada

San Joaquin Valley

San Joaquin

Lake
Tahoe

Great

Basin

Mt. Whitney
14,494 ft
4,418 m

Appalachian

Death
Valley

Mojave

Desert

Lowest Point in
North America
-282 ft, -86 m

Lake
Powell

Colorado

Lake
Mead

Grand
Canyon

Painted Desert

Colorado

Plateau

Mt. Elbert
14,433 ft
4,399 m

+ Pikes Peak
14,110 ft
4,301 m

San Juan Mts.

Front Range

Laramie Mts.

M O U N T A I N S

Niobrara

N. Platte

Sand Hills

Geographical Center
of the 48 Contiguous
United States

S. Platte

Smoky

Arkansas

Red Hills

Black Mesa
4,973 ft
1,516 m

Canadian

Cim

Channel
Islands

Salton
Sea

Imperial
Valley

Colorado

Humphreys Peak +
12,637 ft
3,852 m

Gila
Sonoran

Desert

Salt

Rio Grande

Sangre de Cristo Mts.

Llano
Estacado

Sacramento Mts.

Guadalupe Peak
8,749 ft
2,667 m

Pecos

Edwards
Plateau

Bra

0   400 miles
0   400 kilometers

North Slope
Brooks Range

Yukon

Mt. McKinley (Denali)
20,320 ft, 6,194 m +
Highest Point in
North America

Alaska Range

Alexander
Archipelago

Aleutian Islands

Alaska Peninsula

Kaua'i

Ni'ihau

O'ahu

Moloka'i

Lana'i   Maui

Kaho'olawe

Mauna Kea
13,679 ft
4,169 m

Hawai'i

0   150 miles
0   150 kilometers

ALASKA AND HAWAII:
In addition to the states
located on the main landmass,
the U.S. has two states—Alaska
and Hawaii—that are not directly
connected to the other 48 states.
If Alaska and Hawaii were shown in
their correct relative sizes and locations, the map would not fit on the pages.

Rio Grande

Stretching from the Atlantic Ocean in the east to the Pacific Ocean in the west, the United States is the third largest country (by area) in the world. Its physical diversity ranges from mountains to fertile plains and dry deserts. Shading on the map indicates changes in elevation, while colors show different vegetation patterns.

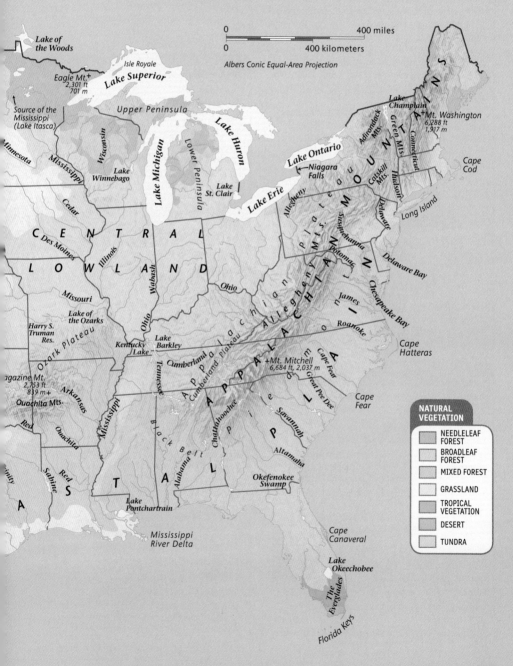

0   400 miles
0   400 kilometers

Albers Conic Equal-Area Projection

Lake of the Woods

Isle Royale

Eagle Mt.+
2,301 ft
701 m

Lake Superior

Source of the Mississippi
(Lake Itasca)

Minnesota

Mississippi

Wisconsin

Upper Peninsula

Lake Michigan

Lower Peninsula

Lake Huron

Lake Winnebago

Lake St. Clair

Lake Ontario

←Niagara Falls

Lake Erie

Lake Champlain

Adirondack Mts.

Green Mts.

+Mt. Washington
6,288 ft
1,917 m

Connecticut

MOUNTAINS

Cape Cod

Catskill Mts.

Hudson

Long Island

Allegheny Plateau

APPALACHIAN

Cedar

CENTRAL

Des Moines

Illinois

Wabash

Ohio

LOWLAND

Missouri

Lake of the Ozarks

Ohio

Harry S. Truman Res.

Ozark Plateau

Kentucky Lake

Lake Barkley

Tennessee

Allegheny Mts.

Susquehanna

Potomac

Delaware

Delaware Bay

James

Chesapeake Bay

Roanoke

Cape Hatteras

Magazine Mt.
2,753 ft
839 m+

Arkansas

Ouachita Mts.

Red

Ouachita

Sabine

Mississippi

Cumberland Mts.

Cumberland Plateau

Appalachian

+Mt. Mitchell
6,684 ft, 2,037 m

Chattahoochee

Black Belt

Alabama

Savannah

Altamaha

Great Pee Dee

Cape Fear

Cape Fear

COASTAL

PLAIN

Okefenokee Swamp

Lake Pontchartrain

Mississippi River Delta

Cape Canaveral

Lake Okeechobee

The Everglades

Florida Keys

NATURAL VEGETATION

- NEEDLELEAF FOREST
- BROADLEAF FOREST
- MIXED FOREST
- GRASSLAND
- TROPICAL VEGETATION
- DESERT
- TUNDRA

THE STATES

From sea to shining sea, the United States of America is a nation of diversity. In the more than 235 years since its creation, the nation has grown to become home to a wide range of peoples, industries, and cultures. The following pages present a general overview of all 50 states in the U.S.

The country is generally divided into five large regions: the Northeast, the Southeast, the Midwest, the Southwest, and the West. Though loosely defined, these zones tend to share important similarities, including climate, history, and geography. The color key below provides a guide to which states are in each region.

Flags of each state and highlights of demography and industry are also included. These details offer a brief overview of each state.

In addition, each state's official flower and bird are identified.

Color Key by Region

Arizona

Area: 113,998 sq mi (295,256 sq km)
Population: 6,482,505
Capital: Phoenix, pop. 1,469,471
Largest city: Phoenix, pop. 1,469,471
Industry: Real estate, manufactured goods, retail, state and local government, transportation and public utilities, wholesale trade, health services
State flower/bird: Saguaro/cactus wren

Arkansas

Area: 53,179 sq mi (137,732 sq km)
Population: 2,937,979
Capital: Little Rock, pop. 195,314
Largest city: Little Rock, pop. 195,314
Industry: Services, food processing, paper products, transportation, metal products, machinery, electronics
State flower/bird: Apple blossom/mockingbird

The FIDDLE is the official state MUSICAL INSTRUMENT of ARKANSAS.

Alabama

Area: 52,419 sq mi (135,765 sq km)
Population: 4,802,740
Capital: Montgomery, pop. 208,182
Largest city: Birmingham, pop. 212,413
Industry: Retail and wholesale trade, services, government, finance, insurance, real estate, transportation, construction, communication
State flower/bird: Camellia/northern flicker

Alaska

Area: 663,267 sq mi (1,717,862 sq km)
Population: 722,718
Capital: Juneau, pop. 32,164
Largest city: Anchorage, pop. 295,570
Industry: Petroleum products, government, services, trade
State flower/bird: Forget-me-not/willow ptarmigan

California

Area: 163,696 sq mi (423,972 sq km)
Population: 37,691,912
Capital: Sacramento, pop. 472,178
Largest city: Los Angeles, pop. 3,819,702
Industry: Electronic components and equipment, computers and computer software, tourism, food processing, entertainment, clothing
State flower/bird: Golden poppy/California quail

Colorado

Area: 104,094 sq mi (269,602 sq km)
Population: 5,116,796
Capital: Denver, pop. 619,968
Largest city: Denver, pop. 619,968
Industry: Real estate, government, durable goods, communications, health and other services, nondurable goods, transportation
State flower/bird: Columbine/lark bunting

Connecticut

Area: 5,543 sq mi (14,357 sq km)
Population: 3,580,709
Capital: Hartford, pop. 124,867
Largest city: Bridgeport, pop. 145,638
Industry: Transportation equipment, metal products, machinery, electrical equipment, printing and publishing, scientific instruments, insurance
State flower/bird: Mountain laurel/robin

Delaware

Area: 2,489 sq mi (6,447 sq km)
Population: 907,135
Capital: Dover, pop. 36,560
Largest city: Wilmington, pop. 71,305
Industry: Food processing, chemicals, rubber and plastic products, scientific instruments, printing and publishing, financial services
State flower/bird: Peach blossom/blue hen chicken

Florida

Area: 65,755 sq mi (170,304 sq km)
Population: 19,057,542
Capital: Tallahassee, pop. 182,965
Largest city: Jacksonville, pop. 827,908
Industry: Tourism, health services, business services, communications, banking, electronic equipment, insurance
State flower/bird: Orange blossom/mockingbird

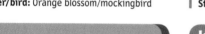

APOLLO 11—
the first MISSION TO THE MOON— BLASTED OFF from FLORIDA in 1969.

Georgia

Area: 59,425 sq mi (153,910 sq km)
Population: 9,815,210
Capital: Atlanta, pop. 432,427
Largest city: Atlanta, pop. 432,427
Industry: Textiles and clothing, transportation equipment, food processing, paper products, chemicals, electrical equipment, tourism
State flower/bird: Cherokee rose/brown thrasher

Hawaii

Area: 10,931 sq mi (28,311 sq km)
Population: 1,374,810
Capital: Honolulu, pop. 340,936
Largest city: Honolulu, pop. 340,936
Industry: Tourism, trade, finance, food processing, petroleum refining, stone, clay, glass products
State flower/bird: Hibiscus/Hawaiian goose (nene)

Idaho

Area: 83,570 sq mi (216,447 sq km)
Population: 1,584,985
Capital: Boise, pop. 210,145
Largest city: Boise, pop. 210,145
Industry: Electronics and computer equipment, tourism, food processing, forest products, mining
State flower/bird: Syringa (Lewis's mock orange)/ mountain bluebird

Illinois

Area: 57,914 sq mi (149,998 sq km)
Population: 12,869,257
Capital: Springfield, pop. 117,076
Largest city: Chicago, pop. 2,707,120
Industry: Industrial machinery, electronic equipment, food processing, chemicals, metals, printing and publishing, rubber and plastics, motor vehicles
State flower/bird: Violet/cardinal

Indiana

Area: 36,418 sq mi (94,322 sq km)
Population: 6,516,922
Capital: Indianapolis, pop. 827,609
Largest city: Indianapolis, pop. 827,609
Industry: Transportation equipment, steel, pharmaceutical and chemical products, machinery, petroleum, coal
State flower/bird: Peony/cardinal

Iowa

Area: 56,272 sq mi (145,743 sq km)
Population: 3,062,309
Capital: Des Moines, pop. 206,599
Largest city: Des Moines, pop. 206,599
Industry: Real estate, health services, industrial machinery, food processing, construction
State flower/bird: Wild rose/American goldfinch

 Midwest Southwest West

Kansas

Area: 82,277 sq mi (213,097 sq km)
Population: 2,871,238
Capital: Topeka, pop. 128,188
Largest city: Wichita, pop. 384,445
Industry: Aircraft manufacturing, transportation equipment, construction, food processing, printing and publishing, health care
State flower/bird: Sunflower/western meadowlark

Kentucky

Area: 40,409 sq mi (104,659 sq km)
Population: 4,369,356
Capital: Frankfort, pop. 25,583
Largest city: Louisville, pop. 602,011
Industry: Manufacturing, services, government, finance, insurance, real estate, retail trade, transportation, wholesale trade, construction, mining
State flower/bird: Goldenrod/cardinal

Louisiana

Area: 51,840 sq mi (134,265 sq km)
Population: 4,574,836
Capital: Baton Rouge, pop. 230,139
Largest city: New Orleans, pop. 360,740
Industry: Chemicals, petroleum products, food processing, health services, tourism, oil and natural gas extraction, paper products
State flower/bird: Magnolia/brown pelican

Maine

Area: 35,385 sq mi (91,646 sq km)
Population: 1,328,188
Capital: Augusta, pop. 19,103
Largest city: Portland, pop. 66,363
Industry: Health services, tourism, forest products, leather products, electrical equipment
State flower/bird: White pine cone and tassel/chickadee

Maryland

Area: 12,407 sq mi (32,133 sq km)
Population: 5,828,289
Capital: Annapolis, pop. 38,880
Largest city: Baltimore, pop. 619,493
Industry: Real estate, federal government, health services, business services, engineering services
State flower/bird: Black-eyed Susan/northern (Baltimore) oriole

Massachusetts

Area: 10,555 sq mi (27,336 sq km)
Population: 6,587,536
Capital: Boston, pop. 625,087
Largest city: Boston, pop. 625,087
Industry: Electrical equipment, machinery, metal products, scientific instruments, printing and publishing, tourism
State flower/bird: Mayflower/chickadee

Michigan

Area: 96,716 sq mi (250,495 sq km)
Population: 9,876,187
Capital: Lansing, pop. 114,605
Largest city: Detroit, pop. 706,585
Industry: Motor vehicles and parts, machinery, metal products, office furniture, tourism, chemicals
State flower/bird: Apple blossom/robin

Minnesota

Area: 86,939 sq mi (225,172 sq km)
Population: 5,344,861
Capital: St. Paul, pop. 288,448
Largest city: Minneapolis, pop. 387,753
Industry: Real estate, banking and insurance, industrial machinery, printing and publishing, food processing, scientific equipment
State flower/bird: Showy lady's slipper/common loon

Mississippi

Area: 48,430 sq mi (125,434 sq km)
Population: 2,978,512
Capital: Jackson, pop. 175,561
Largest city: Jackson, pop. 175,561
Industry: Petroleum products, health services, electronic equipment, transportation, banking, forest products, communications
State flower/bird: Magnolia/mockingbird

The country's **FIRST UMBRELLA** factory opened **IN MARYLAND** in 1828.

COLOR KEY ● Northeast ● Southeast

Missouri

Area: 69,704 sq mi (180,534 sq km)
Population: 6,010,688
Capital: Jefferson City, pop. 43,332
Largest city: Kansas City, pop. 463,202
Industry: Transportation equipment, food processing, chemicals, electrical equipment, metal products
State flower/bird: Hawthorn/eastern bluebird

Montana

Area: 147,042 sq mi (380,840 sq km)
Population: 998,199
Capital: Helena, pop. 28,592
Largest city: Billings, pop. 105,636
Industry: Forest products, food processing, mining, construction, tourism
State flower/bird: Bitterroot/western meadowlark

1. Montana's 200-foot (61-m)-long Roe River is one of the world's shortest rivers.
2. The temperature in Loma, Montana, once rose 103°F (41°C) in 24 hours.
3. Montana's official state animal is the grizzly bear.
4. Glacier National Park in Montana has 131 named lakes.
5. A mummified, 77-million-year-old duck-billed dinosaur was discovered in Montana in 2000.

Nebraska

Area: 77,354 sq mi (200,346 sq km)
Population: 1,842,641
Capital: Lincoln, pop. 262,341
Largest city: Omaha, pop. 415,068
Industry: Food processing, machinery, electrical equipment, printing and publishing
State flower/bird: Goldenrod/western meadowlark

Nevada

Area: 110,561 sq mi (286,352 sq km)
Population: 2,723,322
Capital: Carson City, pop. 55,439
Largest city: Las Vegas, pop. 589,317
Industry: Tourism and gaming, mining, printing and publishing, food processing, electrical equipment
State flower/bird: Sagebrush/mountain bluebird

New Hampshire

Area: 9,350 sq mi (24,216 sq km)
Population: 1,318,194
Capital: Concord, pop. 42,733
Largest city: Manchester, pop. 109,830
Industry: Machinery, electronics, metal products
State flower/bird: Purple lilac/purple finch

New Jersey

Area: 8,721 sq mi (22,588 sq km)
Population: 8,821,155
Capital: Trenton, pop. 84,899
Largest city: Newark, pop. 277,540
Industry: Machinery, electronics, metal products, chemicals
State flower/bird: Violet/American goldfinch

New Mexico

Area: 121,590 sq mi (314,917 sq km)
Population: 2,082,224
Capital: Santa Fe, pop. 68,642
Largest city: Albuquerque, pop. 552,804
Industry: Electronic equipment, state and local government, real estate, business services, federal government, oil and gas extraction, health services
State flower/bird: Yucca/roadrunner

New York

Area: 54,556 sq mi (141,300 sq km)
Population: 19,465,197
Capital: Albany, pop. 97,660
Largest city: New York City, pop. 8,244,910
Industry: Printing and publishing, machinery, computer products, finance, tourism
State flower/bird: Rose/eastern bluebird

● Midwest   ● Southwest   ● West

North Carolina

Area: 53,819 sq mi (139,390 sq km)
Population: 9,656,401
Capital: Raleigh, pop. 416,468
Largest city: Charlotte, pop. 751,087
Industry: Real estate, health services, chemicals, tobacco products, finance, textiles
State flower/bird: Flowering dogwood/cardinal

North Dakota

Area: 70,700 sq mi (183,113 sq km)
Population: 683,932
Capital: Bismarck, pop. 62,665
Largest city: Fargo, pop. 107,349
Industry: Services, government, finance, construction, transportation, oil and gas
State flower/bird: Wild prairie rose/western meadowlark

Ohio

Area: 44,825 sq mi (116,097 sq km)
Population: 11,544,951
Capital: Columbus, pop. 797,434
Largest city: Columbus, pop. 797,434
Industry: Transportation equipment, metal products, machinery, food processing, electrical equipment
State flower/bird: Scarlet carnation/cardinal

PROFESSIONAL BASEBALL was first played in Cincinnati, Ohio.

Oklahoma

Area: 69,898 sq mi (181,036 sq km)
Population: 3,791,508
Capital: Oklahoma City, pop. 591,967
Largest city: Oklahoma City, pop. 591,967
Industry: Manufacturing, services, government, finance, insurance, real estate
State flower/bird: Mistletoe/scissor-tailed flycatcher

Oregon

Area: 98,381 sq mi (254,806 sq km)
Population: 3,871,859
Capital: Salem, pop. 156,244
Largest city: Portland, pop. 593,820
Industry: Real estate, retail and wholesale trade, electronic equipment, health services, construction, forest products, business services
State flower/bird: Oregon grape/western meadowlark

Pennsylvania

Area: 46,055 sq mi (119,283 sq km)
Population: 12,742,886
Capital: Harrisburg, pop. 49,673
Largest city: Philadelphia, pop. 1,536,471
Industry: Machinery, printing and publishing, forest products, metal products
State flower/bird: Mountain laurel/ruffed grouse

Rhode Island

Area: 1,545 sq mi (4,002 sq km)
Population: 1,051,302
Capital: Providence, pop. 178,053
Largest city: Providence, pop. 178,053
Industry: Health services, business services, silver and jewelry products, metal products
State flower/bird: Violet/Rhode Island red

South Carolina

Area: 32,020 sq mi (82,932 sq km)
Population: 4,679,230
Capital: Columbia, pop. 130,591
Largest city: Columbia, pop. 130,591
Industry: Service industries, tourism, chemicals, textiles, machinery, forest products
State flower/bird: Yellow jessamine/Carolina wren

South Dakota

Area: 77,117 sq mi (199,732 sq km)
Population: 824,082
Capital: Pierre, pop. 13,860
Largest city: Sioux Falls, pop. 156,592
Industry: Finance, services, manufacturing, government, retail trade, transportation and utilities, wholesale trade, construction, mining
State flower/bird: Pasqueflower/ring-necked pheasant

 **COLOR KEY** Northeast Southeast

Tennessee

Area: 42,143 sq mi (109,151 sq km)
Population: 6,403,353
Capital: Nashville, pop. 609,644
Largest city: Memphis, pop. 652,050
Industry: Service industries, chemicals, transportation equipment, processed foods, machinery
State flower/bird: Iris/mockingbird

Texas

Area: 268,581 sq mi (695,624 sq km)
Population: 25,674,681
Capital: Austin, pop. 820,611
Largest city: Houston, pop. 2,145,146
Industry: Chemicals, machinery, electronics and computers, food products, petroleum and natural gas, transportation equipment
State flower/bird: Bluebonnet/mockingbird

TEXAS is the only state that allows residents to VOTE FROM SPACE.

Utah

Area: 84,899 sq mi (219,888 sq km)
Population: 2,817,222
Capital: Salt Lake City, pop. 189,899
Largest city: Salt Lake City, pop. 189,899
Industry: Government, manufacturing, real estate, construction, health services, business services, banking
State flower/bird: Sego lily/California gull

Vermont

Area: 9,614 sq mi (24,901 sq km)
Population: 626,431
Capital: Montpelier, pop. 7,868
Largest city: Burlington, pop. 42,645
Industry: Health services, tourism, finance, real estate, computer components, electrical parts, printing and publishing, machine tools
State flower/bird: Red clover/hermit thrush

Virginia

Area: 42,774 sq mi (110,785 sq km)
Population: 8,096,604
Capital: Richmond, pop. 205,533
Largest city: Virginia Beach, pop. 442,707
Industry: Food processing, communication and electronic equipment, transportation equipment, printing, shipbuilding, textiles
State flower/bird: Flowering dogwood/cardinal

Washington

Area: 71,300 sq mi (184,666 sq km)
Population: 6,830,038
Capital: Olympia, pop. 47,266
Largest city: Seattle, pop. 620,778
Industry: Aerospace, tourism, food processing, forest products, paper products, industrial machinery, printing and publishing, metals, computer software
State flower/bird: Coast rhododendron/Amer. goldfinch

West Virginia

Area: 24,230 sq mi (62,755 sq km)
Population: 1,855,364
Capital: Charleston, pop. 51,177
Largest city: Charleston, pop. 51,177
Industry: Tourism, coal mining, chemicals, metal manufacturing, forest products, stone, clay, oil, glass products
State flower/bird: Rhododendron/cardinal

Wisconsin

Area: 65,498 sq mi (169,639 sq km)
Population: 5,711,767
Capital: Madison, pop. 236,901
Largest city: Milwaukee, pop. 597,867
Industry: Industrial machinery, paper products, food processing, metal products, electronic equipment, transportation
State flower/bird: Wood violet/robin

Wyoming

Area: 97,814 sq mi (253,337 sq km)
Population: 568,158
Capital: Cheyenne, pop. 60,096
Largest city: Cheyenne, pop. 60,096
Industry: Oil and natural gas, mining, generation of electricity, chemicals, tourism
State flower/bird: Indian paintbrush/western meadowlark

 ● Midwest ● Southwest ● West

STUMP YOUR PARENTS

GEOGRAPHY ROCKS QUIZ

Are your parents geography geniuses? Quiz them on this chapter's content to measure their worldly knowledge.

ANSWERS BELOW

1 There are almost _____ countries in the world.
- **a.** 170
- **b.** 200
- **c.** 285
- **d.** 17 million

2 A 500-carat diamond was recently found in which country?
- **a.** Botswana
- **b.** Canada
- **c.** South Africa
- **d.** Blingtown

3 Where is "James Bond Island"?
- **a.** United Kingdom
- **b.** Maldives
- **c.** Thailand
- **d.** Hollywood

4 The 56-foot (17-m) Larry the Lobster is a popular attraction in _____.
- **a.** Australia
- **b.** Canada
- **c.** U.S.A.
- **d.** Bikini Bottom

5 True or false? Monaco is the world's smallest country.

6 The Galápagos Islands are located off the coast of which country?
- **a.** Madagascar
- **b.** Ecuador
- **c.** Peru
- **d.** El Salvador

ANSWERS:
1. b; 2. c; 3. c; 4. a; 5. False. The smallest country is Vatican City; 6. b

HOMEWORK HELP

Finding Your Way Around

Every map has a story to tell, but first you have to know how to read one. Maps represent information by using a language of symbols. Knowing how to read these symbols provides access to a wide range of information. Look at the scale and compass rose or arrow to understand distance and direction (see box below).

To find out what each symbol on a map means, you must use the key. It's your secret decoder— identifying information by each symbol on the map.

90°N (North Pole)

Latitude

Longitude

LATITUDE AND LONGITUDE

Latitude and longitude lines (above) help us determine locations on Earth. Every place on Earth has a special address called absolute location. Imaginary lines called lines of latitude run west to east, parallel to the Equator. These lines measure distance in degrees north or south from the Equator (0° latitude) to the North Pole (90°N) or to the South Pole (90°S). One degree of latitude is approximately 70 miles (113 km).

Lines of longitude run north to south, meeting at the Poles. These lines measure distance in degrees east or west from 0° longitude (prime meridian) to 180° longitude. The prime meridian runs through Greenwich, England.

SCALE AND DIRECTION

The scale on a map can be shown as a fraction, as words, or as a line or bar. It relates distance on the map to distance in the real world. Sometimes the scale identifies the type of map projection. Maps may include an arrow or compass rose to indicate north on the map.

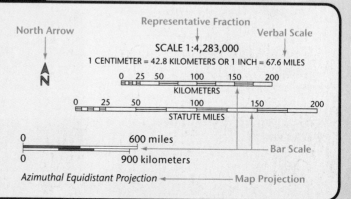

North Arrow

Representative Fraction

Verbal Scale

SCALE 1:4,283,000
1 CENTIMETER = 42.8 KILOMETERS OR 1 INCH = 67.6 MILES

N

0   25   50   100   150   200
KILOMETERS

0   25   50   100   150   200
STATUTE MILES

0   600 miles
0   900 kilometers

Bar Scale

Azimuthal Equidistant Projection ◄——— Map Projection

GAME ANSWERS

What in the World?, page 161

Top row: **tiger, octopus, butterfly.**
Middle row: **jellyfish, snail, chameleon.**
Bottom row: **turtle, hermit crab, zebras.**

Movie Matches, page 163

A–I, B–L, C–J, D–N, E–V, F–X, G–S, H–Q, M–P, O–Y, R–U, T–W.
K is the one whose best friend is stuck in line at the restroom.

Signs of the Times, page 164

Sign **#4** is fake.

Picture-Perfect Fun Park,
pages 152–153

Animal Jam, page 154

Crazy Colors, pages 166–167

We Gave It a Swirl, page 157

1. ladybug, 2. chimpanzee, 3. snake, 4. giraffe, 5. monarch butterfly.

Find the Hidden Animals,
pages 158–159

1. C, 2. J, 3. H, 4. A, 5. K, 6. D, 7. G, 8. I, 9. F, 10. E, 11. B.

Bark Park, page 168

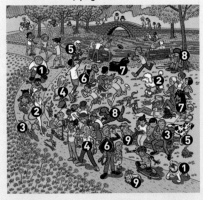

Your World 2014 (8–17)
p. 14 "Floating Vacation" by Cathy Lu; all other articles in section by Sarah Wassner Flynn

Awesome Adventure (18–35)
pp. 20–21 "Dare to Explore" by C.M. Tomlin and Sarah Wassner Flynn; p. 22 "Island Adventure" by Catherine D. Hughes; p. 23 "Mystery in the Skies" by Sarah Wassner Flynn; pp. 24–25 "Crystal Cave" by Jennifer Cutraro; p. 27 "Deep-Sea Explorer" by Scott Elder; p. 28 "Avalanche!" by Scott Elder; p. 29 "How to Survive..." by Rachel Buchholz; pp. 30–31 "Extreme Action Sports" by Sarah Wassner Flynn; p. 33 "How to Take Great Photos" excerpted from *The National Geographic Kids Photo Field Guide* by Neil Johnson

Amazing Animals (36–101)
pp. 38–39 "What Is Taxonomy?" & "Vertebrates"/"Invertebrates" by Susan K. Donnelly; pp. 40–41 "Giraffe Hangs with Goat" & "Dog Loves Owl" by Kitson Jazynka; p. 41 "Raccoon Adopts Cat" by C.M. Tomlin; p. 42 "Critter Creations" by Kitson Jazynka; p. 43 "Animal Myths Busted" by C.M. Tomlin; pp. 44–45 "Play Like a Dolphin" by Elizabeth Carney; pp. 46–47 "Ocean Superstars" by Ruth A. Musgrave; pp. 48–51 "Meet the Penguins" and "Supershark Awards" by Ruth A. Musgrave; p. 52 "Mystery of the Disappearing Frogs" by Fiona Sundquist; p. 53 "5 Cool Things About Koalas" by Crispin Boyer; pp. 54–55 "The Fox Next Door" by Karen De Seve; p. 56 "Meerkat City" by Graeme Stemp-Morlock; p. 57 "Wild Dogs of Africa" by Crispin Boyer; pp. 58–59 "6 Tips Every Polar Bear Should Know" by David George Gordon; p. 60 "Rock-a-Bye Monkey" by Ruth A. Musgrave; p. 61 "Will the Red Panda Survive?" by Fiona Sunquist; p. 61 "Saving the Blue Iguana" by Jennifer Weeks; p. 62 "5 Cool Things About Harp Seals" by Sharon Thompson; p. 63 "Panda Shake-Up" by Ruth A. Musgrave; pp. 64–65 "Horse" and "Serval" by Scott Elder, "Harbor Seal" by Kitson Jazynka; pp. 66–67 "Big Cats" by Elizabeth Carney; p. 68 "Cheetahs: Built for Speed" by Fiona Sunquist; p. 69 "Snow Leopard Secrets" by Karen De Seve; pp. 70–71 "Think Like a Tiger" by Aline Alexander Newman; p. 72 "Leopards: Nature's Supercats" by Crispin Boyer; p. 73 "Lions of the Kalahari Desert" by Fiona Sunquist; p. 74 "5 Cool Things About Butterflies" by Erin Whitmer; pp. 76–77 "Bizarre Insects" by Sarah Wassner Flynn; pp. 78–79 "5 Silly Pet Tricks" by Margaret J. Krauss; pp. 80–81 "Lifestyles of the Rich and Furry" by Bridget A.

English; pp. 82–89 "20 Cutest Animals of 2014" by Sarah Wassner Flynn, Jen Rini, and Elisabeth Deffner; p. 90 "What Killed the Dinosaurs?" nationalgeographic.com; pp. 90–93 "Prehistoric Time Line" & "Who Ate What?" by Susan K. Donnelly; p. 92 "What Color Were Dinosaurs?" by Sarah Wassner Flynn; p. 94 "Dino Classification" by Susan K. Donnelly; p. 99 "Flying Monsters" by Johnna Rizzo

Wonders of Nature (102–123)
p. 104 "Weather and Climate" by Mark Bockenhauer; p. 105 "Weather Comparisons" by Kathy Furgang; pp. 106–107 "Freaky Weather" by Douglas E. Richards; p. 108 "Hurricane" by Renee Skelton; pp. 109–110 "Tornado!" & "Wildfire!" by Sarah Wassner Flynn; p. 111 "Tsunami Heroes" by Scott Elder; pp. 112–113 "The Water Cycle" by Kathy Furgang; p. 116 "Coral Reefs" by Crispin Boyer; p. 118 & pp. 120–121 "How Does Your Garden Grow?" & "Biomes" by Susan K. Donnelly

Culture Connection (124–149)
p. 128 "What's Your Chinese Horoscope?" by Geoff Williams; p. 130 "Halloween Pet Parade" by Sarah Youngson and Kait Gallagher; pp. 134–135 "Handimals" by B.F. Summers and Kelley Miller; pp. 136–137 "We Are Actually Wax" by Zachary Petit; pp. 138–139 "Piece of Cake" by Sean McCollum; p. 140 "Money and Luck" by Kristin Baird Rattini; pp. 144–145 "World Religions" by Mark Bockenhauer; pp. 146–147 "Mythology" by Susan K. Donnelly

Super Science (170–205)
pp. 172–173 "...Big Bang" by David A. Aguilar; p. 172 "Powerful Particle" by Sarah Wassner Flynn; p. 175 "The Three Domains of Life" by Susan K. Donnelly; pp. 178–179 "Your Amazing Brain" & "Your Amazing Eyes" by Douglas E. Richards; p. 180 "All About You: Birth Order" by Amanda Pressner; p. 181 "All About You: Favorite Snack" by Sarah Wassner Flynn; p. 183 "Body Myths Busted" by Sarah Wassner Flynn; p. 186 "Dwarf Planets" by Sarah Wassner Flynn; p. 187 "Super Sun!" by Sarah Wassner Flynn; pp. 189–191 "Solar and Lunar Eclipses" & "Constellations" by Sarah Wassner Flynn; pp. 193–197 "Rock Stars," "It's a Rocky World!" & "Birthstones" by Steve Tomecek; pp. 198–199 "Cool Inventions" by Cathy Lu; p. 200 "Space Robots" by Douglas E. Richards; p. 201 "GPS" by Sarah Wassner Flynn; pp. 202–203 "Animal Killers Busted!" by Kristin Baird Rattini

Going Green (206–223)
pp. 208–209 "Animal Rescues" by Jennifer Weeks and Scott Elder; pp.

210–211 "Green Inventions" by Cathy Lu; pp. 212–213 "Green Houses" by Sarah Wassner Flynn; pp. 214–215 "Global Warming," by Sarah Wassner Flynn; pp. 216–217 "Pollution," "Declining Biodiversity," & "Habitat Destruction" by David George Gordon; pp. 218–219 "World Energy & Minerals" by Mark Bockenhauer

History Happens (224–255)
pp. 226–227 "Packing for the Afterlife" by Crispin Boyer; pp. 228–229 "The Lost City of Pompeii" by Kristin Baird Rattini; p. 233 "5 Cool Things About Ancient Greece" by Sarah Wassner Flynn; p. 234 "Mystery of the Buried Treasure" by Molly Lyons; p. 235 "Curse of the Hope Diamond" by Kristin Baird Rattini; pp. 236–237 "Secrets of the *Titanic*" by Kristin Baird Rattini; pp. 238–239 "War!" by Susan K. Donnelly/Sarah Wassner Flynn; p. 239 "World War I 100th Anniversary" by Sarah Wassner Flynn; pp. 240, 242–243 by Susan K. Donnelly; p. 241 "George Washington's Real Look" by Cathy Lu; p. 249 "The Indian Experience" by Martha B. Sharma; pp. 250–251 "Civil Rights" by Susan K. Donnelly/Sarah Wassner Flynn; pp. 252–253 "Women Fighting for Equality" by Sarah Wassner Flynn

Geography Rocks (256–337)
pp. 258–263 by Mark Bockenhauer; pp. 264–265 "Wacky World" by Elisabeth Deffner; p. 266 "Zany Hotels" by Kristin Baird Rattini; pp. 268–269 "Is It Real or Is It Legoland?" by Zachary Petit; pp. 270–297 by Sarah Wassner Flynn, Mark Bockenhauer, and Susan K. Donnelly; pp. 298–323 "You Are There!" by Sarah Wassner Flynn; p. 335 "Destination Guide: Washington, D.C." by Sarah Wassner Flynn

All "Homework Help" by Vicki Ariyasu

com; 87, AP Images/Virginamerica/Rex Features; 88 (UPLE), Cabrillo Marine Aquarium/Caters News; 88 (UPRT), Karl Ammann/npl/MP; 88 (LO), Tui De Roy/MP; 89 (UP), Donald M. Jones/MP; 89 (LO), Rina Deych; 90 (UP), Chris Butler/Science Photo Library/PR 90 (CTR), Publiphoto/PR 90 (LO), Pixeldust Studios/NGS; 91 (B), Laurie O'Keefe/PR 91 (C), Chris Butler/PR 91 (D), Publiphoto/PR 91 (A), Publiphoto/PR 91 (E), image courtesy of Project Exploration; 92-93 (CTR), Pixeldust Studios/NGS; 92 (LE), NGS; 93 (UP), Ira Block; 93 (UP RT), Ira Block; 94 (UP), Paul B. Moore/SS; 94 (LO), Andrea Meyer/SS; 95, Franco Tempesta; 96-97, Franco Tempesta; 98 (UP), Julius T. Csotonyi; 98 (LOLE), Nobumichi Tamura; 98 (LORT), Robert Nicholls/AFP/GI/Newscom; 99 (UPLE), Atlantic Productions/ZOO; 99 (LORT), Atlantic Productions/ZOO; 99 (LOLE), Atlantic Productions/ZOO; 99 (BACK), Jason Edwards/NGS; 99 (UPRT), Atlantic Productions/ZOO; 100, Eric Isselée/SS; 100, Paul Nicklen/NGS; 100, Ross Parry; 100, Franco Tempesta; 101, Barry Mansell/NPL/MP

Wonders of Nature (102–123)

102-103, Luka Esenko/National Geographic My Shot; 104, Steve Mann/SS; 105 (UPLE), AISPIX/SS; 105 (UPRT), tiorna/SS; 105 (LE CTR), Warren Faidley/Oxford Scientific/PhotoLibrary/GI; 105 (RT CTR), Sergei Bachlakov/SS; 105 (LOLE), John Burcham/NGS; 105 (LORT), Jessie Jean/Iconica/GI; 106 (LO RT), Spectrum Photofile.com; 106 (LOLE), Photo Researchers RM/GI; 107 (UP), U.S. Navy photo; 107 (LO LE), Sygma/CO; 107 (LO RT), AP Images; 107 (CTR), Jim Demaske/St. Petersburg Times/ZUMAPRESS/Newscom.com; 108, NOAA; 109 (BACK), Carsten Peter/NGS; 109 (RT), Eric Nguyen/Jim Reed Photography/GI; 110 (UP), AP Images; 110 (LO LE), Mark Thiessen/NGS; 110 (LO RT), Rebecca Hale/NGS; 111 (UP), AP Images/The Yomiuri Shimbun; 111 (UP CTR), AP Images/Kyodo; 111 (LOLE), AP Images/Dogwood; 111 (LORT), STR/AFP/GI; 112-113, Bamboosil/age fotostock; 114-115, Jason Edwards/NGS; 114 (LOLE), Brandon Cole; 114 (LORT), Reinhard Dirscherl/Visuals Unlimited, Inc.; 115 (LOLE), Dray van Beeck/SS; 115, Brandon Cole; 116 (LO), GI; 116-189 (Background), John A. Anderson/IS; 116 (UP), Paul Souders/CO; 117 (UP), Vilainecrevette/SS; 117 (CTR), Reinhard Dirscherl/FLPA/MP; 117 (LO), Stephen Frink/CO; 118, PR 119, Rebecca Hale, NGP; 120 (UP), AVTG/IS; 120 (LO), Brad Wynnyk/SS; 121 (A), Rich Carey/SS; 121 (B), Richard Walters/IS; 121 (C), Karen Graham/IS; 121 (D), Michio Hoshino/MP/NGS; 122, Vilainecrevette/SS; 122, Photo Researchers RM/GI; 122, Dray van Beeck/SS

Culture Connection (124–149)

124-125, Mark A. Johnson/CO; 126 (UPLE), CreativeNature.nl/SS; 126 (LOLE), Tubol Evgeniya/SS; 126 (UPRT), catwalker/SS; 126 (LORT), Dinodia/age fotostock; 126-127 (header), Madlen/SS; 127 (UPLE), Elena Schweitzer/SS; 127 (LE CTR), Plutonius 3d/SS; 127 (LOLE), Dinodia/age fotostock; 127 (UPRT), Jeremy Villasis/Demotix/CO; 127 (RT CTR), Zee/Alamy; 127 (LORT), wacpan/SS; 128, Scott Matthews; 130 (UPLE), The Palm Beach Post/Zuma Press; 130 (UPRT), Taylor Jones/Palm Beach Post/Zuma Press; 130 (LO), AP Images/Aaron Favila; 131 (UP), Rebecca Hale, NGP; 131 (LO), Rebecca

Hale, NGP; 132 (UP), Rebecca Hale, NGP; 132-133, Rebecca Hale, NGP; 133 (UP), Jay Talbott/NGS; 134 (UPLE), Mark Thiessen, NGS; 134 (UP CTR), Guido Daniele/Sipa; 134 (UPRT), Christian Schmalhofer/Dreamstime.com; 134 (CTR), Mark Thiessen, NGS; 134 (LOLE), Guido Daniele/Sipa; 134 (LORT), R. Gino Santa Maria/Dreamstime.com; 135 (UPLE), Mark Thiessen, NGS; 135 (UP CTR LE), Mark Thiessen, NGS; 135 (UP CTR), Guido Daniele/Sipa; 135 (UPRT), Donald M. Jones/MP; 135 (LOLE), Mark Thiessen, NGS; 135 (LORT), Guido Daniele/Sipa; 135 (LO), Stockjiggo/Dreamstime.com; 136 (LE), Courtesy of Madame Tussauds, Washington, D.C.; 136 (RT), Courtesy of Madame Tussauds, New York; 137 (UPLE), Courtesy of Madame Tussauds, New York; 137 (UPRT), Courtesy of Madame Tussauds, New York; 137 (LOLE), Courtesy of Madame Tussauds, New York; 137 (LORT), Courtesy of Madame Tussauds; 138-108 (UP), Debbie Goard/Rex USA; 138 (LO LE), Debbie Goard/Rex USA; 138-109 (BOARDER), Goss Images/Alamy; 139 (UP RT), Debbie Goard/Rex USA; 139 (LO), Debbie Goard/Rex USA; 140 (UP LE), Stock Connection/SuperStock; 140 (UP RT), Exactostock/SuperStock; 140 (CTR), Top Photo Corporation/CO; 140 (LO LE), James Urbach/SuperStock; 140 (LO CTR LE), David Knopf/Alamy; 140 (LO CTR), David Doty; 140 (LO CTR RT), Esa Hiltula CC/Alamy; 140 (LO RT), Don Klein/Purestock/SuperStock; 141, Mark Thiessen, NGS Staff; 142, Ocean/CO; 143, IS; 144 (UP), Randy Olson; 144 (LO LE), Martin Gray/NGS; 144 (LO RT), Sam Panthaky/AFP/GI; 145 (LO LE), Reza/NGS; 145 (LO RT), Richard Nowitz/NGS; 145 (UP), Winfield Parks/NGS; 146 (UP LE), John Hazard; 146 (UP RT), Jose Ignacio Soto/SS; 146 (LO), Photosani/SS; 147 (LE), Corey Ford/Dreamstime.com; 147 (RT), IS; 148 (UP), Elena Schweitzer/SS; 148 (UP CTR RT), Scott Matthews; 148 (LE), Courtesy of Madame Tussauds, New York ; 148 (LOLE), Esa Hiltula CC/Alamy; 148 (LORT), Don Klein/Purestock/SuperStock; 149 (UP), Neftali/SS; 149 (UP CTR), Ajay Bhaskar/IS; 149 (LO), Sunil Menon/IS

Fun and Games (150–169)

150-151, DLILLC/CO; 152-153, James Yamasaki; 154, Smart Bomb Interactive; 155 (UP), Alex Hyde/MP; 155 (LOLE), Photodisc/GI; 155 (LE CTR), NaturePL/SuperStock; 155 (RT CTR), Gary718/Dreamstime.com; 155 (LO), CO Premium RF/Alamy; 156, Dan Sipple; 157 (UPLE), Martin Ruegner/Radius Images; 157 (UPRT), Digital Vision; 157 (LOLE), Gerry Ellis/Digital Vision; 157 (RT CTR), Paul Banton/IS; 157 (LORT), Cathy Keifer/SS; 158 (UP), Marcia Griffen/Animals Animals-Earth Scenes/All Rights Reserved; 158 (LE CTR), Julie Larsen Maher © Wildlife Conservation Society; 158 (RT CTR), Kenneth Garrett/NGS; 158 (LOLE), Brandon Cole; 158 (LORT), Patricio Robles Gil/PhotoLibrary/GI; 159 (UPLE), Fred Bavendam/MP; 159 (UPRT), Art Wolfe/GI; 159 (LE CTR), Michael Nichols/NGS; 159 (RT CTR), Anthony Bannister/GI; 159 (LOLE), Fred Bavendam/MP; 159 (LORT), Tim Fitzharris/MP; 160 (UP), Gallo Images-Dave Hamman/GI; 160 (LOLE), Jeff Hunter/GI; 160 (CTR), Skip Caplan/Alamy; 160 (RT CTR), Thomas Marent/ARDEA; 160 (LO), Imagebroker RF/Photolibrary; 161 (UPLE), Kesu/SS; 161 (UP CTR), Stubblefield Photography/SS; 161 (UPRT), Phoric/SS; 161 (LE CTR), Robert Marien/CO; 161 (CTR), Studio

Araminta/SS; 161 (RT CTR), Fedor Selivanov/SS; 161 (LOLE), Joel Sartore/NGS; 161 (LOCTR), Blaz Kure/SS; 161 (LORT), Eric Isselée/SS; 162 (UPLE), Chris Ware; 162 (UPRT), Gary Fields; 162 (LE CTR), Chris Ware; 162 (RT CTR), Chris Ware; 162 (LOLE), Chris Ware; 162 (LORT), Chris Ware; 163, Doug Allen; 164 (UPRT), Thinkstock/Jupiter Images; 164 (UPLE), Index Stock/Jupiter Images/GI; 164 (UP CTR RT), Thinkstock/Jupiter Images; 164 (LO CTR RT), Medioimages/Jupiter Images/GI; 164 (LOLE), Alan Schein Photography/CO; 164 (LORT), Rob Howard/CO; 165, Dan Sipple; 166-167, James Yamasaki; 168, James Yamasaki; 169 (UP), Suzi Eszterhas/MP; 169 (LOLE), Suzi Eszterhas/MP; 169 (CTR), Exactostock/SuperStock; 169 (RT CTR), Fotosearch/SuperStock; 169 (LOCTR), Stephen Dalton/NHPA/Collection/Photoshot; 169 (LORT), Stephen Dalton/NHPA/Collection/Photoshot

Super Science (170–205)

170-171, AP Images/Kai-Uwe Knoth; 172-173 (Background), Take 27 Ltd/PR 173 (A), David Aguilar; 173 (B), David Aguilar; 173 (C), David Aguilar; 173 (D), David Aguilar; 173 (E), David Aguilar; 174, David Aguilar; 175 (E), Marie C. Fields/SS; 175 (D), Fedor A. Sidorov/SS; 175 (F), sgame/SS; 175 (A), Sebastian Kaulitzki/SS; 175 (B), Steve Gschmeissner/PR 175 (C), Volker Steger/Christian Bardele/PR 175 (G), Benjamin Jessop/IS; 176, Simon Fraser/Science Source; 177, Simon Fraser/Science Source; 178, Robert J. Demarest; 179 (UP), Dennis Cooper/CO; 179 (LO), Linda Nye; 180, IT Stock Free/Jupiter Images; 181 (UPLE), foodfolio/Alamy; 181 (UPRT), Lew Robertson/Brand X Pictures/Jupiter Images; 181 (LOLE), Karl Newedel/GI; 181, Susan C. Bourgoin/FoodPix/GI; 182, Blend Images/SuperStock; 183, Brad Collett/SS; 183, Jonathan Halling; 183, Jacek Chabraszewski/IS; 184-185, David Aguilar; 186, David Aguilar; 187 (UP), NASA/Science Faction/SuperStock; 187 (LO), NASA; 188 (B), Tony & Daphne Hallas/PR 188 (Background), Gabe Palmer/CO; 188 (UPRT), Walter Myers/Stocktrek Images/CO; 188 (LORT), NASA; 189 (UP LE), David Aguilar; 189 (CTR), David Aguilar; 190, David Aguilar; 190-191 (Background), AlaskaStock/CO; 191, David Aguilar; 193 (UP), Ralph Lee Hopkins/NGS; 193 (UP CTR LE), Visuals Unlimited/GI; 193 (LO CTR LE), Doug Martin/PR 193 (LO CTR RT), DEA/C. Dani/GI; 193 (LO LE), Michael Baranski/SS; 193 (LO RT), Terry Davis/SS; 194 (UP LE), Panoramic Stock Images/NGS; 194 (CTR), Ted Clutter/PR 194 (UP RT), Charles D. Winters/PR 194 (LO LE), Jim Lopes/SS; 194 (LO RT), Jim Richardson/NGS; 195 (UP LE), Scenics & Science/Alamy; 195 (UP RT), Mark A. Shneider/PR 195 (UP CTR LE), Visuals Unlimited/CO; 195 (UP CTR RT), Carsten Peter/NGS; 195 (LO CTR), Dirk Wiersma/PR 195 (LO LE), Arturo Limon/SS; 195 (LO RT), Goran Bogicevic/SS; 196 (LE), JewelryStock/Alamy; 196 (A), Manamana/SS; 196 (B), Jens Mayer/SS; 196 (G), PjrStudio/Alamy; 196 (H), E.R. Degginer/PR 197 (C), Alexander Maksimov/SS; 197 (D), Biophoto Assoc./PR 197 (E), DEA/C. Bevilaqua/GI; 197 (F), DAE/A. Rizzi/GI; 197 (I), DAE/C. Bevilaqua/GI; 197 (J), DEA/GI; 197 (K), Suponev Vladimir/SS; 197 (L), Mark A. Shneider/PR 197 (UP RT), Palani Mohan/GI; 197 (UPRT), Amritaphotos/Alamy; 198 (UP), Michael Lichter/Solent News/Rex

Rex USA; 198 (LO), AquaOne Technologies; 199 (UP), Solent News/Rex/Rex USA; 199 (LO), Courtesy of Event World; 199, Courtesy of Event World; 200 (UP), NASA/iGOAL; 200 (CTR), NASA/iGOAL; 200 (LO LE), NASA/iGOAL; 200 (LO RT), NASA/iGoal; 201 (UP), SS; 201 (LOLE), Dieter Spannknebel/Stockbyte/GI; 201 (LORT), plainpicture/Kniel Synnatzschke; 201 (UP CTR RT), SS; 201 (RT CTR), SS; 201 (LO CTR RT), SS; 202 (LO), Mark Raycroft/MP; 202 (UP), Stockbyte/GI; 202 (RT CTR), David McGlynn/Taxi/GI; 203 (UPLE), Siede Preis/GI; 203 (UPRT), Theo Allofs/MP; 203 (CTR), Stockbyte/GI; 203 (LORT), Otmar Thormann/Nordic Photos/GI; 203 (LE CTR), Alaska Stock/Alamy; 203 (LOLE), PureStock/GI; 204 (UPLE), David Aguilar; 204 (UPRT), SS; 204 (LOLE), David Aguilar; 204 (LORT), Michael Baranski/SS; 205 (LO), Chris Gorgio/IS; 205 (UP), Rob Marmion/SS; 205, AVAVA/SS

Going Green (206–223)

206-207, Nick Garbutt/naturepl.com; 208 (BACK), Stefano Unterthiner; 208 (UP), Stefano Unterthiner; 208 (LO), Stefano Unterthiner; 209 (BACK), Jamie Veronica, Big Cat Rescue; 209 (LE), Jamie Veronica, Big Cat Rescue; 209 (UPRT), Jamie Veronica, Big Cat Rescue; 209 (LORT), Jamie Veronica, Big Cat Rescue; 210, Solar Impulse/Stéphane Gros; 210, Courtesy of Tango Group Limited; 211, Courtesy of Vivien Muller; 211, Courtesy Brad Jaeger; 212 (UP LE), N55/Wysing Arts Centre; 212 (UP RT), N55/Wysing Arts Centre; 212 (LO), Scot Zimmerman; 213 (UP), WENN/Newscom; 213 (LE CTR), David Rose/Telegraph Media Group Limited 2012; 213 (UPRT), Patrick Bingham Hall; 213 (LORT), Patrick Bingham Hall; 214 (LO), Erlend Kvalsvik/IS; 214 (UP), Paul Souders/CO; 215 (UP LE), Michael DeYoung/CO; 215 (UP RT), Catalin Petolea/SS; 215 (CTR), NASA/JPL; 216 (LE), Stéphane Bidouze/SS; 216 (Background), Mujka Design Inc./IS; 217 (UP), 33karen33/IS; 217, Nick Garbutt/naturepl.com; 218 (LO), AP Images/AP Photo; 219 (LE CTR), Walter Rawlings/CO; 219 (RT CTR), Sarah Leen; 219 (CTR), Richard Nowitz/NGS; 219 (UP), Marc Moritsch/NGS; 219, WENN/Newscom; 220, Rebecca Hale, NGS Staff; 222 (UP), Erlend Kvalsvik/IS; 222 (CTR), WENN/Newscom; 222 (LO), Michael DeYoung/CO; 223, Albo003/SS

History Happens (224–255)

224-225, Frans Lanting/CO; 226 (UP), Victor R. Boswell Jr./NGS; 226 (CTR), DeAgostini/GI; 226 (LO), Sandro Vannini/CO; 227 (UPLE), Leemage/Universal Images Group/GI; 227 (UPRT), Werner Forman/Art Resource, NY; 227 (LOLE), Photographer/NGS; 227 (LORT), Photolibrary.com/GI ; 227 (RT CTR), Kenneth Garrett/NGS; 228-231 (UP), Mondolithic Studios; 229 (UP RT), Seamas Culligan/Zuma/CO; 229 (LO), Roger Ressmeyer/CO; 230 (UPLE), Mika Stock/DanitaDelimont.com; 230 (UPRT), Jon Arnold Images/Danita Delimont.com; 230 (LO), Fengling/SS; 231 (UP), David Sutherland; 231 (LOLE), Kenneth Garrett/NGS; 231 (LORT), Yoshio Tomii/SuperStock ; 232, Tibor Bognar/CO; 233 (LO), Photoservice Electa/SuperStock; 233 (UP), James L. Stanfield/NGS; 234, Art by Daniel Dociu/Source: Kevin Leahy, Portable Antiquities Scheme; 234 (LORT), Robert Clark; 234 (LOLE), Robert Clark; 234 (UP), Robert Clark; 235 (UP RT),

Index Stock Imagery/Jupiterimages/GI; 235 (CTR), Chip Clark/NMNH/Smithsonian Institution; 235 (LO), Superstock, Inc./SuperStock; 236, Disney Enterprises, Inc./Walden Media, LLC; 236-237, Corey Ford; 237, Mark Thiessen, NGS; 237 (UPRT), Ocean/CO; 238-241, AP Images/Adam Butler; 239 (RT), Library of Congress; 240 (UP), Scott Rothstein/SS; 241, ©1993 Mort Künstler, Inc.; 241 (UP LE), mack2happy/SS; 241 (BACK), Courtesy of the Mount Vernon Ladies' Association; 241 (UP CTR), Courtesy of Partnership for Research in Spatial Modeling (PRISM), Arizona State University; 241 (LE CTR), Mount Vernon Ladies' Association; 241 (RT CTR), Courtesy of the Mount Vernon Ladies' Association; 241 (LO LE), Courtesy of the Mount Vernon Ladies' Association; 241 (LO RT), Courtesy of the Mount Vernon Ladies' Association; 242 (UP), AleksandarNakic/IS; 242 (LO), Stephen Coburn/SS; 243 (LO), Gary Blakely/SS; 243 (UP), S. Borisov/SS; 244 (B), WHHA; 244 (C), WHHA; 244 (D), WHHA; 244 (E), WHHA; 244 (F), WHHA; 244 (G), WHHA; 244 (H), WHHA; 244 (I), WHHA; 244 (A), WHHA; 245 (A), WHHA; 245 (B), WHHA; 245 (C), WHHA; 245 (D), WHHA; 245 (E), WHHA; 245 (F), WHHA; 245 (G), WHHA; 245 (H), WHHA; 246 (A), WHHA; 246 (B), WHHA; 246 (C), WHHA; 246 (D), WHHA; 246 (E), WHHA; 246 (F), WHHA; 246 (G), WHHA; 246 (H), WHHA; 246 (I), WHHA; 246 (J), WHHA; 247 (A), WHHA; 247 (B), WHHA; 247 (C), WHHA; 247 (D), WHHA; 247 (E), WHHA; 247 (F), WHHA; 247 (G), WHHA; 247 (H), WHHA; 248 (A), WHHA; 248 (B), WHHA; 248 (C), WHHA; 248 (D), WHHA; 248 (E), WHHA; 248 (LO RT), The White House; 248 (LO), The White House; 249, Tom Till/SuperStock; 250 (LO), Bettmann/CO; 250 (UP), Bettmann/CO; 251 (UP), AP Photo/Gene Herrick; 251 (LE CTR), Central Press/GI; 251 (RT CTR), Topham/The Image Works; 251 (LO), Central Press/GI; 252 (UP LE), Women's Suffrage, 1920 The Granger Collection, New York/The Granger Collection/Art Resource, NY; 252, History/alamy; 253 (UP RT), The Bloomer Costume. Lithograph, 1851, by Nathaniel Currier. The Granger Collection, NY/The Granger Collection/Art Resource, NY; 253, Frontpage/SS; 254, Chip Clark/NMNH/Smithsonian Institution; 254, Mondolithic Studios; 254, Ocean/CO; 254, Yoshio Tomii/SuperStock; 255, Alessia Pierdomenico/Reuters/CO

Geography Rocks (256–337)

256-257, Funkystock/age fotostock; 259 (CTR CTR), Maria Stenzel/NGS; 259 (LO CTR), Bill Hatcher/NGS; 259 (UP), Carsten Peter/NGS; 259 (RT CTR), Gordon Wiltsie/NGS; 259 (LO LE), James P. Blair/NGS; 259 (CTR LE), Thomas J. Abercrombie/NGS; 259 (LO RT), Bill Curtsinger/NGS; 264 (UP), Francisco Martinez/Alamy; 264 (LO), Zhang Bingtao/Xinhua Press/CO; 264-265 (BACK), Rolf Haid/dpa; 264, Xinhua/Landov; 265 (UPRT), Jean-Christophe Godet/GI; 265 (LO), Mike Greenslade/Australia/Alamy; 266 (LO LE), The Jumeirah Group; 266 (LO RT), © Denis Oudendijk Refunc.NL; 266 (UP), Hulio Hulio; 266 (BACK), The Jumeirah Group; 267 (UP), Andy Rouse/naturepl.com; 267 (CTR), Reinhard Dirscherl/GI; 267 (LO), David B. Fleetham/SeaPics.com; 268-269, Jonah Light; 268 (UPLE), blickwinkel/Alamy; 269 (LO), Courtesy of LEGOLAND Florida; 269 (UP), Courtesy of LEGOLAND Florida; 270, David Pluth/NGS; 271 (LO), THEGIFT777/IS; 271

(UPLE), Pete Oxford/npl/MP; 271 (UPRT), CB2/ZOB/WENN.com/Newscom; 271 (LE CTR), Loic Poidevin/naturepl.com; 271 (LO CTR RT), Kevin Schafer/The Image Bank/GI; 271 (UP CTR RT), Eric Nathan/Gallo Images/GI; 274, Konrad Wothe/MP; 275 (UPLE), Jack Stein Grove/Danita Delimont.com; 275 (LOLE), FLPA/David Tipling/age fotostock; 275 (UPRT), Carsten Peter/NGS; 275 (UP CTR RT), National Geographic RF/GI; 275 (LO CTR RT), Keith Szafranski/IS; 275 (LORT), Yva Momatiuk & John Eastcott/MP/NGS; 278, ssguy/SS; 279 (LO), David Edwards/NGS; 279 (UPLE), DLILLC/CO; 279 (LOLE), porkrithap/SS; 279 (UPRT), Ilin Sergey/age fotostock; 279 (RT CTR), Nik Wheeler/Alamy; 279, CO/SuperStock; 282, David Wall/Danita Delimont.com; 283 (UPLE), Cusp/SuperStock; 283 (LOLE), Galaxy Picture Library/Alamy; 283 (UPRT), Gerry Pearce/Alamy; 283 (LO CTR RT), Mika Stock/Danita Delimont. com; 283 (LO CTR RT), Jeff Hunter/The Image Bank/GI; 283 (LORT), Mitsuaki Iwago/MP/NGS; 286, Lonely Planet/SuperStock; 287 (LO), Peter Wey/SS; 287 (UP), Paul Thompson/Danita Delimont.com; 287 (LOLE), LianeM/SS; 287 (UPRT), SS; 287 (UP CTR RT), Annette Hopf/IS; 287 (LO CTR RT), Diego Lezama Orezzoli//CO; 290, PhJon Arnold Images/Danita Delimont. com; 291 (UPLE), W. BERTSCH/Robertstock; 291 (LOLE), Jim Reed/Jim Reed Photography - Severe &/CO; 291 (UPRT), Jenny E. Ross/CO; 291 (UP CTR RT), Matt Gibson/SS; 291 (LO CTR RT), benlarhome; 291 (LORT), David Rose/SS; 294, Frans Lanting/CO; 295 (UP), John & Lisa Merrill/DanitaDelimont.com; 295 (LOLE), AP Photo/Ricardo Moraes; 295 (UPRT), Johnny Haglund/Lonely Planet Images/GI; 295 (UP CTR RT), Pete McBride/NGS; 295 (LO CTR RT), Jason Edwards/NGS; 295 (LORT), Bernardo Galmarini/Alamy; 301, Cubo Images/SuperStock; 304, Wolfgang Kaehler/SuperStock ; 307, dovate/IS; 308, Lukasz Pajor/SS; 312, Steve Elmore/GI; 315, B.S.P.I./CO; 318, Mark Van Overmeire/SS; 321, Frank Lukasseck/CO; 334 (LO), PhotoDisc; 334 (UP), Panoramic Images/GI; 334 (UPLE), William Randall/IS; 334 (RT CTR), Harold G Herradura/Flickr/GI; 335 (UPRT), Greg Balfour Evans/Alamy; 335 (CTR), zrfphoto/IS; 335 (LE), Solent News & Photo Agency; 336, CB2/ZOB/WENN.com/Newscom; 336, Mike Greenslade/Australia/Alamy; 336, Wolfgang Kaehler/SuperStock

Published by the
National Geographic Society

John M. Fahey
Chairman of the Board and Chief Executive Officer

Declan Moore
Executive Vice President; President, Publishing and Travel

Melina Gerosa Bellows
Executive Vice President; Chief Creative Officer, Books, Kids, and Family

Prepared by the Book Division

Hector Sierra, *Senior Vice President and General Manager*
Nancy Laties Feresten, *Senior Vice President, Kids Publishing and Media*
Jay Sumner, *Director of Photography, Children's Publishing*
Jennifer Emmett, *Vice President, Editorial Director, Children's Books*
Eva Absher-Schantz, *Design Director, Kids Publishing and Media*
R. Gary Colbert, *Production Director*
Jennifer A. Thornton, *Director of Managing Editorial*

Staff for This Book

Robin Terry, *Project Manager*
Mary Varilla Jones, *Project Editor*
James Hiscott, Jr., *Art Director*
Ruthie Thompson, *Designer*
Lori Epstein, *Senior Illustrations Editor*
Kris Hanneman, *Illustrations Editor*
Hillary Moloney, *Illustrations Assistant*
Sarah Wassner Flynn, *Contributing Writer*
Michelle Harris, *Researcher*
Sara Zeglin, *Digital Content Producer*
Ariane Szu-Tu, *Editorial Assistant*
Carl Mehler, *Director of Maps*
Michael McNey and David B. Miller, *Map Research and Production*
Stuart Armstrong, *Graphics Illustrator*
Callie Broaddus, *Design Production Assistant*
Michael O'Connor, Grace Hill, *Associate Managing Editors*
Joan Gossett, *Production Editor*
Lewis R. Bassford, *Production Manager*
Susan Borke, *Legal and Business Affairs*

Manufacturing and Quality Management

Phillip L. Schlosser, *Senior Vice President*
Chris Brown, *Vice President, NG Book Manufacturing*
George Bounelis, *Vice President, Production Services*
Nicole Elliott, *Manager*
Rachel Faulise, *Manager*
Robert L. Barr, *Manager*

In Partnership with
NATIONAL GEOGRAPHIC KIDS Magazine

Julie Vosburgh Agnone, *Vice President, Editorial Operations*
Rachel Buchholz, *Editor and Vice President*
Catherine D. Hughes, *Senior Editor, Science*
Photo: Kelley Miller, *Senior Editor*; Lisa Jewell, *Editor*

Art: Eileen O'Tousa-Crowson, *Art Director*; Julide Obuz Dengel, *Designer*; Stephanie Rudig, *Digital Design Assistant*
Editorial: Andrea Silen, *Associate Editor*; Nick Spagnoli, *Copy Editor*; Kay Boatner, *Assistant Editor*
Administration: Bianca Bowman, *Editorial Assistant*; Tammi Colleary, *Business Specialist*
Production: David V. Showers, *Director*
Online: Anne A. McCormack, *Director*

CELEBRATING
‹125›
YEARS

The National Geographic Society is one of the world's largest nonprofit scientific and educational organizations. Founded in 1888 to "increase and diffuse geographic knowledge," the Society's mission is to inspire people to care about the planet. It reaches more than 400 million people worldwide each month through its official journal, *National Geographic*, and other magazines; National Geographic Channel; television documentaries; music; radio; films; books; DVDs; maps; exhibitions; live events; school publishing programs; interactive media; and merchandise. National Geographic has funded more than 10,000 scientific research, conservation, and exploration projects and supports an education program promoting geographic literacy.

For more information, please visit www.nationalgeographic.com, call 1-800-NGS LINE (647-5463), or write to the following address:
NATIONAL GEOGRAPHIC SOCIETY
1145 17th Street, N.W.
Washington, D.C. 20036-4688 U.S.A.

Visit us online at nationalgeographic.com/books

For librarians and teachers: ngchildrensbooks.org

More for kids from National Geographic:
kids.nationalgeographic.com

For information about special discounts for bulk purchases, please contact National Geographic Books Special Sales: ngspecsales@ngs.org

For rights or permissions inquiries, please contact National Geographic Books Subsidiary Rights: ngbookrights@ngs.org

Paperback ISBN: 978-1-4263-1118-5
Hardcover ISBN: 978-1-4263-1119-2
ISSN: 2153-7364

Printed in the United States of America
13/QGT-CML/1